DAUGHTER
of the PACIFIC

DAUGHTER
of the PACIFIC

by YOKO MATSUOKA

HARPER & BROTHERS   PUBLISHERS   NEW YORK

TO FATHER AND MOTHER
in affection and gratitude

CONTENTS

JAPAN

I ~

THE LATE autumn sun, reflected through the remaining leaves of the lilac bush, makes an intricate pattern on my dormitory window in this tranquil Boston suburb. As I watch it ever changing, my mind goes back, seeking to retrace the thirty-four years of my life. It is like standing on a mist-covered hill, waiting for the air to clear. Two figures become increasingly distinct—that of my seventy-year-old mother and the other of my eight-year-old daughter, Seiko—who are waiting for my return to Tokyo. As every crease in Mother's face becomes plainer, the mist below seems to break. Seiko's big brown eyes, showing her intense trust in me and her determination to penetrate through the haze, seem to be asking, "Which way now?"

Mother was my age when she married Father, who was one year older. The last several years have mellowed her egg-shaped face, and in her kimono she now looks like an ordinary Japanese grandmother who married young and spent all her adult years just caring for her family. When young, she was a determined-looking woman, however, one who always carried her head straight to show that she was afraid of nobody, not even men. Although she has shrunk considerably, she was then well over five feet—taller than the average. Her feet are large for a Japanese woman, though mine are even larger. There is a saying in our country, "The big feet are stupid." Mother's penetrating eyes show she is obviously an exception.

From her wedding photograph I can see that she was intelligent and proud, but neither beautiful nor dainty. Everything about her marked her as an old maid in a country where woman's only purpose was to marry young and have many children. I have always admired Father for choosing an old maid who was a working woman.

A newspaperman and a university lecturer, with a degree from a

Japanese university and an M.A. from the University of Wisconsin, Father must have had a wide range of choice in picking his bride, so it interested me to know how he came to marry Mother. When I asked him about this as a child, Father answered with his pet story: "Well, I was walking on a Tokyo street one day and saw a lonely-looking woman. So I married her, and that is your Mother."

Mother was more serious when she told me, "Your Aunt Hani [Father's eldest sister] introduced me to your father. I had been working for her magazine *Fujin-no-tomo* [a monthly for women] since 1912, when I returned from America."

Neither Father nor Mother told me that it was a love marriage, not an arranged one. Somehow I have never asked that blunt question, but have always assumed that it was so.

I did not appreciate fully the unconventionality of their marriage until I became old enough to realize the part which tradition and custom play in our society.

Father and Mother purposely chose the day of bad omen for their wedding in order to show that superstitions meant nothing to them. The Japanese calendar has good days and bad days for weddings, for the announcing of engagements, for funerals and other occasions. Even today these superstitions are rigidly followed by many people, particularly among the country population. Some abide by them because they are superstitious; others because they do not want to be different. Father and Mother chose the seventh day of the seventh month, the worst possible day for a wedding. This is the day Vega and Altair meet across the Milky Way. According to the legend which originated in China, Vega, the weaver, and Altair, the herdsman, incurred the wrath of the Heavenly King. So the King separated them, putting one on each side of the Milky Way, and permitted them to meet only once a year on the seventh day of the seventh month. The story goes that if you marry on this particular day, you are destined to be separated. Father and Mother proved a most happily married couple despite this ill omen.

The following year I was born, causing much discomfort to Mother, I understand. In fact the birth was so difficult that it had to be decided whether the doctor should save Mother or the baby. Mother used to explain in a tone of apology: "As Father was away at that time on a trip to South America, Aunt Hani and I had to make the decision, and we told the doctor that I should be saved." If I had had any voice in the matter, I would have agreed.

In the process of saving Mother, I too was saved. But since that day my head has the shape called by the Japanese "the coin purse head." It looks like a coin purse upside down—a rather long peak at the top and sloping on both sides. I have always been glad I was born a girl so that I would not have to wear men's hats—particularly the straw hat, which fits me better sideways than the proper way.

Naming a baby in Japan is almost as important as naming the royal babies in England, for every name has a definite meaning. In my family it was Father who named me *Yoko*—the Child of the Ocean—because he was traveling on the Pacific Ocean at the time I was born. The seventh day after birth is customarily reserved for the ceremony of naming, comparable to christening in the West, for which the baby is taken in a red silk kimono to the near-by shrine. But I don't believe Mother abided by this custom.

In our country it is customary to ask, "What year were you born?" rather than "When were you born?" There are twelve animals which respectively designate each year—the mouse, the cow, the tiger, the rabbit, the dragon, the snake, the horse, the sheep, the monkey, the chicken, the dog and the boar. I understand these were the animals which followed Buddha—the Oriental Noah's animals. There is a superstition that girls born in a particular "horse" year are so aggressive that no man wishes to marry them. Fortunately, this falls only once every sixty years. The last one was 1906. Undoubtedly there are many unmarried women in Japan who were born in this fateful year. The year 1916, in which I was born, was the "dragon" year, to which no such superstition is attached.

The earliest photographs taken of me were a series of twelve, showing me in my bath. The Japanese bathtub—although there are all shapes and sizes—is at least three feet deep. One washes outside the tub before getting in to soak. The whole family bathes in the same tub of hot water. Mother decided that this was not hygienic for the newborn babe and had a small American-style tub made. The photographer from Aunt Hani's magazine took the sequence to show how a baby should be bathed, and this series of pictures was published, including one with Mother putting diapers on me.

The last one in the series shows Mother holding me—all bathed and dressed in a white cotton kimono about twice my length. To dress babies in white was also something new at that time. As only the dead wear white in Japan, it had been customary to dress babies either in red or yellow. For sanitary reasons, Mother was among the first to break the custom and advocated its use in *Fujin-no-tomo*. With thin black hair and a nose which can be distinguished only by two small dots at the end, I look like any other Japanese baby in that picture.

Mother also advocated the use of a crib. Usually the Japanese baby is carried on the mother's back or laid in a quilt on the *tatami* floor. (*Tatami* is a thick mat—three by six feet—made of dried grass and used as floor covering.) Mother had a wicker crib made with four small wooden wheels so that it could be wheeled around anywhere in the house. It looked like a big shopping basket without the handle. Kwoko, my first sister, born a year and a half after me, modeled this crib. The picture of her sucking her bottle of milk in the wicker basket was also published in the magazine.

The name *Kwoko* means the Great Child. Father explained that since I was named the Child of the Ocean, he did not want to give my sister a name which meant anything smaller than an ocean, lest she should feel inferior to me. By the time the third girl was born, Father must have run out of characters which meant anything greater than *kwo*, for he named his third and last *Reiko*, the Diligent Child.

2 ~

IN MY earliest memory of him, Father was smoking a corncob pipe which he had brought back from America. He was dressed in an old black silk kimono with unusually large family crests in white on both sleeves. That kimono must have belonged to his grandfather, for it was no longer fashionable to have the family crest larger than coin size. Wearing a pair of large round spectacles rimmed with tortoise shell and holding a fat Waterman pen, another acquisition from America, he looked as though he had just come out of a pawnshop.

His room in our small house in Tokyo was a combination newspaper office, library, and museum. His large rectangular business desk, which is older than I and can barely hold together now, was set in the middle of the room. Father kept enough of its surface clear for writing his articles and lectures, but the rest was covered with big and small dictionaries, newspaper clippings, stacks of books, an ivory penknife, an ink bottle, a dozen or so varieties of pipes stuck in a wooden container, usually a box of American cigars, a brown leather cup holding dice, and a copy of Confucius' *Analects*, which he had been made to memorize from the age of five. The desk was the only "off-limits" place in our house for everybody including Mother, who was always neat and tidy. He often said, "I know exactly where everything is on my desk, so please don't touch it." I now repeat the same words, but hasten to add, "You know, I inherited the trait from Father," particularly when Mother is around.

All around this room bookshelves had been built. A large portion of those books were on Formosa and Korea, as Father's special field was colonial policies. There was a set of books on Theodore Roosevelt. Father had a great liking for this man, which I always thought was largely due to his efforts in terminating the Russo-Japanese War of 1904-5. Father accepted this American President as a "true friend of Japan."

Father's collection of books included many on the League of Nations and Woodrow Wilson. Considering the differences between Wilson and Roosevelt, it seems odd that Father was equally impressed by both. He talked a great deal about the League of Nations. I am sure he was aware of the weaknesses of the League machinery, yet he always spoke of it with much hopefulness. However, he had one misgiving which he never forgot to mention: "The Japanese delegate at the Peace Conference insisted that the Covenant of the League should include a clause on racial equality, but much to our disappointment it was voted down." Some Western scholars have expressed the opinion that the Japanese delegation were playing a shrewd game of politics when they introduced this proposal, but I feel sure that Father and many others were sincere.

There was one shelf of books by or on Fukuzawa Yukichi, the foremost liberal of the Meiji era (1868-1912) and founder of the Keio University—the oldest in Japan—where Father studied economics. Father told me many stories about his teacher, but one particularly remains in my mind. "Fukuzawa-*sensei*,"* Father used to say, "wrote, 'There is no person above you and no person below you.'"

I was interested to discover recently that, despite his belief in the equality of men, Fukuzawa-*sensei* did not seem to be critical of the unique status held by the Japanese Emperor until 1945. Certainly Father never believed that the Emperor was a god, but he also apparently accepted his position as an integral part of Japanese polity. At least that is the impression he gave me. Unfortunately, I was not critical enough during Father's lifetime to discuss the problem with him.

Almost half the books in Father's library were in English, the other half in Japanese, and a few in French. Conspicuous exceptions to his books on social sciences and biographies were his Bible, which he seemed to know as well as his Confucius' *Analects*, and a copy of the Koran.

On top of these books were all sorts of straw coolie hats which Father had collected from Formosa, China, Java and Malaya. On one shelf stood a brass container about three inches high. A thin tube, slightly longer than the container itself, extended from its top and curved at the tip. Father said this was an opium pipe, but never demonstrated how it was smoked. On another shelf was a small grayish-tan vaselike object. The neck was too long and narrow and the bottom was not stable enough for a vase. There was no painting or writing of any sort, and I always considered it an extremely uninteresting ornament. But Father valued it for its age and because he had brought it back from a South American coun-

* *Sensei* means teacher. Literally the two characters mean "born before you," and originally were applied in this sense. This form has also been used, however, when it is wished to address someone with respect.

try which he visited in the year I was born. This was the only object which stood the heat and survived unchanged in color and shape when our home was burned in the air raid of April 14, 1945.

In one corner of the wall hung a sword about two and a half feet long, curved like the crescent moon, with a beautifully carved ivory hilt. Father was proud of this sword, and whenever he had a little *sake* (rice wine), he told how he came to possess it.

"This was before you were born," he would begin, "when I was a government official in Formosa. There were some head-hunters in the mountains of that island, and they were causing a great deal of trouble. I was commissioned by the governor general to subdue them.

"My superiors and colleagues advised me to be well armed. Well, after some thought, I decided against that. Because if you were armed, the head-hunters would surely think you had come to harm them; therefore, they would be certain to attack you. In that case you would need a whole army, and—no negotiation. But if you went unarmed, the chances were that they would not harm you. So I went deep into the mountains completely unarmed, accompanied only by a native guide." Father would pause for a moment and sip the golden-colored *sake* from a tiny porcelain cup.

"The chief head-hunter welcomed me and gave me a big feast. He liked me so much that he offered me his daughter to be my wife. Mind you, I was still a bachelor then. But this, you see, I did not accept." With that he would again pause and grin. "The chief gave me that sword instead. Yes, that is the head-hunter's sword.

"The chief admired my neck," Father always added, "and he really looked sorry that he could not have it. You see, when head-hunters acquired heads, they displayed them on a shelf, like so many pumpkins. If the neck was narrow and thin, the head would not stand very well. So they valued heads like mine, with short, thick necks."

Even as a child, I thought this story a little too colorful to be true, but I was impressed by the tactics Father used in his negotiation.

There were also two other swords in Father's study, much longer than the head-hunter's sword. Each was carefully wrapped in yellow cotton cloth. Father was truly proud of them for they were the samurai swords handed down from his ancestors.

Although the swords originally belonged to the Matsuokas of the third or fourth generation back, our ancestors can be traced back to the twelfth century. It seems silly, but in a feudal society, where names with prestige carried much weight, a family line was known back to the time of some famous character. This was particularly true of the samurai, the small ruling class at the top of the feudal hierarchy until the Meiji Restoration of 1868.

Although Father never showed off his samurai ancestry nor believed in its superiority, as many others did for many decades after the Restoration, he could not hide a childlike pride and joy when he told the famous legend concerning the founder of our line. Hatakeyama Shigetada was known for his kindness. In one of the battles Shigetada carried his horse down a steep hill because he did not want the animal harmed! This would sound a little exaggerated even to the Society for the Prevention of Cruelty to Animals. The story was in our grade-school textbook as an example of samurai chivalry.

Father always referred to himself as a *heimin*, a commoner. Yet he was peculiarly proud of his samurai background. Sportsmanship, courage and etiquette he attributed to the samurai training. He disliked intensely an "unmanly" man, the opposite of the true samurai. When Prince Konoye, Japan's prime minister intermittently from 1937 to 1941, seemed to lack courage, Father's comment was, "That is the trouble with the nobility." When money-making seemed to be the only concern of one of Father's friends, he said disapprovingly, "Well, he comes from a merchant family." To my father the samurai represented all the virtues, although he deprecated the hierarchical structure upon which this ruling class sustained itself.

I never knew how high my ancestors ranked under the feudal lord, Nambu, but they must have been in the upper third. Since he was the oldest son, Father inherited all the considerable Matsuoka property when he became the head of the family upon his father's death. Father used to say that his land was too large to walk around, and that he had to ride a horse when he inspected it. However, I did not realize until after this last war that the fifty-odd acres of land which Father owned put him in the upper 3 per cent bracket of landowners in a country where an average farm is only two and a half acres. I was flabbergasted to discover in 1946 that Father, who always complained that he put more money into the land than the land earned, would have been one of those "absentee landlords" removed by the American Occupation under the democ- ratization program. I realized that absentee landlordism played a large part in the maintenance of semifeudal oligarchy in Japan, but it was incongruous to think of my own father as an obstacle to Japan's "democracy." He not only believed that "all men are created equal," but implemented that idea in everyday life.

We did not have to face the problem of land reform in the postwar period, however. Father was forced to sell the land during the war to the Japanese Imperial Army, which converted it into an airfield. Since Japan's surrender in 1945, the American Army of Occupation has occupied this field.

Mother also was born into a samurai family. Unlike Father's family, Mother's held a subordinate position directly under the *Bakufu*, or Shogunate. The *Bakufu* was the central government ruling Japan through the feudal lords, who had jurisdiction over local territories. Although the Emperor was the formal head of the feudal hierarchy, the Shogunate possessed the actual temporal power during the three hundred years preceding the Meiji Restoration. This Restoration, because of internal dissension and the pressure from Western powers to open Japan for trade, ended the regime of the Tokugawa Shogunate.

Mother's family followed the last Tokugawa Shogun from Edo (Tokyo) to Shizuoka eighty miles southwest of Tokyo when he evacuated Edo Castle before the newly established Meiji Govern- ment took over. Although the Tokugawas themselves lost not wealth so much as political power by the Restoration, the lesser samurai under the Shogunate suffered the total loss of their source of income. And yet, many of these lesser samurai were not ready to engage in "lower" professions such as agriculture, the arts, or trade to earn their daily bread. Mother's family was no exception.

I have not forgotten the story of Mother's younger brother, which exemplifies the feeling of samurai families trying to keep up their prestige. This uncle of ours has an excellent voice, particularly suited for *yokyoku*, or the classical Japanese singing. When he was a child, one of the two famous *yokyoku* families, the Kanze, wanted to adopt him.

The Japanese classical arts—theater, singing and dancing—have been and still are carried on by established families. If their own children are good enough, they are trained from childhood in the family's particular profession. But if they do not meet the standard, qualified children are adopted into the family. After one has entered a profession in this way, his position and livelihood are secured.

My grandmother refused the offer by the Kanze family on the ground that to lower one's position was a shame which no samurai could bear. Mother would always comment after telling this story, "Your uncle would have been much better off as a professional *yokyoku* singer than a perennial high-school teacher, but your grandmother just could not see the son of a samurai become an artist."

Mother remarked how strange it was that people clung so tenaciously to the old traditions and values after the social structure which produced them had collapsed. Yet she herself later faced this same conflict of emotions when one of her own daughters, Reiko, wanted to become an actress.

It was partly due to this financial difficulty in Mother's family that my grandmother worked as the dean of women at a mission college in Tokyo. The teaching profession had always been considered respectable and this position did not constitute a shame. The Aoyama-Gakuin, where she worked, was founded by my grandmother's cousin, Sen Tsuda, in 1873—one year after compulsory education was adopted in Japan. In Mother's words, "This first Methodist college was started in a Buddhist temple because that was the only space available, and Uncle Tsuda's first pupils were his wife, son and daughter."

In my childhood I heard a great deal about Uncle Tsuda from Mother. He sent his daughter, Umeko, to the United States in 1871 to study with the first group of five women enrolled under the sponsorship of the Japanese Government. Umeko, the youngest member of the group, was only nine then. She later studied at Bryn

Mawr College and, after her return to Japan, founded Tsuda College, one of the finest women's colleges we have.

I understand that Uncle Tsuda was one of the first to introduce into Japan such American vegetables as tomatoes, celery, cabbage and parsley. Mother used to say, "When I was a child, these vegetables were still very rare, and I often visited the Tsuda family to get a taste of the foreign vegetables from their garden. I thought they were delicious."

Mother admired the unorthodoxy and pioneering spirit of Uncle Tsuda and respected her Cousin Umeko. She was proud to have them among her relatives. But Grandmother discouraged her from being intimate with the Tsudas after they became socially prominent. According to Grandmother, who was the proud daughter and wife of a true samurai, it was in bad taste to treat one's famous relatives intimately because that would look as though one was showing off. Had the position of the two families been reversed, it would have been all right to treat them as relatives. "What peculiar vanity!" was Mother's comment.

Uncle Tsuda encouraged Mother to receive higher education. After graduating from the Aoyama-Gakuin college in 1905, Mother managed to come to America, where she studied English literature in a night school while helping her brother in business in New York City. She stayed seven years.

There were photographs of her taken in the United States with her hair gathered upward in the style of the early twentieth century, wearing a long full-skirted dress with a high neckline and long tight sleeves puffed at the shoulders. As a child I thought Mother looked nice in Western dress, and asked why she no longer wore it. "When I was leaving America," she replied, "your uncle told me that I must wear kimonos upon returning to Japan. Otherwise, I would not only find it difficult to obtain a job, which I needed badly, but I would not be accepted by society." So when Mother went back to Japan in 1912, she discarded her American wardrobe. I do not know whether that had anything to do with her getting a job. She was successful in finding one in the office of Aunt Hani's *Fujin-no-tomo* and also a teaching position in a girls' high school in Tokyo.

[13]

3 ~

MY FIRST memory of Mother is watching her rush off to work, leaving me with the maid. She has often said, "I always hurried home to find your round face squashed against the window in our veranda, watching for me." Mother translated many children's stories from English for *Fujin-no-tomo*, so I was brought up on "The Three Little Pigs," "Little Red Ridinghood" and "Cinderella." Another favorite bedtime story was called "The Golden Window." It went something like this:

There was a boy who lived on top of a hill. At sunset he would look out to see a house on top of another hill far away. The window in that house shone like gold. He always wished his windows also were of gold. One day he went down the hill and up another hill to see this golden window. When he reached there he found, much to his disappointment, that it was just a plain window like the one at his house. Then he looked across to his house and, behold, its window was shining gold.

There was a small lawn in front of our house surrounded by narrow green bamboo trees, which shut us off from the street. Here Father taught us to wrestle in Japanese style. On sunny warm days, we would dress like professional wrestlers—just a piece of cloth tied around our waists. I remember how we three children looked forward to Sundays when Father was at home to play and roughhouse with us.

Kwoko was most quick to learn these boyish games. She proved to be the healthiest and naughtiest of the three sisters. Reiko, the baby of the family, was an adorable child with her long curly hair and fat cheeks, but she cried easily. She would cry when Father threw her on the floor in a wrestling match, so he would manage to lose two out of three games with her. Reiko never developed the endurance of Kwoko, but had and still has the most congenial disposition. We used to say that it was because she was born in the "sheep" year. Kwoko and I often fought each other, but neither of us fought with Reiko.

[14]

Kwoko used to call me *O-ne-chan*, or Honorable Big Sister. It is the custom in Japan that elder brothers and sisters are so addressed by the younger ones, and not by their first names. This is only one of many deferences. Those who are born before you or those whose social rank is superior to yours have their own form of respect. There are many variations of "I" and "you," and one must learn the proper usage, according to circumstances. In speaking of the members of one's own family to other people, one uses a deprecatory form such as "my stupid wife" or "my stupid younger brother," but never "my stupid husband" nor "my stupid older brother." The latter are simply "my husband" and "my older brother." On the other hand, if one is referring to persons related to the one addressed, he must say "the honorable husband of yours" or "your honorable wife." Moreover, there is a difference between men's language and that used by women. Women who use men's language are considered vulgar.

There are two schools of thought as to whether we really mean "honorable big sister" when we say "*O-ne-chan*," or whether this form has become so much a part of the language that it is wrong to attach any special meaning. I don't think we can say it is one or the other. Although a great deal of the original meaning still survives, something has been lost.

My father apparently believed that the use of these honorary prefixes from childhood would gradually condition one's attitude toward others in a feudalistic way. One day he told Kwoko, "Yoko is not superior to you just because she was born first. Why don't you call her by her first name, as she does you?" Since then Kwoko and Reiko have called me by my first name—something still unusual in Japan. For the same reason we were never taught to use a particularly polite language to our parents. We talked to them as we would to friends, though we did call Father *O-to-san*, or Honorable Father, mainly because there was no simpler form of address. I think this is one instance where the word "honorable" has lost its literal meaning.

I can now appreciate Father's independence in bringing up his daughters according to what he believed to be right. When he returned home from the United States in 1918, as a member of the

Japanese Economic Mission led by Baron Megata, he saw me sitting properly on the floor, legs folded beneath me, eating a meal with chopsticks. I have been told that he asked Mother then to buy a stool for me so that I would not have to sit on the floor. Father said, "It is much more important for her to have nice straight legs when she grows up."

To learn to sit properly on the floor, and for a considerable length of time, is still the first lesson for many Japanese girls. This position is basic to the Japanese etiquette, as there are no chairs in a Japanese house. If a girl sits on the floor with her legs in front of her, she is considered boyish. If a woman sits with her legs sticking out at the sides, she is called loose. Thus one had to take the risk of being called unladylike in order to have nice straight legs.

All this consideration did not make my legs very shapely, and I shudder to think how they would be if I had been made to conform to custom. Father often commented, "At least you ought to be thankful that you are not as bowlegged as many Japanese women." Indeed I am, particularly since I wear Western clothes all the time.

Although Mother agreed with Father in principle, I think she was a little reluctant to see us become completely unconventional or eccentric. It was probably because he pursued such a liberal policy in bringing up his children that Mother was a strict disciplinarian.

She could not say, as most Japanese mothers do: "Sit properly on the floor. Otherwise you will be laughed at." "Hold your chopsticks this way. Otherwise nobody will marry you." "You must receive good grades at school so as not to bring shame to the family." Instead, Mother would say: "Hold your chopsticks this way because it is the proper way." "It's bad not to finish your homework first." She extended this to more fundamental things in life. It was "bad" to be selfish, and it was "good" to be kind. As I remember, "to laugh at people" and "to lie" were the worst kinds of behavior.

Normally in a Japanese family the father is the one to be held in awe and feared, and the function of the mother is to soothe the father and spoil the children in his absence. However, in our family it was Mother who scolded us every time we misbehaved. We children nicknamed her *oni-baba*, or Demon Grandma.

One memorable event while we lived in Tokyo was the great

earthquake of September 1, 1923. I happened to be in Karuizawa, the summer resort one hundred miles northwest of Tokyo, with my Aunt Hani and her family. It was noon and I was sitting on the kitchen floor of the Hani cottage, helping my cousins prepare lunch. We all heard a deep sound somewhere—something like thunder, but not from the sky. Then there was a weird sensation as though a big worm were crawling up my legs. We jumped up and went outside to see Mount Asama, a near-by volcano. Though Asama had been inactive, we all thought it was going to erupt. That evening the news of the earthquake in the Tokyo area reached us. That night we could see a tinge of ripe persimmon red in the eastern sky. We knew Tokyo was burning.

Father was away at Sakhalin, accompanying an expedition of scientists. Only Mother and my two sisters were in Tokyo then. Mother has described what happened this way: "First I thought the movement was sideways, but soon I realized it was up and down. I ran to the room where Reiko was playing. She was sitting on the *tatami* floor with her usual wide grin and saying, 'Look! the house is rocking like a big ship.' It was only when I grabbed her to go outside that she began to cry." (We had been told that the earthquake with horizontal movement is not as serious as the one whose movement is vertical.) Luckily no one in the family was injured, and there was little damage done to our house.

Mother discarded her kimonos completely at this time when she had to travel through the devastated areas of Tokyo on behalf of *Fujin-no-tomo*. Elevated trains and trucks, which the city of Tokyo provided, were the only means of transportation available and the kimono, wrapped around her tightly to the ankles and with its long sleeves, was not serviceable. She gave away all but her wedding kimono to victims of the earthquake. From that time on she wore Western clothes until about the middle of the last war when *mompe,* a Japanese counterpart of trousers, became the only sensible garment to wear.

While Mother was away on her assignment, she left Kwoko and Reiko with the Andos, who lived only a block from our house. Mr. Ando, a painter who had never been able to earn very much from his work, was one of Father's university friends, and Mrs. Ando, more talented than her husband, often played with us and took care of us.

I still remember Mother's first Western dress. It was a dark brown woolen skirt, hanging straight down to three inches above her ankles, and a tan silk blouse of hardly any shape. It was quite modern and daring for a woman of Mother's age to be so attired, and I used to look upon her with mixed pride and shame because she looked different from other mothers.

A dress not only permits more movement, but it can be washed and ironed more easily than a kimono, which has to be ripped apart and sewed together again every time it is cleaned. Since dresses were more convenient and serviceable, Mother considered that it would be extravagant to keep up both a Western and a Japanese wardrobe.

She insisted that we follow the same practice. As soon as we grew out of the baby stage, she dressed us in Western clothes exclusively. Most urban children owned both kimonos and Western clothes. And I remember being rather envious, although not as much so as Kwoko, of the colorful kimonos other children wore, particularly on New Year's Day.

I consoled myself by reasoning that my dresses were cut more smartly and made of better cloth than other children's. Kwoko's reaction was more direct and less restrained. When given the topic "What I want to be when I grow up" in first-year composition class, she wrote that she wanted to be a countess, wearing a beautiful silk kimono and a pretty parasol.

This startled Mother, who later confessed, "I did not expect such superficial vanity from one of my children. But this made me realize that children long for what they do not have at home. It is certainly much more sensible not to maintain duality, but I feel we can't be rational about everything. I was afraid that you might seek elsewhere to satisfy your desires if I kept my rule. That was why I made each of you a kimono."

That was a beautiful kimono—made of muslin delaine, with pale pink cherry blossoms on a pastel blue background.

[18]

Obviously for a different reason, Mother let Father do as he pleased in the matter of clothes. He always wore a Western business suit to work and relaxed in a kimono at home.

4 ~

FATHER WAS transferred to the Osaka office of the *Mainichi Shimbun*, one of the three largest newspapers in Japan, in December 1923, and the whole family moved to Osaka the following spring just in time for the reopening of school. I remember Mother complaining while packing: "I wish Father would stop accumulating all this junk." Our family moved many times after this, and Father's "junk" kept increasing.

I was a sickly child when we lived in Tokyo. A bad case of measles and pneumonia kept me out of school more than half of my first year. Thus when we moved to Osaka, Mother had to decide whether she should put me in the first grade with my sister Kwoko, or start me in the second grade without much knowledge of the first year of schooling. She decided it would be bad for my morale to be in the same class as my younger sister, and so put me in the second grade. This meant I had to do a great deal of catching up.

The small private school, called the Lark-Hill School because it stood on top of a hill named Skylark, was coeducational and considered progressive. Although the official textbooks approved by the Ministry of Education had to be used, the school had considerable freedom in arranging its curriculum. Besides the usual grammar-school subjects—Japanese language, arithmetic, history, geography, composition, morals, calligraphy, singing, drawing and gymnastics—we had a class in English taught by an American missionary. The first two years in this English class were spent learning the alphabet and *Romaji*,* the Romanized way of writing the Japanese lan-

* The use of *Romaji* was strongly urged by the first American Education Mission, which made a study of the Japanese educational system in the spring of 1946 in order to liberate the Japanese from learning thousands of complicated Chinese characters. In the middle of the 1920's the teaching of *Romaji* in a grammar school was quite rare.

guage. We also learned such simple English words as "good morning," "good-by," and "thank you," along with some songs in English —"London Bridge Is Falling Down" and "The Ten Little Indian Boys." I remember this English class as my favorite and I liked the teacher, who spoke a little Japanese with an accent.

Mother visited my classes to see how the subjects were being taught, and went over the lessons with me every afternoon when school was out to make sure that I understood. This was something of an ordeal, but there was no way of escaping. Mother was a strict and rather impatient teacher, as well as a disciplinarian. It did not take me long to catch up with the other children, and soon I began to receive good grades. But Mother never relaxed her vigilance; she made me do my homework before I could go out to play. And I never had the nerve to disobey.

I enjoyed school, except for two subjects which I disliked intensely. One was calligraphy, and the other morals. Until the postwar educational reform, both subjects were required in grammar school as well as in middle school. Good handwriting is considered a sign of education and culture in our country. Quite unlike the symmetrical regularity of handwriting common to American copybooks, calligraphy is an art acquired only by many hours of practice with brush and India ink. First you must learn to sit properly—in an erect and unchanging position. Then you pour a few drops of water in the inkstone on the right-hand side of the desk. Bending your wrist back and forth with an even motion you rub the ink stick on the stone. The ink must be quite dark; a grayish shade is permissible only in writing letters of condolence. The brush must be held properly before it is dipped in the well of black ink. With the left hand placed on the desk in front of you, you write, slowly moving the whole right arm. You must not refill the brush while in the midst of writing a character. There is a definite line of motion in writing every character, not to be interrupted nor changed.

It was not difficult for me to concentrate on arithmetic, but I was frustrated watching my hand draw a character which I knew did not look right and which I was unable to perfect. This clumsiness I never had the patience to overcome. I always felt that my time could be better spent on something else.

Perhaps the American Education Mission, when it recommended that calligraphy be eliminated from the grammar-school curriculum, reasoned that in the atomic age more time should be spent in teaching the rules of science and logical reasoning than mental calm and patience. Twenty years from now I will not be so ashamed of my bad handwriting as I am today, because the next generation will not be trained in this art. Yet I know I shall miss something when that day comes. Is it sentimentalism? I don't believe so. As much as I value rational thinking, I do not think that rationality and aestheticism are mutually exclusive. But perhaps one has to be sacrificed for the time being in order to emphasize the importance of the other.

Morals was also important to the school curriculum in prewar days. Loyalty to the Emperor, filial piety, and other virtues were taught in this class. I remember how confused I was by the stories in the textbook on morals; they sounded so anachronistic. There is the famous story of Ninomiya Sontoku, which every child in Japan read to learn the virtues of diligence and perseverance. Sontoku was born in extreme poverty, the eldest of many children. He got up earlier than anyone else in the family and kindled the fire under a kettle of rice every morning. With the light of this fire Sontoku studied. Every day he went to gather wood from the mountain to help the family. While he was walking to and from the mountain he read his books. By studying every minute of the day, he became a great scholar, despite his poor background. A statue of a ten-year-old boy with a big bundle of wood on his back, holding a book with both hands, was a common sight in many schoolyards—to remind the children what they could be if they tried.

As example of a good wife there is another story. Yamanouchi Kazutoyo was a poor samurai, so his wife took sewing jobs at night after he had gone to bed. She saved her earnings in secrecy in a small narrow drawer in a wooden charcoal brazier. A war started between Kazutoyo's feudal lord and some other lord. Being a samurai, Kazutoyo was obliged to fight for his lord, but he was too poor to buy a horse, which he wanted. At this crucial moment his wife presented him with the money which she had saved and enabled him to go to war on a horse.

To me these stories had no reality, idealism or imagination. My confusion found expression when I said to Mother one day: "Mother, I don't think I am poor enough to have virtues." I did not understand, moreover, why Kazutoyo's wife saved money in secrecy. At our home Mother always discussed financial problems with Father. To my remark Mother only smiled, and suggested a great deal of outside reading, which I realize now played an important part in shaping my thinking.

From the fourth grade on I read more than children's stories. I was particularly interested in translations of foreign books. I wept through *Uncle Tom's Cabin*, and when its movie version came to Japan, Mother took the three of us to see it.

Mother herself translated many works by Charles Dickens. I read *Nicholas Nickleby* and Eliot's *Silas Marner*. But perhaps Victor Hugo's *Les Misérables* made a deeper impression on me than any other book during this period. I tackled it in full when I was in the sixth grade. I cannot say that I understood it all, but it opened my eyes to problems and attitudes which could not be found in our textbooks on morals. It was not diligence and perseverance alone which made men learned and resulted in a better society. It would be much better if children of Sontoku's ability were given a proper opportunity to study despite their poverty. Mother took us to see the movie of *Les Misérables*, too, when it came to Osaka.

I never tired of reading, especially detective stories, although Mother several times objected. I read all of Sherlock Holmes, and many of Poe's mysteries.

In Japan the 1920's were called the era of liberalism and democracy. But remembering those free and comfortable days of my childhood in Osaka, I recall uncomfortably something which does not fit into the picture.

There were two popular games which we played almost every day at the Lark-Hill School. One was called Destroyer and Submarine. The game was played by two teams. Each team had a head who was called the battleship. The other members of the team were divided into equal numbers of destroyers and submarines. The destroyer could kill the enemy submarine; the submarine could kill the battleship; the battleship could kill the destroyer. The object of the game was to get the enemy battleship. If this game were as popular in postwar Japan as in those days, I am sure Western anthropologists could call it a militaristic remnant, since they say that all social phenomena are indicative of something basic to the thinking of a people.

In the other game a child bounced a rubber ball to the accompaniment of a song. The object was to see who could bounce the ball for the longest time without a break. Instead of counting one, two, three, and so forth, we sang. The song was made to rhyme with the numbers one to ten. It went something like this:

> The negotiation broke down,
> And the Russo-Japanese War began.
> The Russian soldiers ran away fast;
> The Japanese soldiers fought until their death.
> Fifty thousand enemies were attacked;
> Except six, all were killed.
> In the battle of July eighth
> We went as far as Harbin
> And took the head of Kropotkin.
> Big Banzai to Admiral Togo.

Obviously this song originated after the Russo-Japanese War of 1904-05. It is amazing that its popularity had not waned during the following two decades. I am sure we sang it not because we liked the words, but because it rhymed nicely. As far as I was concerned —and I feel certain that most of my friends felt the same way—the song had no meaning. Undoubtedly the Western anthropologists would have something to say about this too.

It was Mother's idea to send us to a Sunday School conducted by the American missionary who was teaching us English. The class was held at her house and more than a dozen children went regularly. We heard the stories of Jesus and learned to sing hymns—some of them in English. "Jesus loves me this I know" was the first hymn I remember. At first I thought the stories of Jesus were American fairy tales. America was the only Western country which had any reality in my mind, and since Christianity was a Western religion, I linked the two together. It was a shock when I discovered that Jesus was a historical character and a Jew, not an American.

[23]

As I was going through some old copies of *Fujin-no-tomo* recently, I came across an article written by Mother entitled "Children's Prayers," in which she mentioned her daughters' first prayers.

"Reiko's first prayer," Mother wrote, "was 'God, please make us rich.'" Mother explained that it was probably because our neighbors on Skylark Hill were all of the upper class that Reiko—then five— felt conspicuously different.

Kwoko prayed: "God, I'd like to know what you look like. Please let me see you." "This child," Mother remarked, "has always been more interested in natural sciences than any other subject at school."

"Yoko, on the other hand," Mother continued, "prayed: 'God, I am grateful for this food and for thy protection.' Yoko never forgets to thank God for all the things she has. She is a gentle child."

This remark brought back something that has been lost, and it hurt me as though Mother had touched an old wound. I was considered "gentle and kind" in those days. This was before circumstances forced me to be on my own and pushed me into competition with others. It is more than nostalgia I feel about these words.

5 ~

IT WAS when I was in the third grade of the Lark-Hill School that Father invited Viscount and Viscountess Nambu to a mushroom hunt. The suburb of Osaka is known for *matsutake*, or pine mushrooms, which grow only under a certain kind of pine tree. The ancestors of the Viscount had been the feudal lords to whom the generations of Matsuokas were subject. Father referred to the Nambus as *tonosama*, "my lord," and *okusama*, "my lady," and not as viscount and viscountess, the titles given them after the Meiji Restoration.

To a child born in the Taisho era (1912-26), the word *tonosama* connoted only one thing—a man wearing an old feudal costume with a crown which looked like a black teapot, and two swords on his side, just as pictured in storybooks. *Tonosama* was something which belonged to the remote past. Therefore, when I went to the near-by streetcar station with Father to welcome the *Tonosama* and the *Okusama,* I expected to see them in such a costume. I was astounded to find the *Tonosama* in a dark blue Western suit and the *Okusama* in a regular Japanese silk kimono. After I was introduced, I ran back to the house and excitedly reported, "Mother, they are not different from any of us!"

It struck me as very strange that Father and Mother treated the Nambus, who looked like ordinary human beings, with such deference as I had never seen before. The Viscount and Viscountess responded with the polite condescension peculiar to those who were born "superior."

The Nambus and our whole family set out for a near-by mushroom mountain. The late September sun was still high in the sky when we reached a small *chaya,* or tea shop, at the entrance of the mountain forest. There we were met by a guide, a wrinkled man in farmer's attire with a large bamboo basket upon his shoulder. He led the way into the forest.

Tall red-pine trees shut out the sunlight, making the air cool and moist. Myriads of pine needles fallen to the ground gave the rich, buoyant feeling of a thick rug. The guide showed us that it was beneath this rug of pine needles that mushrooms were hidden. It was a thrill to uncover slightly damp pine needles and find soft brown mushrooms like so many small umbrellas, some folded and some opened. With a slight push by your fingers at the root, they fell on your palm.

Apparently this was the first time the Nambus had been on a mushroom hunt. There were soft but high-pitched exclamations from Viscountess Nambu, who hunted with much enthusiasm. Of course, we children were full of excitement and gathered as many mushrooms as we could in the small bamboo basket given to each of us. Mother was the slowest of all. When I teased her afterward that she was not a good mushroom hunter, she said with all seriousness: "The way you people picked, particularly the Okusama, worried me no end. I did not know whether Father had brought enough money." It had never occurred to me that we had to pay.

After the baskets were filled, the guide led us to a small picnic ground. Over a pine-needle fire, he cooked rice and broiled the mushrooms, each wrapped in a piece of dampened Japanese rice paper so that it would not be burnt. There is nothing so appetizing under a clear autumn sky as steaming white rice with fresh mushrooms tinged with the odor of burning pine needles and dipped in *shoyu* (soya bean sauce) mixed with citron juice. This must have cost Father more than he could afford, for I do not remember such an extravagant mushroom hunt any other time.

This show of deference by Father for his *Tonosama* and *Okusama* was unusual. Within his own family, he was quite consistent in advocating equality, even at the risk of conflict with the conventions of Japanese society. He never expected that he should be the first to bathe, or that Mother should stay up until he returned in the evening, although these are still commonly accepted customs. Whenever we had guests for dinner (and they were usually Father's guests), Mother and we children always ate with them. We were served just as many dishes as Father and the guests. In many Japanese families, the wife only serves the meal and never appears at the same table with guests. In rural areas, and to some extent in urban homes, women and children eat in the kitchen while the men entertain themselves in the best room of the house. My parents considered it a part of our education to eat and talk with their guests. At least, we learned not to be shy with people because they were older or because they were men.

One of the many guests Father brought home for dinner was Hitomi-*san*. She was a young woman in her early twenties. When she first visited us, she wore, like a country high-school girl, a short black serge skirt and a middy blouse, which she had outgrown, and her long black hair was twisted into a knot in the back. It was hard to believe that this was the famous Olympic champion, the first Japanese woman to take part in those games. Her height—five feet six or seven—was unusual for a Japanese woman. Her well-developed muscles and her long, narrow face reminded you of a good race horse.

The *Mainichi* had hired her as a sportswriter, and that was how my father came to know her.

She received an ovation perhaps unknown to any other woman in Japan when she returned from Holland in 1928. Immediately afterward, the *Mainichi* sponsored a meeting where she spoke of her experiences and showed a moving picture of the Olympic games. Our whole family attended. The most impressive scene to me was when the national flags were hoisted and the national anthems sung at the conclusion of each race. I think it was in the 100 meters that Hitomi-*san* came in second. As I saw the rising-sun flag slowly lifted on the second mast, I felt a lump in my throat. This was the first time the sight of our flag had moved me.

Hitomi-*san* often visited us while we were living in Skylark Hill in Osaka. We children always wanted to stay up later than our bedtime when she came. Knowing well how we felt, and how Mother felt about our bedtime, she would come up to our room and tell us stories as we went to sleep. She was completely untouched by her fame, and I admired her greatly. My ambition in life for the following few years was to become an Olympic champion.

KOREA

6 ~

I REMEMBER there was much discussion between my parents as to whether or not they should take us children to Korea. My father's appointment as vice-president of the *Keijo Nippo*, the Japanese Government-sponsored newspaper in Seoul, was made with the understanding that he would return to Japan proper within three or four years at the most.

We were all in the Lark-Hill School at that time, and Mother was sure she could not find a better educational institution for us in Seoul. Somehow Korea seemed such a remote and backward place. Kwoko and I dreaded the thought of going there. Furthermore, we thought it would be enterprising to be left alone with our aunt, Mother's eldest sister, and a maid.

Finally, however, it was decided that the whole family was to move to Seoul. Father insisted that it was more educational for the children to travel and to see a different country even if the school there might be inferior. I suspect that beneath this reasoning lay his wish to have us around for more wrestling bouts, while Mother was more concerned about what might happen to our discipline and behavior if we were left alone. At any rate I am glad we went to Korea, for the experiences there served to widen my outlook, particularly when Japan's turn came to be occupied.

The trip to Seoul, which took thirty-six hours from Osaka, was exciting. This was the first time we had traveled first class. We had been accustomed to take second, but perhaps the prestige of my father's position in Korea demanded that we travel in style. The conductors and porters seemed exceptionally polite, and even to a child of eleven this noticeable difference in service was pleasing.

At every station where the train stopped, we saw a number of

[31]

policemen and railroad officials standing at attention. This was a performance reserved for members of the Imperial Family, cabinet ministers or men of similar rank when they traveled. We learned from the porter that a Korean prince, apparently going back to Seoul for his vacation, was occupying the next compartment.

When Japan annexed Korea in 1910, the members of the Korean royal family were brought to Japan and were likewise "annexed" into the Japanese Imperial Family. In fact Prince Yi, the would-be heir to the throne in Korea if the power situation in Asia had taken a different course, married the prettiest of all eligible Japanese princesses.

A few years later Father was invited by Prince Yi to his palace in Tokyo. As they walked about the grounds, he commented on the exceptional beauty of the garden. To this the Prince replied, "After all I traded a country for it." Father was rather surprised at this cynical but candid comment, and when he reported it to us he weighed every word as though he wanted us to remember it.

This young prince on our train was related to Prince Yi. Kwoko, Reiko and I had never seen a prince before. Since we were told by Mother that we should not talk to royalty, and it was impolite to peek, we went out into the narrow corridor outside our compartment to play and ran back and forth in front of the prince's stateroom, hoping that he would come out. To our astonishment he did not wear the robe and crown which princes wore in fairy tales or in pictures we had seen. Unlike other high-school students in Japan, who always wear student uniforms except when they have on a cotton kimono, he wore a regular Western-style suit. We could see that the prince was completely bored by a stuffy-looking chamberlain, who followed him everywhere, but he was not free to talk to us, nor we to him.

When we went into the diner, the prince and his chamberlain sat at the next table, and I took every chance to observe him. In the first-class diner the food was cooked only in Western style. (In the diner where the second- and third-class passengers were served, one had a choice of Japanese or Western cooking.) Soup was served in a big dish. We had been taught at home to eat with knives, forks and spoons. So we proceeded with a big soup spoon, tipping the

[32]

dish slightly in the proper direction. I looked out of the corner of my eye to see how the prince was doing. He was not only handling his spoon in the wrong way but eating with a loud "slurping" sound. To make a slurping noise is the proper thing to do when eating Japanese noodles and soup. That is the way to show one's appreciation of the food. Some people say you don't know the real taste of noodles unless you slurp them down without chewing the noodles. However, it was disillusioning to discover that a prince did not know the European etiquette of eating. I looked at Kwoko, and our eyes met with a smile.

7 ~

KOREA SEEMED very foreign—with a different language, a different dress, and different scenery. The white costumes worn by the men and women appeared particularly strange, for, as mentioned earlier, it is only the dead who wear white in Japan. Here the women carried heavy loads—often such breakable objects as jars—on their heads. They balanced the load with a unique hip movement, making the long white skirt wrapped around the body wave in irregular lines when they walked. And when one arm was stretched upward to support the bundle, you could see where the short white blouse went up to uncover the lower part of the breast.

It seemed Korean women invariably had good posture owing to this custom of carrying things on their heads. The women parted their straight black hair in the middle, and wore it pomaded and tied in a knot at the back with only one big pin, usually made of some kind of metal. Girls also wore theirs parted in the middle, but in pigtails. Even when many Japanese women began to have permanent waves, most Koreans preserved this orthodox style. The men wore trousers, tied at the ankle, and a white blouse cut in the same way as the women's. Their winter dress was thickly padded. The rubber shoes, which looked like ballet slippers, came off easily, for Koreans, like the Japanese, remove their shoes when they enter a house.

From the port of Pusan we motored to a near-by hot spring, where we spent a day resting. The hotel was a regular Japanese inn with a Kyoto-style garden—pines, stones and pagodas arranged in orthodox fashion. It was just like Japan—sitting on the *tatami* floor, eating slices of delicate raw fish served by Japanese maids. Somehow a Japanese dinner is not complete without raw fish—usually the tunny—and even the mountainside inns include it among the other dishes. I imagine even geisha were available. All the best hotels in Korea were owned and operated by Japanese for Japanese guests.

From Pusan to Seoul the expanse of bare mountains and miles of irregular line of paddy fields were a contrast to the tree-thick green mountains and hills and rolls of rectangular paddies we knew in Japan. Father told us that the Koreans cut the trees from the mountains for their fuel faster than the government could plant them.

Whenever the train passed rivers or streams, we invariably saw Korean women washing. They sat beside the water, placing the white cloth on a rock and pounding it with a wooden club. They used no soap. Like the Japanese kimono, the Korean costume is ripped apart when washed, spread on the grass to dry, and then sewed together again. No clothesline is used since the theory is that clothes bleach better on the green grass.

At one station before we reached Seoul, my father's secretary, a Korean wearing European clothes and speaking perfect Japanese, came to the train to welcome us. Mr. Ryu was extremely polite and made a bow in excellent Japanese style. He took care of our baggage, so the only thing we had to do when we arrived in Seoul was to behave like well-disciplined children.

Seoul, the capital of Korea, was surrounded by a stone wall similar to the Great Wall in North China. In ancient times this protected the city from probable enemy invasions. The wall had collapsed in places, but one could still observe a line of beige on the summit of North Mountain beyond the white marble Government Building. The four large stone gates to the south, north, east and west were originally the only entrances to the city, and their heavy wooden doors used to close every evening. The West Gate had been destroyed, but the others still stood magnificently to tell the story of workmanship more than five hundred years ago.

8 ~

THE *NANDAIMON* primary school was named after the famous Great South Gate, located nearby. This was a public school for Japanese children. In Korea segregation was maintained in education except at the university level. Mother has told me that the Japanese parents had to pay very heavy school fees, whereas public schools for Korean children were free. All the subjects in both schools were taught in the Japanese language, and if I remember correctly the Korean children were not permitted to use the Korean langauage in school.

I feel sure that the logic of colonial policy demanded the teaching of the same subjects to the Korean children as to the Japanese, and that they were taught to respect and revere the Japanese national polity. It was only recently I learned from an article in *The New Yorker* concerning the first woman member of the Syngman Rhee cabinet in South Korea that this was probably centered around the idea of "Emperor worship." She said that her first arrest by the Japanese police was for poking holes in the eyes of a photograph of the Japanese Emperor. To a Korean he apparently symbolized Japanese tyranny.

There were no private schools for Japanese children in Seoul, and since the Great South Gate School was nearest to where we lived, all three of us went there. It happened that the children of those who held high positions were enrolled there, too. Among my fifty classmates were a daughter of the president of the Chosen Railroad (which was owned and operated by the Japanese Government), a daughter of the governor of the Seoul area, and a daughter of the director of the Oriental Development Company (a semigovernmental corporation which, I later learned, invested heavily in real estate and virtually monopolized the good farmland in Korea).

Although coeducation existed in public grammar schools, boys and girls were usually separated into different home rooms, and so my classmates were all girls. When there were not enough pupils to have

[35]

two classes, the boys sat on one side of the room and the girls on the other. Since boys and girls never played together, it was not strange that I did not come to know a single boy at the Great South Gate School.

I was surprised to discover that the children acted according to their father's rank. Ohmura-*san*, the daughter of the president of the Chosen Railway, assumed an air of leadership not only because she received the highest marks, but because she lived in the third largest official residence in Korea, next to the vice–governor general's. The girls whose fathers held important positions in the government or were rich businessmen followed her around. I, too, could have belonged to this upper class. But as I began to compete for the highest marks with Ohmura-*san*, the spirit of rivalry grew between us, and my pride did not let me remain in a subordinate position. I soon found myself the leader of another group of girls whose fathers were either low-class officials, poor merchants or rickshaw men. During the noon recess hour these two groups fought bitterly in the Destroyer and Submarine game. Needless to add, Ohmura-*san* was the battleship of one team and I the battleship of the other.

I felt this competition keenly, and I was aware that Ohmura-*san* took it just as seriously. Our home-room teacher must have been conscious of so open a feud, but he pretended not to know. I can now understand why he pursued this hands-off policy. Like other low-rank government employees, he was at the mercy of the ruling class. Although neither Ohmura-*san*'s father nor mine would have been outraged by any discipline the teacher may have felt compelled to exercise, if that was what their children deserved, apparently experience had taught him not only to be discreet but to flatter the upper-class children by giving them high marks. I thought then that we were smarter than other children, but I feel certain now that the teacher was liberal about our grades.

Once a year the governor general or the vice-governor general inspected the schools. The day before this annual inspection the pupils scrubbed and dusted the school building with particular care, and the teacher told us again and again how to behave. One year Vice-Governor General Ikegami and his party of officials came to inspect our school. As they entered the classroom, led by the principal, the home-room teacher shouted, *"Kiotsuke!"* or "Attention!" We all stood erect in a soldierlike manner without cracking a smile. At the proper moment the teacher again shouted, "Bow!" and we all bowed. Then he told us to sit down and continue doing whatever we had been doing.

The vice–governor general was a chubby man with a big beer stomach and wore narrow gray trousers that accentuated his figure. His face was red—from too much drinking, I presume—and not a bit handsome. When he entered Reiko's room, a mixed class, one boy snickered at the sight of him, starting off two others. At this improper and discourteous behavior the color faded from the teacher's face, and he stood speechless with shame. After the official party left the school, this instructor handed in his resignation. It was the only possible apology for such a show of disrespect.

A week later the whole school assembled in the auditorium to hear his farewell speech, in which he said that he regretted his failure as a teacher. When he had finished, only the sobs of his former pupils were heard in the large barren room. I felt very sorry for the unfortunate man, but I was then too much a part of this whole social structure to be able to feel indignant toward such a sense of values. My sisters and I were relieved to learn later that he was able to find a place in one of the schools for Korean children. His position was definitely lowered by this transfer, but at least he did not have to starve. I hate now to think how rigorously he must have trained his Korean pupils not to repeat the same "mistake."

In the north corner of the schoolyard was a cement structure about four or five feet high with an iron door in front. The roof slanted in such a way as to suggest a Shinto shrine. This was the place where the photographs of the Emperor and the Empress were enshrined. These photographs were called *go-shinei* or the "honorable true image." All public schools were required by the Ministry of Education to have the *go-shinei*, while private schools could have them upon request. The photographs were considered sacred as they were the "true image" of the Emperor, who was "sacred and inviolable" according to the Constitution. They were kept in a fireproof building, to be taken out only on special occasions. And we were to bow respectfully every time we passed by this "shrine."

The Ministry of Education required all schools to hold ceremonies on national holidays, when the *go-shinei* was taken out of the cement hut with the utmost care and placed in the auditorium. New Year's Day, Birth of the Nation Day (February 11), the Emperor's birthday and the birthday of the Meiji Emperor were the four most important national holidays. The children dressed in their "Sunday clothes," women teachers in formal kimonos bearing their family crests, and men teachers in striped trousers and morning coats. On the stage in every school auditorium was a shelflike affair which usually had maroon colored draperies in front. The *go-shinei* was placed here during the ceremony. The climax came when the principal with his white-gloved hand would pull the cord attached to the draperies to unveil the sacred photographs before which we were to bow at an angle of more than ninety degrees.

Another important part of the ceremony was the reading by the principal of the Imperial Rescript on Education, the basis for formal education in Japan issued by the Emperor Meiji in 1890. The rescript prescribed loyalty to the Emperor, and filial piety and conformity to the traditions of the past as the foundation of education. As all these were "sacred" words, we bowed our heads in prayerlike fashion during the reading.

I still remember one chilly afternoon when the whole student body at the Great South Gate School stood in the schoolyard rehearsing for the reception of the new photographs of the Emperor and the Empress. We lined up from the school gate to the main entrance of the building in so many neat rows. The "honorable true image" was to be brought from the Government Building in an automobile, accompanied by Japanese government officials. We were told that it was not necessary to bow at a ninety-degree angle as we did during the ceremonies; this time we were to bow at forty-five degrees, our faces turned toward the automobile as it entered the gate and following it in that position from the gate to the main entrance. It was the duty of the gym teacher to give the orders.

"Attention!" he screeched.

Silence fell on the air and we stood like so many tin soldiers. Since the school could not afford to hire an automobile for rehearsal, the principal came in at this point through the gate on a bicycle traveling at approximately the same speed one would expect from the automobile the following day.

The next order came: "Bow!"

A thousand small black heads plunged at forty-five degrees with two thousand brown eyes intently following our principal, puffing along on his old bicycle, until he reached the entrance. This was repeated over and over again until he was assured that his pupils would behave with due respect and without an "incident."

9 ~

THE JAPANESE in Korea lived in a society of their own. True, there were Koreans working in my father's newspaper office, and Father invited them to our house for dinner just as he invited the Japanese men who worked under him. But they were never family friends; rather they were Father's business acquaintances. Our neighbors were Koreans, but we children never played outside the high wall which surrounded our house. The only Koreans I came to know well were our Korean maid, whom we called *omoni* (meaning "mother" in Korean but used by the Japanese when addressing their Korean maids), and her son, our houseboy, whom we called *chonga* (meaning "unmarried man").

All the large stores were under Japanese control, and we normally went to them for shopping, since they were located in the center of the town and were also much cleaner than the Korean shops. Better hotels and restaurants were frequented more by the Japanese than the Koreans, not because there was any official segregation, but perhaps because most Koreans did not have the means nor the desire to patronize them. As far as I remember, there was no official policy of segregation in public places such as streetcars, trains, parks, beaches, ball stadia and theaters. Except for a very few unusual individuals, however, the Japanese and the Koreans lived in two separate worlds although side by side.

Segregation was maintained, even in Christian churches, not by law but by custom. This did not seem particularly extraordinary to

[39]

me, a child, since the rest of society was that way. But I remember how it appalled Mother when we first arrived in Seoul. She said, "After all, we worship the same God, and the church is the place of worship." Had I been older, I might have questioned: "Then why do you go to the same Japanese church every Sunday and send us to its Sunday School?"

When I try to piece together bits of life in Korea from memory, I think Mother did try to break the pattern of that society. Unfortunately, her efforts were drowned by much larger tides of circumstances than I at that time could be aware of.

One day Mother took us to visit a Korean girls' mission school. The only thing I remember about that occasion is that we were chased out of the school by the students as soon as we entered the compound. At another time she took us to a rummage sale held by the Korean YWCA. The silent hostility expressed by the women was so frightening that we got out of the building as quickly as possible. These episodes aroused my indignation. After all, it was so obvious that we wanted to be friendly. And yet these Koreans did not have the grace even to be polite. I refused to call them Christians and came to believe that "the Korean Christians were the most anti-Japanese element" as the "old Korea hands" kept saying.

Since then I have learned that people are not born hateful, fearful, ungracious or unchristian. Their attitudes are molded according to what they hear, what they see and what they experience. I realize now that there was ample reason for the Koreans to feel hostile toward the Japanese. On the other hand, I cannot deny the sincerity and good intentions of people such as Mother in trying to meet the problem. The hatred of the Koreans toward the Japanese is understandable, but their crude expression of it only confused the sincere Japanese as to the real cause of the problem, which was the Japanese rule itself.

American missionaries, too, were divided into two groups—one serving the Japanese Christians and the other the Korean Christians. Those working with the Koreans refused to do anything for the Japanese.

Mother wanted us to learn English while we were still children. She was particularly concerned that I should not lose all I had learned at the Lark-Hill School. Although she herself could teach, she insisted on getting an English-speaking person for us and decided to ask one of the American missionaries working for the Koreans.

The thought of taking private lessons from an American was rather exciting and I had looked forward to it. So it was a bitter disappointment when Mother told me: "She says she cannot teach you because her service here is for the Koreans and not for the Japanese." Although puzzled, Mother kept telling me, "You know she is really a good person." Nevertheless, from that moment on I held a prejudice against all American missionaries working for the Koreans. It lent credence to the belief that American missionaries were partly responsible for the anti-Japanese sentiment of the Korean Christians.

Several months later Mother discovered why this missionary refused to associate with the Japanese. Mother and a few other English-speaking Japanese in Seoul had started a Japanese-language school for the foreign residents there. The school was held in the evenings in the Japanese Methodist Church and many missionaries working for Koreans, including the one who refused to teach me, attended. As Mother told it to me: "They were very cordial and even friendly at the language school. But whenever I met them on the streets they were invariably cold—almost impolitely so. One day I took the courage to ask that missionary why they behaved in such a way. She was frank enough to tell me that if they befriended the Japanese, the Koreans would immediately think of them as Japanese spies and this would alienate them. She added that they had to be careful even in attending the language school lest they should be looked upon with suspicion by the Koreans."

As Mother told her story, her eyes fixed somewhere far away, I remained unconvinced, insisting that a missionary ought to be more "Christianlike."

10 ~

WHEN WE first arrived in Seoul, the Japanese who were "old Korea hands" told Mother that Korean maids ate so much it would be best to limit their bowls of rice. Moreover, they added, it would be unwise to spoil them with good food, since this would make them unhappy when they returned home. Accordingly, many Japanese gave their servants only rice and *kimchi*, the normal Korean diet.

Kimchi is the Korean national dish made of Chinese cabbage, scallions, red pepper, garlic, and dried fish, chestnuts or other ingredients added according to taste, pickled together with salt water in a big jar. Just before the cold weather sets in, the Korean housewife makes a year's supply for the whole family. The dark brown jars about three feet high which stand in front of the mud huts contain this main dish, and the wealth of the family can be counted by the number of *kimchi* jars which surround the house. The unique odor of Korea, which can be rather nauseating to one not accustomed to garlic, is produced in these jars.

Mother did not approve of the idea of giving different food to the maids and insisted that everybody in the family eat the same. Anything that would not go around she divided among us children. This was an unusual practice even in Japan proper. In many Japanese families the father is served the best food the family can afford; the mother and children eat more simply, and the maids most simply.

We were also told that the Koreans could not be trusted; that they stole anything if given the slightest chance. One Japanese kindly suggested to Mother that it would be wise to test the maid's honesty during the first few days of her employment. He said with an air of authority: "Leave some money here and there in the room where she is to clean. If she does not steal it, then it is all right to hire her. But you must continue this for at least a week or so, for some of them already know the trick. It is much better to do it this way than later have to turn her over to the police."

Although Mother thanked him politely for his advice, she never did try this ruse on our Korean maid. Her comment afterward was: "How can you do that to anybody!" Although we could trust our *omoni* and *chonga* completely, we had to be constantly on our guard against others. The doors were locked at all times, washing watched on the line, and pocketbooks held tightly in public places —something we never had to do in Tokyo or Osaka. The Japanese proverb, "Always think of a stranger as a thief," seemed to be substantiated in this colony of ours.

Even to a child the Koreans seemed dirty and unsanitary. They pushed and pulled to get on the streetcar, spat indiscriminately, blew their noses with their hands in public places, and urinated everywhere. Many of them had ideas of a prescientific age, particularly in regard to medicine. Dysentery, typhoid and smallpox were common. As they were afraid of doctors, and hospitals represented the place to die, these contagious diseases spread rapidly everywhere. Whenever there was an epidemic, the Government sent health officers to various street corners and gave free inoculations to everybody who passed by. But many Koreans feared them and tried to avoid those corners as much as possible.

During an epidemic of smallpox, our *omoni* and *chonga* refused to go to the hospital to be vaccinated. I remember our otherwise quiet *omoni* wailing to Mother, "Ma'am, inoculation—I am frightened." Mother finally decided to ask the doctor to come to our house, and in front of our *omoni* and *chonga* she and we children received the vaccination. Still fearful, but reluctantly convinced that it was not going to kill them, the maid and her son finally submitted. Theirs "took" so well that I can't help but wonder what the consequences would have been if they had refused.

That is why when "old Korea hands" insisted that "Koreans are untrustworthy and ignorant and therefore must be kept in their proper place," I soon grew to accept such statements without question. I became convinced of the inherent inferiority of the Korean people and took pride in the high principles and superior knowledge of the Japanese—"We wouldn't do that, would we?"—I would still believe all this if my faith had not been shattered by the behavior of our own people in postwar Japan.

I I ~

FOR MANY Japanese life in Korea was easy and comfortable compared to what they had known in their homeland. Government officials were provided with residences which rented at low rates. Those who could afford only one maid in Japan had two in Korea. Some wives of high officials used government automobiles for their private travel, but nobody complained. I suppose I also would have taken that sort of thing for granted if my father had not been so strict about what was official and what was not. For example, even when there was ample room in his automobile, he never let us ride with him to the baseball games sponsored by the *Keijo Nippo*. We three sisters always took trams.

Even the lowest and poorest Japanese had millions of lower and poorer people to look down upon here, and that no doubt sustained their superiority. Perhaps these incentives were necessary to induce Japanese to live in Korea, for it was a dirty, cold and remote place where they could so easily be forgotten by the "proper" people in Tokyo.

The Japanese colony, which was concentrated mostly in Seoul, moved strictly according to protocol. The personalities of the governor general and the vice–governor general had a great deal to do in making the rest of us feel comfortable or uncomfortable within that limited framework.

Admiral the Viscount Saito, who was the governor general when we first arrived in 1927, represented the cultured and liberal school of the Japanese Imperial Navy. He and the Viscountess both understood English. I have the impression that both were respected and liked by many in Korea, including the foreign residents. If this cultured admiral had any defect, it was his calligraphy. Even I could tell that he was not very skillful with the brush and ink. His writing lacked the strength of an artist and suggested a dignified but amiable fat man who did not have enough exercise. As a matter of fact, that was just the way he looked.

I am sure it was the liberal attitude of the Saitos which induced Mother to take us along when she paid courtesy calls at the governor general's residence. The children in an autocratic society do not count socially unless they happen to be chosen as playmates for the offspring of those in authority. Since neither the Saitos nor the Kodamas, the vice–governor general and his wife, had any children, it was most unusual for us to accompany Mother on those visits. Mother took us, I think, partly for our education and partly because our presence would provide her with subjects for conversation—such as our schooling and what we wanted to be when we grew up. She was never skillful at the art of social chitchat. Whatever her purpose was, we looked forward to those visits, which occurred only once or twice a year, because the Saitos and the Kodamas always gave us beautiful presents such as crystal necklaces and leather handbags. But after they left Seoul, this practice of taking us along was not continued.

General Yamanashi and General Ugaki, who succeeded Viscount Saito, were more Spartan in their approach. Like the Saitos, they, too, honored the nonofficial Japanese residents of Seoul by attending the Christmas party—the most important social event of the year—sponsored by the Rotary Club, of which Father was an active member. But somehow their khaki uniforms and leather boots and dangling swords did not harmonize with the spirit of the party as the Viscount's well-fitted plain navy uniform.

Nor did the new vice-governor general, Ikegami, fit into the formal but friendly atmosphere created by the Saitos and the Kodamas. Unlike the polite, polished and suave-mannered Count Kodama, Mr. Ikegami was uncouth and exorbitantly proud of anything Japanese. In fact, it was after his visit to the Great South Gate Primary School that Reiko's teacher resigned.

Mother's habit of wearing Western dresses apparently displeased His Excellency, for he told Father it was a disgrace and that Mother should be wearing kimonos. However, Mother never yielded to this fancy, and Father stuck by his stubborn wife. Perhaps this was an expression of their protest against a ruthless and rigid society. When I realize how inconsequential this sort of resistance was, in proportion to the risk involved—for it could have resulted in Father's discharge —I become acutely aware of the immense power which the rulers exercised under such a social system.

12 ~

FOR JAPANESE children the entrance to middle school was an important step toward adolescence. Compulsory education ended with completion of the primary school's six grades, and the five-year middle school represented the first hurdle before reaching that bottle-neck of the elite, the university. For those who could afford higher education, the last half of the sixth grade was spent in preparation for the entrance examination to middle school. Most of those who did not enter middle school went to a business school.

Formal education ended with the middle school for most girls, who then prepared themselves for marriage by learning the art of flower arrangement, the tea ceremony, sewing and cooking. Thus the choice of a secondary school was as important as the choice of a college would be in America.

For me the decision had been reached even before I entered grammar school when my aunt, Mrs. Hani, started a middle school and junior college for girls in Tokyo in 1921. Attending this school would mean living away from home, but in my mind its prestige was a more important consideration. Moreover, I wanted to get away from the uncomfortable competition and favoritism at the Great South Gate Grammar School, and I knew that if I went to one of the two middle schools for girls in Seoul, the same atmosphere would prevail. Therefore, with mixed feelings of relief and superiority, I told my homeroom teacher and my classmates that I was going away to school in Tokyo.

However, the distance from Seoul to Tokyo—two days and two nights—suddenly loomed very large, and I began to feel apprehensive at the idea of being completely on my own. I sought strength in religion and decided to be baptized. This was the first big decision in my life which I made all by myself. Mother was happy that I chose this path, and Father, I guessed, was glad that I made up my own mind.

I left for Tokyo in March 1929 to enter Jiyu-Gakuen, or the School of Freedom.

SCHOOL OF FREEDOM

13 ~

FATHER ACCOMPANIED me to Tokyo and delivered me with my suitcases to the Hanis. Although a dormitory room was available, Aunt Hani wanted me to stay with her family. My aunt's first comment was: "My dear, you have acquired that peculiar continental complexion, tannish-yellow without much luster. It's been only two years since you went to Seoul, has it not?" I had not noticed this change, but perhaps the drier and colder climate of Korea had brought it about. From my aunt, who does not know how to flatter others, this was a hearty welcome.

Aunt Hani always took an interest in me—more so perhaps than in my two sisters—and wanted to educate me. Perhaps it was because she never saw eye to eye with my father that she wanted me to be like her rather than like him. Or perhaps the fact that I look more like her than either of her daughters contributed to her liking me.

I resented being told that I looked like Motoko Hani (although I wanted people to say I resembled Father, who had many of her features), for I considered my aunt one of the most insignificant-looking women I knew. Less than five feet, she is small even for a Japanese. I, being five feet three inches, am taller than the average.

Aunt Hani does not have the delicate fragility which often characterizes a tiny person. Her high cheekbones, round cheeks and rather high forehead, now wrinkled like a dried prune, and the determined way she walks, suggest a farmer who would plant and harvest regardless of the weather.

She is a little deaf in one ear and her failing eyesight makes her peer at you with one eye closed, as though she were looking through an old microscope. Her eyes do not have that look of seeing-through-you which is characteristic of many brilliant people. Rather, they

[49]

often appear puzzled and surprised. If she were wearing a cotton kimono and a pair of *mompe,* you might almost think her illiterate.

Sometimes she takes advantage of her appearance. I can still hear her joyful chuckle when she reported: "In a streetcar coming home today I sat next to a young man who started to smoke. When I noticed that he looked rather wicked and defiant, I knew it would do no good to remind him of the rule. So I changed my tactic, and pointing to the 'no smoking' sign, I asked, 'What does that say?' He had to put out his cigarette before he read it to me!"

My uncle, Yoshikazu Hani, is a striking contrast to my aunt, who is six years his senior. He is as tall and handsome as a *kabuki* actor. There is something about him, however, that is dignified and unapproachable, and I have always kept at a respectful distance.

Motoko Hani was born in 1873 in Hachinohe, a small town in the northern tip of Japan. According to Father, from their childhood Aunt Hani was the most brilliant of two girls and two boys in the Matsuoka family. In her autobiography she wrote: "My hands were slower and more clumsy than the average; my mind more precise."

As a child she excelled in Japanese literature, Chinese classics, arithmetic and abacus, but sewing, calligraphy and drawing were so difficult that they were "painful" to her. Aside from her clumsiness, she attributed her inferiority in such subjects to bad teaching, which imposed "only forms and not the substance of the subject."

Apparently this gap between her superior and inferior qualities has been of great concern to her. "If the gap between the two is prominent," she wrote, "that person tends to be unbalanced. On the other hand, if one's abilities are more or less balanced, it is difficult for him to discover his characteristics. The school and the home must foster children's superior abilities, but must not discard their prominent inferior qualities which, too, must be and can be developed." The all-round person which Jiyu-Gakuen purposes to produce is undoubtedly based upon this belief.

Aunt Hani was eager for further schooling, and at the age of sixteen she went to Tokyo, accompanied by her grandfather—making part of the trip by rickshaw and sled, since the railroad had not been extended that far north in Honshu Island.

After three years of schooling and teaching in Tokyo she married, with parental consent, a man of her choice. When her marriage ended unsuccessfully, she was determined not to let her family know until she could establish herself.

If she was not to ask the aid of her friends the most easily available job was as a maid, and this she became in the home of Dr. Yayoi Yoshioka, the founder of the Tokyo Women's Medical College, from which my sister Kwoko later received her degree. Aunt Hani's dream was to write novels and she felt this experience would be profitable for such a career, but looking back upon those days, she reflected: "At first I felt heroic about becoming a maid, but I soon discovered it was excruciating."

When Dr. Yoshioka saw that Aunt Hani was no ordinary servant, she encouraged her to find other jobs. Although she soon found a teaching position, her ambition to become a writer was still uppermost in her mind. Thus she jumped at a want ad in one of the Tokyo dailies for a proofreader. But when a janitor at the newspaper office boldly told her that only a man was wanted, she left her application and letter, saying that she had been asked to deliver them. Apparently the editor was impressed by her letter and was willing to test her ability.

Aunt Hani proudly recalls that day in her book: "The editor told me that not even men could proofread so accurately." She was employed immediately. Soon she began to write feature stories, which were also praised. On her interviews she never took notes. "I had an extraordinarily good memory," she writes, "and people called me a reporter with hell-ears." Thus was born the first newspaper woman in Japan. She had established herself in only six months after her divorce.

It was at this newspaper office where she met Yoshikazu Hani, also a reporter. Together they pioneered in the field of magazine publishing and together they founded the school Jiyu-Gakuen in 1921 when Keiko, their second daughter, was ready to enter middle school.

14 ~

THE SCHOOL of Freedom was an expression of revolt against the system of formal education in Japan, which Aunt Hani believed gave out knowledge only for the sake of learning. To her the ideal education is that which can be immediately implemented in everyday life and which is based on the Christian principles as she interprets them.

"To think, to live and to pray" is the motto of Jiyu-Gakuen. My aunt has often said: "A school must not stop at being a place where knowledge is supplied. A real school must be an organization having a life of its own, where students find themselves making progress day after day in their ideals and thoughts, and where they go higher and higher by applying to practical life what they have learned."

I understood that it was to symbolize the freedom of Jiyu-Gakuen that Aunt Hani discarded the idea of a traditional boxlike school building and asked Frank Lloyd Wright, who had built the Tokyo Imperial Hotel, to design her school. From the room I shared with Keiko, I had a full view of the main building. Like the famous hotel, which since Japan's surrender has served as a billet for VIP's and high Occupation personnel, the school has a flat, low roof and lies extended on the ground in a lazy U shape like a caterpillar. After thirty years, it now looks like a worn-out California ranch house, but in 1929, when I went there as a student, the green slates still matched the meticulously cared-for lawn and contrasted brilliantly with the light walls. Among the dark wooden houses of Tokyo, the Western architecture of the whole Hani establishment with its cream-colored walls and many large windows produced the effect of something fresh and modern.

Appropriately, the entrance examination for Jiyu-Gakuen is, like its ideals and architecture, different from most middle schools. Applicants are divided into groups of not more than twelve girls, and to each group Aunt Hani herself gives three hours of written and oral examinations. Stress is put upon a composition entitled "Why I Want to Enter Jiyu-Gakuen," which is required of each student. I have

[52]

forgotten what I wrote then, but I do remember my answer to one of the questions on my written examination: "Whom do you consider to be the greatest persons in the world?" I wrote only two names— my father and Aunt Hani! This was not a joke as I did not possess such a sense of humor, and my aunt knew it. Nor was it flattery since I was naïve and honest, and my aunt knew that. Both the Hanis and my parents were astonished by my reply.

The first day of school in Japan is characterized by a ceremony in which the student body and teaching staff welcome the incoming class. At Jiyu-Gakuen, not only does Aunt Hani give a talk, but older students also make short speeches of welcome. Aunt Hani may also ask questions of the newly admitted students.

When my class of thirty girls was received, I was among those my aunt picked extemporaneously for questioning. "Yoko," she asked suddenly, "do you think Jiyu-Gakuen, the School of Freedom, has rules?"

To be singled out so abruptly before a large audience froze my mind. Obviously, "The school has no rules" would be too simple. On the other hand, it did not seem quite right to say, "The School of Freedom has rules." I could not detect what was in her mind. My face was getting increasingly hot, and without really knowing what I was saying, I answered meekly, "The School has a rule that it has no rules."

It must have sounded as though my reply was the result of keen observation and thinking, for my aunt seemed proud of the "wisdom" displayed by her thirteen-year-old niece. I never had enough courage to tell her that I really did not deserve her praise.

Most of the Jiyu-Gakuen girls at that time came from upper middle-class homes with educated parents. Tuition was higher than in most middle schools, and their parents of course agreed with Mrs. Hani's ideas of "progressive education."

Unlike most schools, Jiyu-Gakuen does not require uniforms. The reason given for uniforms in all public schools and many private institutions in Japan is that it prevents competition in clothes. The rich and the poor are therefore indistinguishable—an expression of equality rather than of uniformity. Mrs. Hani, however, decided against them, for she reasoned that individuality would be hampered by such a rule. Hence we could wear any Western dress we chose. Kimonos were not permitted. I usually wore a middie or sweater with a skirt during the winter, and a cotton dress when it was warm.

Most of us wore our hair bobbed. This was considered modern then. Only a few had pigtails, a style which was more common among students of other middle schools.

The school day began at 7:50 in the morning throughout the year. If it was not raining, the whole student body assembled on the dot in the schoolyard in front of the auditorium. There for several minutes we did our morning exercises, led by a fellow student. Jiyu-Gakuen was among the first few schools in Japan to adopt Danish gymnastics. In contrast to the more military exercises of German type, Danish gymnastics are smooth and rhythmical. Although my ambition to be an Olympic champion had dimmed slightly by this time, I enjoyed them.

At eight o'clock the first-year pupils led the procession into the auditorium. Since Christianity was inseparable from Mrs. Hani's idea of ideal education, the half hour of morning service which followed was considered an important feature of the daily life at Jiyu-Gakuen. On this occasion my aunt (and my uncle, too, sometimes) read and discussed the Bible.

Some sarcastic critics have called Mrs. Hani's belief "the Hani sect of Christianity." As far as I remember she never attended church. Rather she held Sunday services in the dormitory with her students during the school year and in her home with her family during vacations. I rarely saw her read any book other than the Bible. It seemed that her belief was based solely upon the Scriptures, interpreted in the light of her own experiences and not on her knowledge of theology or other Christian writings.

The students took part in the service. A representative from each of the eight classes, serving in rotation, sat on the platform with Mr. and Mrs. Hani, and made a short talk, perhaps giving her impression of the passage read that morning. I did not look forward to the days when I had to get up on the platform, although my turn came only once a month.

These morning services played an important role in my life. They, more than anything else, served to strengthen my faith in Christianity.

[54]

The fact that I had had no contact with other religious beliefs may have contributed to my uncritical acceptance, but perhaps it was due more to living with Aunt Hani whose unshakable faith left no room for philosophical exploration. "What is God?" He was omnipresent and omniscient, the Creator of all. And in Him alone two and two could be made more than four. It was beyond reason; it was faith. With the knowledge and experience of a thirteen-year-old, I believed this.

These morning services had another function besides the teaching of religion. This was to report how well we were keeping the schedule of "good living."

Aunt Hani believed vehemently that "good living" is the foundation of progress and the basis of a "good society." "Good living" for each individual meant first of all regular hours. Consequently, each student was obliged to follow a daily schedule. My day began at six A.M. when I arose, dressed, made my bed, cleaned my room, and had breakfast in time to be inside the school gate by seven-fifty. Classes over, I left the school before three o'clock to study for two hours. After that I had my domestic duties—since there were two maids in the Hani household, I was given only the task of keeping the entrance hall clean. Eight o'clock was bedtime.

Each student had a card which told how she spent the day. If she got up five minutes later than her schedule, she must mark it down. If she was not outside the school gate before the three o'clock bell stopped ringing, she must give herself a black mark. If her dress was not neat, if she had a hole in her sock or a button off her coat, a black mark went in the column headed "attire." The tidiness of desk and room was similarly recorded. And anything from a little sore throat to a broken arm was noted in the column under "health."

Each student handed in her card the first thing in the morning and a class representative totaled the record before the morning service. The class records, in turn, were given to the vice-president of the student government who announced them to the school. Therefore, we knew unfailingly how many students had been absent, late, less than a hundred per cent healthy, or lax in getting to bed on time the night before. Those who had black marks were obliged to stand up. An explanation might be asked for some unaccountable lapse. If the reason given sounded plausible, the student body excused the culprit.

Although there were no punishments for black marks, the knowledge that the school was watching your every step brought such a pressure that any deviation from schedule created a feeling of guilt. If one believed implicitly, this atmosphere of "good living" was not too uncomfortable, but if there was a shadow of doubt in one's mind, the discipline held little freedom.

15 ~

DURING MY first year at Jiyu-Gakuen I followed this "good living" program religiously. Even Mother's strict discipline had not had such inflexible rigidity, but as I considered my aunt among the greatest people in the world I never thought of questioning its validity.

Therefore, I was shocked to encounter emphatic opposition from Father when I tried to impose this same rigid schedule upon my family during my first summer vacation in Seoul.

Father said rather impatiently: "It is all very well to budget your own time; to divide household tasks among yourselves. But remember I have my own work and social obligations which I must meet. It is wrong to think that my way of living is 'bad' because I don't happen to live as 'regularly' as you do."

Coming from a person who had always been patient and never scolded us, this comment struck me with the force of an explosion. I found myself confronted with two sets of ideas which could not be reconciled. Although I continued my schedule at school, Father's words remained in my mind as a big question mark.

I think it was in my second year at Jiyu-Gakuen that Aunt Hani suggested to the teachers that it would be a good idea if they, too, followed this program of "good living." I remember in particular an argument she had with one of the art teachers, an eminent painter who had the habit of working late at night and sleeping late in the morning.

"I should think you would do better work if you planned your daily life more regularly," Aunt Hani told him in front of the whole student body.

"Mrs. Hani," he retorted, "creative work cannot be done mechanically from nine to twelve in the morning and one to five in the afternoon."

"I find that one's work, including creative expression, is conditioned by daily good living," she insisted.

Aunt Hani reasoned that she accomplished her work by such a schedule, so why not others? She could do so, of course, because her life centered around Jiyu-Gakuen and there was little need for her to go outside the school grounds.

As official textbooks required in public schools were not used in Jiyu-Gakuen, Mrs. Hani had to pay the high price of not having her school accredited by the Ministry of Education.

The class in literature was a striking example of Aunt Hani's teaching methods. Instead of giving us the Japanese classical literature, as in other schools, she started us with one of her own books and the Japanese translation of *The Blue Bird*. Aunt Hani personally taught this class. Then we read in translation *Little Lord Fauntleroy,* Ibsen's *A Doll's House*, Chekhov's *The Cherry Orchard*, and Dostoevski's *The Brothers Karamazov*. Apparently these were the books which had impressed Aunt Hani in her youth. The literary diet was the more peculiar since most students did not read much beyond the assignments.

Aunt Hani conducted another class, called "discussion," which was comparable to the morals class in accredited schools. Its chief purpose was self-examination. I can see my aunt now walking into the rectangular classroom promptly as the bell rang and searching out everybody with her one eye closed. She never stood in one place long, but walked along the aisles as she talked. In this class the students were free to discuss anything, but for the most part we criticized ourselves and each other. The discussion might start by a student saying:

"Sato-*san* and Suzuki-*san* are very friendly, but they are not that way with the rest of us. I don't think that is the right attitude to take."

Mrs. Hani always listened intently—often nodding her head. She would ask Sato-*san* and Suzuki-*san* how they felt about the matter, and the discussion would follow. But Mrs. Hani always had the answer as to what was right and what was good.

One day the discussion turned on me. A girl raised her hand, was recognized and said: "Yesterday I was going to Minamisawa with Yoko-*san*. We were a little late, and as we neared the station the train was pulling in. Yoko-*san* realized this before I, but without saying anything to me she started to run for the train. Although we made it, I think she should have warned me. I think she is a little too individualistic and not considerate enough of others."

Aunt Hani nodded as though she agreed a hundred per cent, and went on to expound this point. "Too individualistic and not considerate enough of others." This was probably an apt criticism of me then, and I am sure it was more apt later when I became the bread-earner in my family.

This class was much more meaningful to me than the morals class for the reason that the discussions applied directly to our daily conduct. Although in retrospect Aunt Hani's ideas of right and wrong seem arbitrary, I have to remind myself that at that time I too was certain as to what was right, what wrong; what was good and what bad.

This early habit of analyzing myself, I think, prevented me from being a carefree youngster. Constant emphasis on making progress day after day did not leave much room for relaxation and hearty laughter.

Practical knowledge was considered all-important. Abstract theories and the deductive method of teaching were deplored. Therefore, instead of a course in the social sciences, once a week a class in newspaper reading was conducted by Uncle Hani. Each student would bring a copy of the *Asahi Shinbum,* a Tokyo daily with a circulation of over three million, to school. Appropriate articles were selected by Uncle Hani for reading, and he would then interpret the news. But to girls with no background knowledge of government, politics, or economics, the day-by-day happenings were only isolated phenomena, unrelated to one another or to any body of information. In many cases we did not understand them even as isolated facts. Sometimes Uncle Hani would ask us which story we considered important. I could always answer that, not from the content of the story but by its location in the paper.

I remember the morning in 1930 when we learned that our Prime Minister was shot in the Tokyo station. The newspaper boy's voice crying "Extra! Extra!" had a quality of excitement which made me —the daughter of a newspaperman—jump. It heralded something very unusual. This was the first time that news which had no personal meaning for me stirred my emotions. I was physically a little sick in my stomach. That day in the newspaper class we learned that Yuko Hamaguchi had been the second commoner to become prime minister of Japan. The fact held no significance for me then, nor did I have a hint that this attempt on his life was part of a chain of events leading up to the military control of our country in the following decade.

A nursery which Mrs. Hani started on the school campus was another example of learning by observation and practical implementation. Students took turns working there with an instructor. By observing children, the students were expected to arrive at an understanding of behavior patterns with practically no background knowledge of psychology. To Aunt Hani learning theories was meaningless, and anyone with the power to observe could discover the rules.

On the middle school level (equivalent to the junior high in America), cooking, sewing, washing, cleaning and other household chores took a relatively large portion of the classroom time. I could never learn to like these subjects, particularly sewing, which in Japan is all done by hand. I considered it a complete waste of time to learn to make a kimono, especially as we wore Western clothes exclusively. During the first semester of the first year we were required each day to sew three straight lines on a piece of white cotton cloth one meter long. This was the most onerous task of my school life. I am more grateful that we also learned to mend stockings, to make buttonholes, to wash clothes with a minimum of soap, to press and iron, for these skills have been useful. Still they do not deserve the time I was required to spend at school learning them.

Cooking was the most enjoyable of the household subjects, perhaps because it involved more action—cooking a meal for the entire school. Aunt Hani's idea was not to make fancy cakes and dishes for showing off at home. Cooking was no experiment with us; it was the real

[59]

thing. If we burned the rice or put too much salt in the vegetable, that was what three hundred people had to eat for their lunch.

On the cook day assigned to our class, immediately after the morning service we waited in white cotton aprons and kerchiefs for the teacher, Nakasone-*sensei,* to burst into the classroom and direct us in operations for lunch. It must be ready at twelve sharp, and hot.

Nakasone-*sensei* was talkative but very likable. Her ready laughter seemed to brighten the rather dimly lighted kitchen. She always gave us the recipe for five people—the normal family—and also for three hundred people. "Now, children," she would say, "remember the proportion of seasoning for five is different from that for three hundred people. If you just multiplied the ingredients by sixty, the food would be uncomfortably tasty.

"There are certain things you must learn from the beginning," she would caution us. "And don't let this go in one ear and out the other. When you are boiling greens, never start with cold water. Heat the water to the boiling point, then put the vegetable in without covering the container. Never cook greens too long. They should retain that certain crispness. When done, put the vegetable in a bamboo basket and pour cold water on it quickly. Don't ask me why, but that will keep that fresh appetizing green. Greens are no good if they are wilted.

"And, children, never put seasoning in until the vegetables are already soft. Vegetables don't cook after you add sugar and *shoyu* (or soy bean sauce). And never, never put in the *shoyu* first. Sugar is always the first; otherwise, you will taste only the *shoyu.*"

Nakasone-*sensei* was a good commander-in-chief when it came to directing an army of thirty girls. She saw to it that we wasted neither time nor energy.

In this cooking class, we also learned how to estimate calories and how to plan nutritious, but inexpensive menus. At lunchtime a representative of the class which prepared the meal reported the total and individual costs of the meal and the number of calories in that lunch. After lunch was over, we washed the dishes and cleaned the kitchen, as there were no janitors at Jiyu-Gakuen.

Another teacher who helped relieve the sometimes too-serious atmosphere of the school was Shiraishi-*sensei,* my first English teacher.

Having studied in Canada, she always dressed in Western style and wore shoes with high heels. Not only that, but she would never wear the same dress two successive days. Her hair was permanented, and she always had on a good deal of make-up. This was the kind of modernism which my aunt and uncle disliked. Consequently, many girls at school eyed Shiraishi-*sensei* with silent criticism. I must say she did stand out rather noticeably in that company of girls who used no make-up, always wore flat heels, and whose clothes though clean and pressed fitted like coarse sugar bags.

Like Nakasone-*sensei*, Shiraishi-*sensei* had a good sense of humor. Her laughter, though not ladylike according to Japanese orthodox standards, was nevertheless refreshing.

Saturday in the school calendar was art day. Several eminent painters and sculptors—including Tsuruzo Ishii who is now president of the Tokyo Art School—came to the school that day, and all the students did something: painting, modeling in clay or weaving. Mrs. Hani believed that anybody could be taught anything, and as the purpose of education as she saw it was to make an all-round person, in Jiyu-Gakuen everyone learned to paint, to sing and to play a musical instrument. However, she herself did not paint or play, and sang off key.

Art day was the one time during the week when the well-kept lawn in front of the main building was open to students. Then at noon hour the work of the morning was displayed on the walls of the dining hall. After lunch the visiting artists commented or criticized. Although I never excelled in anything I had to do with my hands, I enjoyed those Saturdays. Somehow, sitting on the grass under the sun and quietly painting gave me the joyous feeling of being outside my cage.

The annual art exhibition, when the students' work was displayed and sometimes sold, and the concert in which the whole student body participated were two famous events at Jiyu-Gakuen. When I was there our music teachers were all professional singers and as outstanding as the art teachers in their fields. Viscount Konoye, the younger brother of Prince Konoye, often conducted the Jiyu-Gakuen choir.

Although occasional tests were given in English, mathematics, literature, and science, there were no final examinations. At the end of the year, the student body gathered in the auditorium to hear praise, criticisms, and suggestions from the teachers. I remember a comment made by my algebra teacher: "Matsuoka-*san* excels in that she learns quickly, but she is not meticulous enough with her notebook. I would almost call it untidy. Now Oguri-*san* is just the opposite."

At this Aunt Hani nodded her head and muttered, "Ah! that is so. That is a very apt point."

The grade card given at the end of the year was like a thin notebook. Each teacher made an entry, suggesting what the student could do to improve herself. It was my sewing teacher who wrote: "Your mind seems to move more quickly than your hands."

Mother laughed at this and said, "My! what a polite way of saying you are clumsy with your hands."

Unlike other schools, Jiyu-Gakuen never flunked its students. However, these public comments by teachers and the self-examination by students served as incentive and pressure to study.

16 ~

IT WAS the purpose of Jiyu-Gakuen to develop each student into a well-rounded person and to help her apply her knowledge and skills to everyday living. However, my father (and many others) felt that Jiyu-Gakuen often failed to give students the strength to stand on their own feet outside of school. Jiyu-Gakuen girls could do many things. And they were serious, industrious, and useful as good soldiers would be. But their knowledge was too limited. Father held that "the biting knowledge of many things does not prepare you to know anything," and "to know one thing deeply enables you to understand other things as well."

Although despising pedantry just as much as Aunt Hani did, he believed that a certain amount of formal knowledge was essential in learning to think. It was a question of choosing, he said, whether knowledge would conquer your mind or your mind digest the knowledge. But the tools had to be acquired before independent thinking was possible.

He was also concerned about the Jiyu-Gakuen girls' attitude that only theirs was the right way of life. I remember his saying, "Aunt Hani is an exceptionally brilliant woman. But when girls acquire only her dogmatism and not her brilliance, it is hopeless."

When my father died in 1944, Aunt Hani said to me: "The trouble with your father was that he was too wise." I think I know now what she meant.

Like Mrs. Hani, Father too was a person of principles. But unlike her he never imposed his ideas and beliefs upon others. Rather he tried through practice to induce those around him to respect the same principles he did. Despite the odds against his winning many converts to his way of thinking, Father kept his faith in human rationality.

To one like Mrs. Hani, who not only lives by her principles but commands others to do the same, a liberal like Father must have appeared to be evading the issues. "Too wise" was, I think, the kindest expression this honest woman could have used.

When I compare my father and my aunt, this appears to be the greatest difference between them. Although they respected each other, neither compromised. In Mrs. Hani were the fire and zeal which Father lacked, and in Father the tolerance and learning which she failed to acquire.

Although I would not name them as the greatest individuals in the world today, I have loved and admired them both. Perhaps my sympathies are more on Father's side, for there is an ego in my aunt which repels sympathy. In myself I find the influence of both my father and my aunt, and the result is not too well-balanced. The fact that I possess the almost reckless enthusiasm of my aunt but lack her inflexible faith, plus my adherence to my father's cosmopolitan outlook without his restrained wisdom, has made me on occasion jump around like a rodeo horse.

It was not coincidental that we three sisters left Jiyu-Gakuen without having finished its seven-year course and chose to go into three widely different fields. I did not realize then, as I do now, how carefully we had been prepared from childhood to follow our own particular bents. Only recently Mother explained in these words: "Your Father and I wanted each of you to have the ability and strength to walk by yourself. It was not easy to draw out your talents and let you choose your own paths."

Mother reminded me how naughty Kwoko was as a child. She never studied very much at school, except for natural sciences which she liked. Instead of doing her homework, she would spend her time raising a grasshopper. When she was in the fifth grade, she mentioned that she wanted to be a surgeon. My parents thought it was probably one of her passing dreams. But when she really seemed fascinated watching Dr. Wada, a surgeon in Seoul, they began to think seriously that this might be a possible field for her. After that they took every opportunity to encourage her. Thinking that the kind of education Jiyu-Gakuen offered would not prepare her well for a medical college, they transferred her after her third year to the Aoyama-Gakuin— from which Mother herself had been graduated.

From the Aoyama-Gakuin, Kwoko entered the Tokyo Women's Medical College, the oldest women's medical college in Japan. She has become an obstetrician and gynecologist since then, and particularly enjoys surgical work.

"Reiko," Mother said, "had a good voice as a child. We took her to a well-known singer, who advised us to bring her back again when she was sixteen." Unfortunately, Reiko injured her health when she was thirteen and took years to recover. While convalescing she became interested in the theater and in writing plays. Although she was talented, Mother and Father felt that she needed more fundamental education than Jiyu-Gakuen was able to provide. So Father talked with Aunt Hani, and Reiko entered the Tokyo Women's Christian College, where she studied Japanese literature. When she finished her four years there, Reiko was determined to get a job with a professional theatrical troupe. Mother would have preferred to see her a writer rather than an actress, but she had promised Father not to interfere with what we girls chose to do. Later in a letter to me she said, "A playwright would be all right, but an actress is still looked upon by many as not respectable."

Reiko joined the theatrical troupe and worked in the scenario department. Although she has taken up other work since then, she has kept her professional interest in the theater.

Unlike her stories of my sisters, Mother's story concerning me is not something to be taken out of the lower drawer and aired with complacency. It does not completely belong to the past; it still belongs to the future.

"You remember that the Oriental Exclusion Act became law in the United States in 1924," she told me. "The Act excluded not only future emigrants from the Oriental countries, but also barred entrance to the wives, parents, and children of Orientals already settled in the States.

"This action appeared so unfair to me that I wanted to appeal to the women of America. But my English was inadequate; I could not express my thoughts fully in that language. So I wrote my appeal in Japanese and asked one of Father's friends, a brilliant man and an alumnus of Yale, to translate it for me. He replied, however, that he could not do it because he was a businessman. What he meant was that a translation which reproduces mere words without complete understanding of the underlying emotions would not convey my real thoughts. Ever after that Father and I hoped very deeply that one of our children would be able to speak and write English fluently enough to carry our thoughts and ideas to the American people.

"But of course, we did not know which of you would be most suitable for such a career.

"You remember we often took walks together in the evenings while we were in Osaka and also in Seoul. Whenever Father talked about international politics, the League of Nations or the World Court, you showed more interest than the others. In fact you seemed eager to learn about these things. I believe your hope for international organizations and your desire to work for one began to develop during this period.

"By the time you were twelve Father and I had decided to send you to America to study. It was his firm belief that the only way to master a language was to go to the country where it was spoken when one was still young—if possible, before the age of sixteen."

AMERICA

17 ～

IT WAS during the summer vacation of 1931 that Father first proposed that I go to America. What could be more exciting to a fifteen-year-old than a trip abroad! Without hesitation I answered, "Of course!"

The thought of leaving home for several years, of living among people whose language and customs were unfamiliar, did not worry me in the slightest. It was not that I had so much confidence in myself. Rather it was confidence in the world, which was an outgrowth of the faith nurtured at Jiyu-Gakuen. I am appalled when I realize how inexperienced and immature I was then. Now the truth seems to be that I knew too little to worry.

American-Japanese relations took a decisive turn for the worse at this time, due to the "Manchurian Incident" of September, 1931. On the eighteenth, following an explosion near Mukden on the Japanese-owned South Manchurian railroad, the Japanese Army, holding the Chinese responsible, moved into their garrisons and forced them to withdraw. Although officially minimized as only an "incident," it was reported in the newspapers that public opinion in America was so aroused that a boycott of Japanese goods was being considered, and some even discussed the possibility of war between the two nations. Many friends of my family were doubtful as to the wisdom of sending me to America at this time. Father, though not so pessimistic as to the eventual outcome of the Manchurian affair, was concerned very much over the growing bitterness in American-Japanese relations and insisted that this was all the more reason why I should go to help promote understanding. For myself, I was too excited about the trip to let these thoughts disturb me.

While in Seoul my parents had learned that Miss Bertha Starkey,

[69]

an American missionary working for the Japanese Methodist Church there, was returning to America for a furlough in the summer of 1932. They asked her if she would take me back with her, and she consented. Although Mother's brother and his wife were in Los Angeles at that time, my parents decided that since I was going to the United States to study the language and the people, I should be away from the Japanese. Cleveland, Ohio, where Miss Starkey was going, represented to my parents a type of true American city with no Japanese influence whatsoever.

When my family returned from Korea to Tokyo in December of that year, Father converted his savings into dollars. He had a choice, either to build a house which the family needed or to send me abroad. Father said, "It is much more important to build a person than to build a house." So it was decided that the family would rent a small house in order to make my trip possible. It was indeed an expensive project. Not many Japanese parents would spend so extravagantly for a girl's education.

In order for aliens to enter the United States on a student visa, the following requirements had to be met: one must be over fifteen years of age, able to understand and speak English well, be accepted by an accredited school, and be capable of financing oneself so as not to become a liability to the government.

I was over fifteen, Father was able to pay all my expenses, and it was not difficult to find an accredited school in Cleveland. The only rub was that I had to pass a test in English given by the American consul general. My three years of English at Jiyu-Gakuen had enabled me to sing "Old MacDonald had a farm, E-I-E-I-O! . . ." and to say a few simple things, but I could not carry on a conversation. Several days were spent rehearsing with Mother some obvious questions and answers.

"What is your name?"

"My name is Yoko Matsuoka."

"What is your status?"

"I am a student."

"What school are you going to attend?"

"I am going to attend Cleveland Pre-pa-ra-to-ry School." This was

[70]

one of the few private accredited schools of high school level in Cleveland to which alien students were admitted.

"How old are you?"

"I am sixteen."

If the consul general asked much else, I would be certain to fail. Obviously a person whose vocabulary was so limited would not be able to gain much from American schooling. But on the other hand my purpose in going to America was to learn the language. Father decided to talk to the consul general before the test was to be given, and he was wise enough to arrange for my interview during the noon hour so that most of the people working in the Consulate would be out for lunch.

I was perspiring under my arms and my hands were getting wet as I entered the Consulate. I prayed to God that I would pass the test. Poor God must suffer from millions of prayers of this kind. The consul general came into the big front room, which was almost deserted, sat on the edge of a desk in the middle of the room and motioned me to a chair in front of him. I had the impression that he was chewing gum. He was extremely casual, not a bit like the formal diplomat I had pictured in my mind.

Dangling his feet in front of me, he asked the expected questions. Then in the same manner he inquired, "Where were you born?"

This I had not rehearsed with Mother. I thought for a moment and replied triumphantly, "I was born in a hospital." A wry smile spread over his bored face, and I could hear the laughter of Miss Starkey, Father and Mother in the back of the room. The consul general dismissed me at this point, and I passed the test!

18 ~

WHEN MY passport and visa were ready, Father took me to the Ise Shrine, where the Sun Goddess, the first ancestor of the "unbroken lineage" of Japanese Emperors, is enshrined. This was the Japanese mecca, which the Japanese visited before launching on any great undertaking. It was the custom for the newly appointed prime minister and other cabinet ministers to pay their respects to the Shrine before commencing their duties of office. People of lesser position did the same. I don't believe Father wanted me to observe the tradition so much as he wanted me to see this most revered shrine. The trip to Ise took almost ten hours on the train from Tokyo.

Father and I made another trip, to his home town, Hachinohe, fourteen hours in the opposite direction from Ise. This was to bid farewell to our ancestors—another Japanese custom, perhaps a part of what the Westerners call ancestor worship. It is in effect no more than a visit to the family cemetery.

The Japanese cemetery is usually located near a Buddhist temple, not a Shinto shrine. Although our ancestors did not belong to any sect of Buddhism, the family cemetery occupies a lot belonging to a Buddhist temple.

Dozens of cryptomeria—all must have been hundreds of years old—surrounded this ground. No sunlight peeked through, the place was dark and conspicuously quiet. No wonder that most Japanese ghost stories take place in cemeteries. Protected from the wind but not from the rain and snow, the edges of rectangular stones had been rounded and the writings on some had become almost indistinguishable. Dark brownish green moss covered the ground and seemed to absorb the rustling of my silk dress. Carefully I placed green incense in front of each stone and lighted it with a candle flame. Streaks of light gray smoke curled up slowly into the air, leaving that odor which is peculiarly Oriental. This was my farewell to the Matsuokas who had lived before me.

Father wanted me to call on Viscount and Viscountess Saito, the former governor general of Korea and his wife, to say good-by. Unexpectedly the Viscount had been appointed Japan's prime minister to succeed Premier Inukai, who was killed by a group of young navy officers, army cadets and civilian rightists. This assassination in 1932 is known as the May 15 Incident. Mr. Inukai, then in his seventies, had been the head of the Seiyukai, one of the two major political parties. He was the last of the "party premiers," and his assassination led the country another step toward military control.

The Viscount was obviously too busy to receive me, but the

Viscountess let us know that she would be glad to have me call at their premier's official residence.

Mother, Kwoko and Reiko went with me. There is not much I remember about the visit except the room in which the former prime minister was shot to death. Viscountess Saito led us through a long, well-polished corridor to an iron door which separated the main part of the house from the Japanese part, where Mr. Inukai and his family had lived. Pointing to the door, she said, "It can be shut by pushing a button, but evidently they did not have time to close the door before the officers rushed in."

We followed her into the room. Serene and dignified, the Viscountess always spoke in a quiet, soft voice with a restrained politeness and impassiveness which showed her upbringing in a high samurai family. But even she seemed a little moved as she explained: "The *tatami* had to be changed because of the bloodstain."

It was an ordinary Japanese room with a carefully dusted table in the middle, whose polished black surface reflected the white of the *shoji*, sliding doors made of light frame and paper. More than two weeks had passed since the murder, but the odor of incense was still noticeable in the air.

When these visits had been paid, I was ready to leave.

There were several ways of reaching America. I would have loved to go by way of Hawaii to Los Angeles where the Olympic games were to be held that summer. But the northern route would be shorter, though rough and less interesting. Miss Starkey suggested that we get off the boat at Vancouver and enter the United States through some remote Canadian border town. She said in explanation: "You will be confronted with the immigration officer at any point of entry. They are usually most difficult at San Francisco and Los Angeles, less so at Seattle, and least fussy at the Canadian border." This seemed a wise suggestion in view of my scanty knowledge of English.

It was a cloudy day when I left Yokohama on the *Hiyemaru*, a Japanese steamer. Wearing a white silk dress which came just below my knees, a pair of brown flat-heeled shoes and a brownish beret set straight on bobbed hair, I must have looked much younger than my age. In my left hand I held a large bouquet of red roses, which hid half my face, and with the other hand I threw dozens of colored paper tapes to my family, friends and former classmates gathered on the pier. The tapes made a rainbow connecting the ship and the people below. As the deep, sad whistle signaled the ship's departure, all the hustling and bustling stopped. Suddenly I became uncomfortably aware of my unknown future. I looked at Mother in the crowd down below. Holding the blue paper tape which bridged us, she wiped her eyes unashamedly. Then I burst into tears and could not stop. I looked at Father, but he was not looking at me. Being a true samurai, he kept his face toward Miss Starkey.

All was blurred. I clung tightly to the blue tape. It was June 16, 1932.

19 ~

AFTER TWELVE days of cold and rough sea, the white houses and green trees of Vancouver Harbor looked warm and welcome. The Canadian Pacific from Vancouver sped us through the Rockies, whose tall, erect evergreens were such a contrast to the small and twisted pines of Japan, a reminder of the vastness of the American continent. The train ended its journey in Chicago near midnight of July 2. Here for the first time I stepped on the soil of the United States.

I had heard a great deal about Chicago as the city of gangsters. Just before I left Japan, the newspapers had given much space to the kidnaping of the Lindbergh baby. Thus it was with a feeling of adventure—a combination of fear, courage and anticipation—that I followed Miss Starkey into the dark streets outside the terminal building. The tall silent buildings on both sides made it seem as if I were walking inside a well—a feeling one would never experience in Tokyo where the tallest building was less than ten stories high. The lights on the street cast curious shadows, and I imagined myself to be the heroine of a detective story. I fully expected—and hoped— to hear either gunshots or the scream of a woman. Nothing happened—not even the sound of a fire engine. It was a great disappointment!

Next day in Cleveland we were welcomed by Miss Starkey's brother and his family. It was a Sunday, and the first thing we did was to attend church in a large stone Gothic structure with lustrous stained-glass windows. I was reminded of the Buddhist temples at home, dark yet colorful and filled with incense, rather than of the Japanese Christian churches there, which in their simplicity looked much like Quaker meeting houses. Was it wealth that made the difference? I thought not. Perhaps the difference lay in the fact that in America Christianity was taken for granted. Although a few might question its assumptions, there was no organized opposition. A church therefore had time for the formalities of religion—for the things which have to do with creating a religious atmosphere. In Japan, where Christianity was one of many religions, with comparatively few followers, it had to fight for recognition. And its only weapon was the message it brought of the new "truth." All emphasis was on this message.

After the service an elderly woman sitting in front of us turned around and shook hands, first with Miss Starkey and then with me. I did not understand what she said, but this obviously friendly gesture was a startlingly new experience. Not that I had been taught to believe in the Japanese saying: "Think of a stranger as a thief." Nevertheless, it was pleasantly unsettling to be greeted so affably by someone who had never set eyes on me before.

The Starkey family included Mr. and Mrs. Starkey and their three daughters, ranging from high school to grammar school age. It was fortunate that I was in a home where there were children, for, like any other children, these had neither the imagination nor the politeness to understand my English unless I spoke it accurately. I must have provided them with amusement and helped to boost their egos. They would laugh when I mispronounced a word, and show their teeth in a grimace to teach me how to say it properly. Miss Starkey good-naturedly talked to me only in English, and with painstaking effort would say the same thing in more than one way if I did not understand her the first time. Hence there was not much I could

[75]

do but learn the language. The question was how quickly and how well.

Early in our acquaintance, Dorothy, the youngest of the Starkeys, asked, "Yoko, would you like to read the funnies?" Without knowing what I was getting into, I answered "Yes," because to say "No" would be impolite. Since I could not read the funnies, it was with complete bewilderment that I looked at the pictures. Later, when my knowledge of English was more extensive and I could understand that "Me gotta find-um" meant "I have to find him," and "What sorta fella is he . . . huh?" should read "What kind of a man is he?" I was surprised to find that the funnies are not really funny at all— not to my sense of humor anyway. It chagrined me to discover that they have such a big part in the pattern of American culture, and not only the nine-year-old Dorothys but many grownups and some college graduates find them indispensable to relaxation.

I remember my first Fourth of July. The Starkeys took me to Euclid Beach, and there they introduced me to popcorn. Its salty taste and crispness reminded me of Japanese rice powder cookies and I enjoyed it, but eating while walking in a public place made me self-conscious. That would be considered vulgar at home, and I knew Mother would disapprove. Compared with the solemn ceremonies which marked Birth of the Nation Day in Japan, the fireworks, popcorn and rollercoasters seemed an uncultured way of celebrating the independence of one's country. The constant motion and speed were overpowering to one coming from a land whose aspiration, as expressed in the National Anthem, was to live "until a pebble becomes a rock, aged with moss."

During the summer I accompanied Miss Starkey to various missionary gatherings. It was at Lakeside, Ohio, before the Women's Foreign Missionary Institute, that I made my first speech in America. Wearing a pale orange kimono with a large golden butterfly in front and, about my waist, a bright green *obi* woven with gold and silver thread, which once served for Mother's wedding, I spoke my well-rehearsed sentences:

"My mother studied in the Methodist Mission School in Tokyo, and my father was baptized by a missionary. I can speak English very little. Although we cannot understand each other's spoken language, I am thankful that we can understand our hearts' language in Christ."

The ovation given by nearly a thousand men and women was warm and kind.

It was this belief which made the Church a great part of my life in Cleveland. At first the sermons were beyond my English vocabulary, but I was determined to understand them. Emboldened by the kindliness of Dr. McCombe's face and his firm handshake which sometimes hurt my fingers, I took courage one day to ask him, "Would you explain your sermon to me in simpler language beforehand?" I suppose it would be only natural for a Christian preacher to comply with such a request from an eager follower, but I still think it was most gracious of him to spare those few minutes before the service every Sunday morning for the following several months.

One thing embarrassed me—that was to have Dr. McCombe open the door of his study to let me precede him, even though I knew this was the custom in the West. To one brought up in the gentlemen-first tradition of the Orient—not that I approved of it or enjoyed it—it was most uncomfortable to let a preacher, who was born before me, open the door for me. To minimize my embarrassment I always followed one step behind Dr. McCombe so that he would reach the doorknob before I reached the door. Then as soon as he opened it, I made a hurried exit.

To this day I cannot help having a creepy feeling when an older man, particularly a professor who would rank high in the Oriental social scale, opens a door or holds my coat for me. Worse still is to see men washing dishes!

In spite of my earnestness and diligence, I cannot now remember a single sermon Dr. McCombe preached. I do, however, remember a church bazaar which offered, among various entertainments, a fortuneteller. When Don, a boy in my Sunday school class, invited me to join him in having our palms read, I could only stare at the Gypsy-costumed woman in the little cubicle and say "No thank you" in a stubborn and unfriendly tone. Although I wanted to explain, I could find no words then to say that to me there was a limit to what a church might do in raising money; that fortunetelling was as out-of-place as gambling.

[77]

20 ∿

THE CLEVELAND Preparatory School was another disappointing experience at first. Ever since I had tried to pronounce its name in order to pass my English test in Tokyo, I had dreamed of a beautiful brick building in the midst of a large green lawn surrounded by trees and flowers. It would have an indoor basketball court and a swimming pool. And I would play basketball in real basketball shoes with crepe soles, which I had always wanted in the School of Freedom but which were too expensive for my twenty-*yen* monthly allowance. My dream was miserably shattered when Miss Starkey took me to meet the principal, in an old dirty building facing the Public Square in downtown Cleveland. In a confusion of streetcars, busses, automobiles and always too many people, the school occupied four rooms on the second floor. In addition to Mr. Hopkins there were two women teachers—the entire full-time teaching staff.

The function of the school was to give a high school education to newly arrived immigrants who hoped to become American citizens, and to adult Americans who had missed high school at the proper age and would be self-conscious attending a regular public school. This service the school fulfilled admirably. I found myself to be the only Asiatic and the youngest student in a group which included a Russian choir director—tall and bony; a half-bald German doctor; a short middle-aged Jewish man who looked most at home when he was reading a Hebrew paper; a French girl in her twenties whose coy manner was pathetically contradicted by a flat chest and a big nose, and a few American business girls.

We were an odd assortment. Perhaps the liveliest and noisest class was the English one taught by Miss McArthy, feminine-looking and rather attractive, who introduced us to *Treasure Island*. Hampered by inadequate command of the language in varying degrees, we raised our voices and used our hands and feet in an effort to make ourselves understood.

My greatest difficulty at first was to distinguish between *r*'s and *l*'s, as there are no such sounds in Japanese. "Girl" was perhaps the easiest of the combination, but it took months before I could pronounce "parallel" and "lyric" without concentrating on where my tongue should go next.

Algebra was a cinch, as American teen-agers would say, because I did not need the language to grasp figures and logic. European history and chemistry, on the other hand, were beyond my comprehension. If I read two pages of my history book and understood it in a day, I was doing well. Twenty-four hours were too short for me to thumb through my English-Japanese dictionary for almost every other word in the book.

When the midterm examinations came, my chemistry teacher was good enough to say that I did not have to try. The French girl, who had much less difficulty than I with the language, was also excused. She told me that she was not taking her exam. But I knew what my father would say—"A samurai does not shrink from difficulties."

"At least, a Japanese can be more courageous than the French," I thought, and proudly entered the classroom for the examination with my pocket dictionary in my hand. It was like fighting a lion with bare hands when I found that I could not even read the questions on the blackboard. There was one question which looked simple enough: "What is the difference between a physical change and a chemical change?" The only unfamiliar word was "physical," which I proceeded to look up in my dictionary. My eyes searched— "physic, physical exercise, physician . . ." Baffled and in despair, I went to the teacher and showed my dictionary. I whispered timidly so the other students could not hear: "I think you made a mistake."

His laughter echoed throughout that dirty old room. But I was more relieved than embarrassed to know that he took it with such good humor.

Now that it is all safely folded into the past, I can look at those first months with amazement. What I thought of then as courage seems now to have been mere ignorance—ignorance of my own limitations. Yet my ignorance was part of and inseparable from my faith in God. The two continuously sustained hope and prevented discouragement from defeating me.

[79]

21 ~

A FEW months later, in October, I had my first visitor from home. Aunt Hani, accompanied by her daughter Keiko, had attended the International Progressive Education Conference in Nice that summer, and they came through the United States on their way back to Japan. I joined them in Buffalo and we had a few days together.

I told Aunt Hani how discouraged I was because I felt that my ability was too limited to accomplish my mission. In answer she read me the miracle of the two fish and five loaves of bread. "No matter how small your talent is," she said with confidence, "if you offer it to God He will bless it."

It seems now that faith beyond reason was a prerequisite to my learning. Perhaps empirical knowledge is all one can hope to attain, but broadening the sphere of one's experience seems possible only when one has the faith and courage to try the unknown. Somehow, I have never lost completely my belief in tomorrow.

The belief that God would not bless my talent unless I offered all of it made me work hard. This, I think, invited kindness and encouragement from those around me. Perhaps what I believed to be God's blessings was only the generous help and constant friendship of my teachers and my friends.

Later, while Aunt Hani was visiting me in Cleveland, a teacher from the Shaker Heights Junior High School whom my aunt had met in Nice took us to visit the Shaker schools. The methods of teaching in use there, with emphasis on the applicability of knowledge, impressed my aunt. What attracted me was the highly suburban environment and the cleanliness. Immediately I set my mind on transferring to the Shaker Heights High School at the end of the current year. But there were legal difficulties. I was told that it took the combined efforts of Dr. Bair, the superintendent of the Shaker Schools, and Mr. Newton D. Baker, a former Secretary of War of the United States and a prominent member of the Shaker community, to set aside the restrictions governing alien students and get me the necessary permission. In all this I was particularly impressed by the flexibility of the American Government. The Japanese Government would never have made such an exception to the rules for an unknown foreign girl.

22 ∼

AFTER A year's furlough, Miss Starkey returned to Japan, and I spent my second summer in America traveling with a Japanese friend, Tagawa-*sensei*, who had been my Sunday school teacher in Seoul.

Two personalities we met at Chautauqua, New York, stand out in my memory. One was Norman Thomas. Tall, with silvery white hair and the bluest eyes I had ever seen, he was a powerfully vivacious speaker. But what impressed me most was the reaction of several hundred people who packed the auditorium to hear him. So enthusiastic was the ovation he received that I wrote Father: "I should not be surprised if Mr. Thomas became the President of the United States." Father apparently knew America better than I, for he did not comment.

Mrs. Thomas A. Edison was so quiet that I thought at first she had been subdued by the genius of her husband. But her eyes told another story. In her wisdom she was keenly receptive, but in the most unassuming way. Mrs. Edison heard Tagawa-*sensei* and me speak at one of the meetings in Chautauqua and invited us for tea and later for dinner. It was a thrilling and new experience to be accepted as a friend by one of such wealth and prominence—an experience seldom possible in Japan where the class lines are rigidly observed. After all, she did not know to whose "horse's bone" we belonged.

About this time my parents wrote, saying, "Now that Miss Starkey is gone, we should like you to go to Washington, D. C., and stay with our Japanese friends. We should feel much safer to have you with someone we know." But before the letter reached me I had been enrolled at the Shaker Heights High School, and arrangements had been made for me to live with the Clarke family in the community.

After many days of pondering this problem, I replied to Mother: "I understand how you and Father feel, but my purpose in coming to America was to learn English and to know the American people. I feel sure that I can accomplish this if I stay with an American family rather than with a Japanese family. This is the first time I am going against your advice, and I feel badly, but I trust you will agree with me."

In those days before the institution of air mail service it took six weeks for an exchange of letters. Mother simply said, "Father and I are glad you made your own decision."

23 ~

I WAS the first Japanese to enter the Shaker Heights High School and I was treated with such warmth and kindness as I had never experienced before. During the two years I was there, my tenth-grade class in American literature gave me the most trouble of any subject. Trigonometry and physics made much more sense than Negro literature. Here I was hopelessly lost, as there was no dictionary which would help me with the southern dialect. Neither diligence nor concentration would solve this problem. I can still remember the quizzical but kind eyes of Miss Graham looking into my blank face.

Learning a language is not only memorizing words and rules of grammar. One must be able to feel all the creases in the language. I have learned that there is a distinct difference in feeling when someone writes to me, "Dear Yoko," or "Yoko dear," "My dear Yoko," or simply "My dear." The words are the same, but the subtle change in order or in omission makes all the difference.

Father had told me before I left home, "When you begin to dream in English, then you really are beginning to know the language." I do not know what Freud would say about this, but I think Father's reasoning was right. It was with great eagerness that I waited for the time when I could dream in English. It took a whole year and a half. I do not remember the details of the dream now, but I do remember how excited I was the following morning. Taking two steps at a time, I dashed down to the kitchen and reported to Mrs. Clarke, "At last I dreamed in English!"

24 ~

SHAKER WAS my first experience in coeducation, since I had grown up. This experience led to many confusions. At first the term "boy friend" sounded flippant and in bad taste. Why should a male friend be distinguished from a female friend in such a way? Why not just friends?

Don, a fellow student, often asked me half-teasingly and half-seriously, "Don't you have any boy friends at home, Yoko?" My reply was invariably an emphatic "No," which always produced a quizzical look as though he wanted to say: "I cannot believe you are telling the truth, but if you are, you are indeed a weird animal!"

Perhaps I was—serious, "weird," or immature about the boy-and-girl relationship. I had no sympathy for girls who spent most of their time chattering or sighing over their "dates," or boys who spent all their time with girls. My girl friends at Shaker tended not to be the so-called "popular" type. And while I did make friends among boys, my feeling toward them was not the kind which would lead me to sigh over their photographs.

I cannot remember having a real date while at Shaker except the time I asked the brother of one of my friends to our senior dance. It was exciting and I enjoyed it, but half the pleasure and excitement came from wearing a formal party dress, going out with a college man and coming home after everybody else had gone to bed. In this case I did the asking. If the initiative had come from the other person, I would have been more elated.

In a country where the peculiar custom makes it proper only for men to do the asking and paying, I think women's vanity is unnecessarily flattered by being asked by and seen with a man. Girls might not fuss over dates so much as they appear to if they could reciprocate in a similar manner. But perhaps it is a privilege men would like to keep when women are demanding equality in so many other ways. In Japan "dating" was considered highly improper.

Compared with my Japanese friends, American young people seemed carefree and not a bit serious about life. If they were engaged in a discussion outside their personal affairs, it usually had to do with some technical matter like assembling a radio or repairing parts of an automobile. Very rarely did I hear them talk about religion or philosophy, or practice self-criticism as many Japanese high-school students would do.

In time I came to believe that this was perhaps the greatest difference between the youth of the two countries. I doubt that the difference is inherent in their natures, but rather the result of dissimilar environments. In Japan, where education beyond the grammar-school level is not taken for granted, competition is keen and young people in consequence put thinking before playing. Although not common, there have been reports of twelve-year-olds committing suicide because they were unable to pass the entrance examination to middle school. It is not that the Japanese prefer suicide as some Western writers have implied, but that life is a more serious matter to all Japanese and looks hopeless to many who attempt to solve the riddle of existence.

In America high-school education is for everyone, and almost anyone can go on to a higher institution. The dream of a boy from a log-cabin becoming President, a poor boy becoming a Henry Ford or a John D. Rockefeller, is still current among young people as something which belongs to the present and the future as well as to the past. Thus they are gay, carefree, and sure of themselves.

25 ~

WHEN IT came to choosing a college, I had certain requirements in mind: it must be in the east, as I understood that was the cultural center of America; and preferably a coeducational institution—Japan at that time did not have coeducation on the college level, although there were a few men's universities which admitted women—finally, it must have a good department of social sciences as I wanted to prepare myself for work in an international organization or in journalism. With Japan withdrawn from the League of Nations, my future seemed more likely to be in the field of journalism. Father had warned me, "If you want to go into newspaper work, you should study the social sciences, particularly economics, rather than go to a school of journalism."

I was admitted to Swarthmore College in September 1935. The four years at this small Quaker institution in a suburb of Philadelphia were rich in intellectual stimulus, friendships and good times.

It was a course in philosophy during my freshman year which made me re-examine my faith, so well secured until then. I had believed in the existence of the mind and the soul, the intellectual and spiritual worlds, as separate from each other. Now my position began to look untenable. The Sunday services in the small Protestant churches in Swarthmore did not help me to an answer. So I sought it in the Quaker Meetings, where those so moved stood up to speak— sometimes they sat in complete silence. Those meetings were simple and yet stimulating. But to one accustomed to hymns, chanting and prayers, this was an experience too foreign to be convincing at first.

What was this God in which I had so firmly believed? I wanted to describe Him. If I could not describe Him, how could He exist for me?

With this in mind, I chose for the subject of my term paper in philosophy "What is God?" The result was miserably unsatisfying. Although logically consistent, my God turned out to be cold and unsympathetic. He lacked warmth and vitality, which to me had been among His essential qualities. As this was the best I could do with my limited experience and knowledge, I carefully laid Him aside for the time being.

26 ~

AS MY first college vacation approached, I grew anxious to spend the summer with my family in Tokyo. I had been away from home for four years, and I felt it important to see my parents. Unfortunately, Father could not afford to pay for the trip. Mother wrote, "As much as we regret it, you'd better not try to come home this summer."

I counted my money and decided the trip could be made if I went by coach from Philadelphia to San Francisco and traveled third class on the boat. Although my parents were not snobbish, I knew Mother would be horrified to have me come home in third class on a Japanese boat, as this was considered indecent for unmarried girls of good families. So I decided not to tell them of my homecoming until the boat docked in Yokohama.

With a round-trip ticket and very little money in my bag, I started my westward journey. By choice I took a route through the Grand Canyon, and I have never been so impressed as I was by those ever-changing rainbows of the canyon walls. Beside such sublimity and power, the beauties of Japan are delicate and feminine.

Carrying a bag filled with grapefruit, of which Mother is fond, and a few lemons to chew in case of seasickness, I descended the narrow staircases to the third-class cabin of the *Chichibu-maru*. It held from twelve to sixteen plain wooden bunks—arranged in two tiers in the style of silkworms' shelves. There was only one porthole, and I think the cabin was without cabinets or closets. But after all I had chosen to travel third despite its reputation and I had paid only a little over fifty dollars for my fare.

I was determined not to complain, and I didn't until I discovered that my cabin-mates were of mixed company. And not one of the women was related to one of the men. Apparently we had been put together as carelessly as salt and pepper. The only privacy was afforded by a piece of thin and inadequate curtain around each bunk. While the male passengers sat in complete apathy, the women protested loudly and vigorously. Finally, the occupants of ours and another mixed cabin were rearranged and the sixteen women were put together.

Third class was the only place on the boat where the bath was of Japanese style—public and not private. As everybody bathed in the same water, it was important to get in first. By tipping the boy-*san* in advance, we sixteen women were always called before the men.

This was also the only class where Japanese food was served three times a day. With rectangular wooden tables and benches, which were so crude that one had to be careful of splinters, the dining room looked like one of the cheapest restaurants in Tokyo. The menu, consisting of rice, slightly diluted bean mash soup, a dash of pickles, and perhaps a dish of boiled fish and a few vegetables for dinner, well matched this atmosphere.

I consoled myself that I would land in Yokohama just as soon as the first- and second-class passengers did.

My plan had a setback halfway across the Pacific, however. I was discovered by the chief engineer, whose daughter was attending Aunt Hani's Jiyu-Gakuen. When he found my name on the third-class passenger list, he called me to his office. Solemnly he asked: "*O-jo-san* (honorable daughter), why are you traveling third class?" I explained that I could not afford anything better, but he did not seem to believe me.

"Do your honorable parents know this?"

"No, they don't know that I am coming home."

He shook his head as if to say that a little *o-jo-san* of good breeding should not be playing such a joke. Then he insisted that I wire home to let them know of my arrival. "If you won't, I will," were his final words.

I did not have the courage to tell him that I had thought it would be fun to surprise my family by telephoning them upon my arrival. Moreover, at that time they would have no choice but to welcome me. Although I was quite confident that they would approve my decision to come home, there was nevertheless a slight doubt as to how my samurai father would react. I remembered a story in our textbook on morals about a samurai father who was critically ill but refused to let his son into the house when the boy returned in the middle of his apprenticeship to see how he was. To let such sentimentality disturb one's study was not permissible by the samurai code of life.

So it was with a certain reluctance that I went to the telegraph office, repeating to myself the arguments by which I had justified my trip earlier: No, I am not coming home for any sentimental reason. It is extremely important for me to talk with Father and Mother after so long. My college work will be much more meaningful to me if I spend the summer with them now.

When the next day I received the following wire: "Welcome home.

[87]

We are all eagerly waiting for you," I felt as though the fresh salty air of the ocean had given me several additional inches.

Mother later said how happy they were to receive the news of my visit. "Father was particularly pleased, because you had made up your own mind." Then she added with pride: "That was when your Aunt Hani admitted, 'I think I have lost the game to you in regard to your children's education.'" To Mother this was a great reward, and to me it was an overwhelming challenge.

A few hours before the steamer docked at Yokohama, quarantine and immigration officers were to arrive in a launch. With the rest of the passengers I was leaning against the railing of the ship, watching the approaching boat. Suddenly my eyes came to rest on a brown figure standing erect at the back of the launch. Those slanting shoulders, on which a suit hung as though on a cheap wire hanger, were chokingly familiar. I took one deep breath and looked again. It was Father! I waved, almost in an unladylike manner. And Father recognized me. I could see him nod.

As soon as the ladder was lowered to the floating launch, I ran up to the first-class deck to meet him. I stopped short when I saw him coming toward me swinging his favorite stick. It was not our custom to kiss, and I was too grown-up to be hugging my father. Only a child might do that. It would look odd to shake hands since that, too, was not customary. Yet, it would be too formal to bow. So I just stood smiling and said, "I have returned, Father," the normal Japanese greeting.

He grinned back. "Your mother and sisters are waiting for you at the pier."

How inadequate those words must sound to a Western ear, but we understood and appreciated what was left unsaid.

"How did you get permission to ride on the launch?" I inquired. Somehow I always seemed to bring up the least important subject first.

His grin was wider as he replied, "I have a reporter's pass."

It was obvious that the editor of a Tokyo daily newspaper would not be writing about the happenings of an incoming ship. His tender eyes were saying, "I have abused my privilege for the first time." Returning his smile, I answered him in silence: "I will remember that, Father."

27 ~

SOON AFTER my arrival I was recruited to join the third America-Japan Student Conference, held in Tokyo that summer. This gathering was an attempt to foster better understanding between the two countries, and it had been held alternately in Japan and the United States. The guest country sent about fifty students, selected from various colleges and universities, and the host country provided about twice that number. One important qualification for Japanese students was a knowledge of English, as the conference discussions were carried on entirely in that language.

What first impressed most American students about Japan was the mixture of the old and new cultures existing side by side. They would say to me: "It is so strange to see on the well-paved streets of Tokyo streetcars, automobiles, busses, along with rickshaws and sometimes an oxcart of honey buckets! Then there are the women dressed in kimonos with elaborate hair-dos shopping in French pastry shops and eating in restaurants called, 'Colombin,' 'Mon Ami,' or 'Tricoleur.' It is such an odd combination."

The Japanese would explain, "This is exactly the problem we are facing today. In order to modernize Japan, we must get rid of the old, which is retarding our progress."

This would usually start a heated discussion. Dennis McEvoy, son of the well-known writer J. P. McEvoy, was most emphatic in opposing this view. Shaking his head of short curly hair, so much like the head of the famous *Daibutsu*, a statue of Buddha in Kamakura, he would retort, "There is much good in the old! Japan would not be Japan if you throw away the *Kabuki*, the *Noh*, the tea ceremony and the kimonos. You must keep all the good in the old and discard only its undesirable parts."

"But, Denny," the Japanese students argued, "you must remember that these remnants of an old culture are outgrowths of an autocratic society. For Japan to become a truly modern state, it is necessary that the old be discarded."

[89]

So the discussion would go on and on in conference rooms and on the campus of Waseda University.

As a member of the political discussion group, I was asked to present a short paper on "The Road to Peace." I knew just enough to realize that no simple answer was possible. Lacking time to do the necessary reading for the paper, I chose the easier way of talking with Father. To him the essential factor for maintaining world peace was to have a stabilizing force in the East as well as in the West. This, he believed, would keep the balance of power. Obviously Father had in mind the United States as the stabilizing force in the West, and Japan in the East. It was the logical choice as Japan was the one independent nation in Asia with first-rate power.

This idea, full of wishful thinking, was perhaps the only one tenable to a liberal Japanese who disapproved of the increasing military control of the country and yet could not bring himself to think that it would lead the nation to a major catastrophe. Father could not have been so naïve as to assume that two forces, equally powerful and able to "stabilize" half the world, would not conflict at some point in their interests. Japan had successfully launched her crusade into Manchuria by the summer of 1936, and the whole world was condemning her. To a person like Father, a military expansion was justifiable only so long as it served as a prelude to peace in Asia and consequently peace in the world. And he wanted to think, or rather he was forced to think, that that was what Japan was doing.

28 ~

ACCOMPANIED BY Mother, I paid a visit of condolence to Viscountess Saito before the summer was over. Her husband had been assassinated in February of that year—one of several Japanese statesmen killed by a group of young Army officers. I had learned the news in Swarthmore through the *New York Times*, which flashed a big headline on the first page that particular morning.

Viscountess Saito was dignified and serene as ever. Not a trace of bitterness could I detect in her ivory-like face, except that she looked ten years older than when I had seen her in the spring of 1932. On her right hand was a bullet scar, still painfully vivid, the result of a wound received when she tried to protect her husband. This was the hand which had pointed out to me the *tatami* floor where Prime Minister Inukai was killed four years earlier. I could not know then that these two assassinations were pieces of a continuous thread, and that the spool was still unwinding. I felt righteously indignant toward those who took such barbarous measures to get their own way and was glad to hear at the time that the coup had ended with the execution of the officers responsible, although later it was rumored that several of them were secretly freed in Manchuria on condition that they would not return to Japan.

Prince Konoye, later Japan's prime minister, who was said also to be on the death list, escaped his fate this particular morning. It was said that he received a tip-off. Some of his neighbors reported a truckload of furniture leaving his residence the night before. Apparently he was gone when the insurgents arrived. Whether or not the Prince anticipated the coup has never been proved to my knowledge. But those like my father, who were skeptical of his liberalism, felt that this incident confirmed their belief.

My seven weeks' stay in Tokyo passed only too quickly, but it had proved worthwhile. I felt reassured, particularly through the America-Japan Student Conference, that my American education would not make me a fish out of water in Japan. In fact, I felt I could be quite useful upon my return home. In Mother's first letter after my departure she wrote: "You came and left like a storm. After the fallen leaves are gathered, all is conspicuously quiet at home. Father was glad to know that you are not as missionary-like as your previous letters had indicated."

The following summer Mother visited America as one of the three Japanese delegates to the Pan-Pacific Women's Conference held in Vancouver. This was her first visit to the United States in twenty-five years, and it was the first time since her marriage that she had taken such a long trip away from home. My eyes were full of tears when I hugged her at Vancouver Harbor. It had been only a year since I had seen her, but somehow the sight of Mother always invited tears.

She seemed upset and worried—more so than the other two delegates—over the so-called "Marco Polo Bridge Incident" which had occurred on July 7, five days before. It was a skirmish between the Chinese Army and the Japanese forces stationed in China, but the newspaper reports indicated Japan's determination to push further. The situation looked grave, and we were acutely aware that it was not going to be easy for the Japanese delegates to weather the conference. Mother told me that they had been warned before they left Japan that whatever they said during their trip in the United States would be reported to the Japanese authorities.

Over a hundred women leaders attended the conference from the United States, Hawaii, the Philippines, Canada, China, Australia and New Zealand. It was apparent from the beginning that their sympathies were with China, but all were polite and many even cordial to the Japanese. The Chinese delegates were elegant in appearance and smooth in their approach. This seemed to overwhelm Mother, who was sincere, serious, but shy when it came to speaking English. She was disturbed to find herself pushed into the position of justifying Japan's actions, which she seemed to believe inevitable although she wished very much that a more civilized solution had been possible. Mrs. Gauntlett, a Japanese married to an Englishman, was bilingual and could manipulate the English language adroitly. As chairman of the conference she was in a delicate position, but her wit and nerve, qualities rare among Japanese women, saved many an embarrassing situation for our delegation.

Mrs. Gauntlett made me an associate delegate to the conference. My job was to type the speeches, sometimes to make drafts and do other errands for our delegation. It made me happy and proud that I could be useful in an adult world.

It was not easy to get to know the Chinese women at the conference, but I was in a better position than older members of our delegation to cultivate their friendship because of my naïveté. The Chinese from Hawaii were more approachable than those from China, so I concentrated my efforts on them. Although I never came to know them well enough to give them our ideas on the most touchy subject, by the end of the ten-day conference one of them, Mrs. Zen, a beautiful and intelligent woman, presented me with a small darning kit as a token of our friendship. This meant so much to me that I made a special effort to save the gift with other valuables from the air raids on Tokyo. Even today when I am skeptical of international conferences and personal friendships as the sole basis for understanding among nations, I cannot throw that darning kit into a wastepaper basket although most of the thread has been used.

After the conference, Mother and I traveled together. I took her to meet my former teachers and friends in Cleveland, and to Swarthmore. Here she seemed to absorb every detail of my dormitory room, the trees and flowers of the campus, as though to have a complete picture of the place to take away with her. I can still see her sitting in my old wicker chair, bending slightly to darn my uncared-for socks as I hurried to attend a class. She left Philadelphia late in September for her return journey home.

29 ~

A BOYCOTT of Japanese goods started in American colleges late that fall. My roommate had been born in China and her missionary parents were still there. Naturally she had strong feelings for the Chinese people, and these she never bothered to conceal. Mano was among the first at Swarthmore to wear a "Boycott Japanese goods" pin.

One wintry day when we were walking to our room together, she proudly showed me her pin, the size of a fifty-cent piece. "Don't you think it's good, Yoko?" she insisted.

I made a sound in my throat which might have meant anything: "Hmmn . . ."

It was not that she was needling me and I knew that. She was so proud of doing something which she felt right that she wanted to show off, and I appreciated her truthfulness. However, she did not realize that I, as the only Japanese on the campus, was taking the full burden of the situation upon myself, and it hurt.

Some persons, I think, participated in the boycott movement because they felt it would strengthen the liberal elements in Japan. I felt differently. I thought this would give the militarists all the more reason to insist that they had to protect Japan's interests where they could.

Twitter was another missionary child who boycotted Japan. Although attractive and intelligent, she did not appeal to many boys, so that a date was an event. One Saturday night she was getting dressed up in her one and only party dress to go out with a boy. Like other missionary children, she had very little spending money, and to her dismay she discovered that she did not have a good pair of hose. She came to ask me whether I would lend her a pair. Intentionally I drew out my best pair of silk stockings, obviously a Japanese product, and presented them to her. She tenderly put them on her palm and seemed to ponder. After a few minutes she returned them to me with a sigh and said, "Thanks just the same, Yoko." For that, I appreciated Twitter all the more.

It was at the World Youth Congress, held at Vassar College in the summer of 1938, that I experienced emphatic anti-Japanese sentiment. Drunk with good intentions and self-righteousness, hundreds of young people representing more than half the nations of the world condemned Fascism, militarism and imperialism.

About thirty young Chinese were flown to the conference on the *China Clipper*. These representatives from "war-torn China" were hailed as though they alone were the symbol of resistance against the evils in the world. Among them was a young girl—rather homely and boyish with bobbed hair, wearing a simple blue Chinese cotton dress—who could not speak a word of English. Her qualification for attending the conference seemed to be that her parents had been killed by a Japanese bomb. When I heard this, I felt that I could not look her straight in the eye.

It pained me that a country of which I was a part was responsible for taking the lives of her parents and making her an orphan. Yet it seemed hypocritical for me to shake hands with her and say, "I apologize." I was sorry—perhaps more so than many others at the conference who shook hands with her and patted her on the shoulders. I knew it was against the rule of international law to kill civilians, and that Japan was violating the rules. But wasn't that modern warfare?

[94]

It was easy to say that Japan should be condemned because she was the aggressor. Legally, defensive war was permissible. But the right to decide whether or not a war was defensive was reserved to the nation at war. The Japanese Government, of course, insisted that she was merely defending her legitimate interests and that it was a threat to her national security to have an unfriendly neighbor such as China. Although I felt some other solution was more desirable, I could not be convinced that Japan was all wrong and others all right.

The fervor and excitement of the conference did not sweep me away, but rather made me more sober than before. I kept asking, "How can they be so sure that they are right?" I was disturbed and confused. And when a reporter from *Life* magazine interviewed me, I said with all sincerity: "I don't believe Japan knows how to bring about peace with the assurance shown by the delegates of other countries." When the magazine came out, I saw myself quoted as saying: "Japan does not know how to bring about peace . . ." Although my letter of protest to the Editor was published later, I heard that the Japanese police blacklisted me for this remark.

This, however, did not discourage me from trying to get to know the Chinese students residing in International House in New York after the conference was over. I even made friends with a Korean girl who was notorious for her anti-Japanese sentiment. Some Japanese eyed me coolly for my conduct, but that only made me defiant. "This is the only place where I can come to know these people, and why shouldn't I?" I said. I was outraged when I heard some Japanese call me unpatriotic. But I have somewhat enjoyed the uncomfortable role of being one of the minority ever since.

30 ~

WHEN I was ready to start my junior year at Swarthmore, Father was no longer able to support me even with the tuition scholarship given by the college. It was through Mother's efforts and the kindness of the Umeko Tsuda Scholarship Committee in Philadelphia and in Tokyo that I was granted a thousand dollars to finish my education. This scholarship was established by friends of Mother's "Cousin" Umeko, the first Japanese woman student at Bryn Mawr. Although I never told the scholarship committee of my relationship to Umeko Tsuda, since it is rather remote, Mother and I felt it more than a coincidence when this award was granted to me.

In my senior year at Swarthmore I wrote a thesis on "Japanese Ideas of Sovereignty." Just as I had needed earlier to clarify my ideas on God, so now I wanted to examine for myself the Japanese concept of sovereignty—which, it was claimed, only the Japanese could understand. Yosuke Matsuoka (no relative of mine), who was the chief Japanese representative to the League of Nations at the time of Japan's withdrawal and later our foreign minister, had attempted an explanation in an article he wrote for *Liberty* magazine about this time. To call the Japanese Emperor the organ of the state was like calling a star a bunch of dust, Mr. Matsuoka asserted. It did not convey a true image. According to him, the Emperor was the Emperor and no explanation was possible. I could not accept this. If it takes a Japanese to understand our feeling toward the Emperor, I reasoned, then what makes a Japanese?

I cannot say that I was fully equipped to tackle this problem. I started by assuming that the expression "sacred and inviolable," as applied to the Emperor, could be explained in modern political phraseology. In other words, I accepted his inviolability and set out to examine it. In the course of my reading, I had access to two books which were said to be authoritative but were banned in Japan at the time. Dr. Tatsukichi Minobe, the author, had been a professor of constitutional law at the Tokyo Imperial University, but because he maintained what was known as the "organ theory of the Emperor," his books were forbidden and he himself expelled. For him, the only possible interpretation of Article III of the Japanese Constitution— "The Emperor is sacred and inviolable"—was that the Emperor *as an organ of the state*—being the source of all law—was outside and above it though limited by it in exercise of his authority. This distinction between the Emperor as a person and as an organ of state was not acceptable to those in power, who wanted to make the Emperor a living god. But to me Dr. Minobe's view seemed the only tenable one.

My thesis, which followed his line of reasoning, was submitted to the political science department and helped to earn for me high honors upon my graduation.

All through college I had cherished two secret ambitions. One was to go to graduate school and work for a Ph.D. in political science. The other was to see Europe before Father did. My course was decided when the Japanese YWCA invited me to attend the World Christian Youth Conference to be held in Amsterdam that July. I accepted. One dream was to be fulfilled. The other would have to wait.

EUROPE

31 ~

AFTER SEVEN years it was sad to leave America, which had become my second home. I had made many close friends whom I might never see again. With a through ticket to Tokyo and two hundred dollars in traveler's cheques, I stood on the deck of a Cunard steamer until the last bit of New York's skyline disappeared from sight. Feeling rather dramatic about returning to my mother country, which now seemed slightly unattractive except for my family, I murmured softly, "No one, not in my situation, can appreciate my feeling of sadness at this parting. . . . I now leave, not knowing when or whether ever I may return," a passage from Sherwood's *Abe Lincoln in Illinois*, which I had seen magnificently played by Raymond Massey the night before.

London was the first stop in the long journey. More than anything else I wanted to visit the Parliament. It was on July 10 that I sat in the spectators' gallery and witnessed an event of great import to the history of England and of the world. On this hot afternoon Prime Minister Chamberlain reaffirmed his government's resolve to assist Poland in the event of a German invasion, putting an end at least for the present to all uncertainties which had attended speculations on the subject.

The House was filled as the Speaker, clad in a black robe and a heavy wig, entered to take his seat. If the gallery had not been so deadly quiet, I am sure I should have whispered to the one sitting next to me: "Wouldn't you think he would suffocate in that costume? Isn't it odd that such a civilized country as England should still maintain this sort of rather unsensible tradition!" My second thought was one of slight relief that the Orient was not the only part of the world guilty of sustaining antiquated customs.

The grave, but otherwise emotionless expression on Mr. Chamberlain's bony face remained unchanged while he read his prepared address. Although he had been severely criticized for his "appeasement" before, the present announcement was received not with cheers but with very heavy hearts. Or so I felt.

In contrast to what one might call the unashamed candidness of the Americans, I found the English people painfully restrained and reserved. In America even a stranger would ask me, and often in an accusing tone of voice, about Japan's military expansion. The first question invariably was, "Why is Japan in China?" At first I considered this impolite and rude, but later I came to like such frankness. There was no need to search for unspoken ideas and indignities.

The English were totally different. All England was reported to be outraged at Japan because of the "Peking Incident" in which Japanese soldiers literally pulled down the pants of some British soldiers: for the first time in history, perhaps, the white men had been openly "insulted" by the yellow men in Asia. But not once was I asked to comment on this during my ten-day stay in England.

An Englishman would always smile when introduced, but would never talk about anything more controversial than the weather. Perhaps I looked too innocent and naïve for any enlightening discussion. Perhaps this English attitude was more sensible than the American practice, for neither energy nor emotion was used up. But to me, fresh from America, such extreme politeness was almost painful.

While in London I was invited to the home of some Japanese friends where I met a naval attaché to the Japanese Embassy. After several cups of warm *sake*, this officer began to talk about how much he missed his children. To convey my sympathy in what I thought was the proper manner of conversation, I said with all sincerity, "You must miss your wife, too." To my surprise he replied bluntly: "No, I miss only my children." Then I realized my blunder. I had forgotten that most Japanese men, particularly military men, considered it "sissy" to show attachment to their wives. Even if they loved them they would pretend to care little for them, especially in front of others and more especially to a slight acquaintance.

However, the way this navy man answered me was a little too

emphatic to suggest that he was merely following the normal etiquette of conversation. Moved by the inquisitiveness of an American college graduate rather than the timidity of a Japanese woman, I ventured to ask, "How could that be when you miss your children?" This time he glared at me through his spectacles and answered very distinctly: "The wife exists only to lend her belly."

I had never heard such vulgar and rude language, so completely foreign to my upbringing. It was an insult—a great insult.

In anger I retorted, "Do you mean to say that women exist merely to perpetuate the family line?"

"What else?"

"Well, first of all,"—I was still the American college graduate speaking—"women are human beings and not the tools. Moreover . . ."

I stopped short when I noticed that he was becoming very amused. Apparently, he had never been talked back to by a female in this fashion, and he seemed to think it was a big joke. For the first time in my life I wanted to slap a man—to slap him very hard. Then after indignation subsided, I felt helplessly sad. I would have to face more of his kind at home. I certainly did not look forward to it.

32 ~

PARIS WAS the next stop. Although I did not have the slightest knowledge of the French language, I assumed that English would be understood in tourist centers such as railway stations and hotels. I was astonished and worried, therefore, upon my arrival in Calais, only a hopping distance from England, to find that no one spoke or seemed to understand very simple English—much less Japanese.

It was past ten in the evening when I found myself in the Paris terminus building. There was nothing I could do but hail a taxi to take me to the YWCA residence. The streets seemed unusually dark and quiet as we sped along, and I could think of all sorts of ominous situations. Sitting on the edge of the seat, I prepared myself for the worst.

Finally the taxi stopped in front of a tall iron gate, which had already been closed. The driver motioned me to get out and rang the bell. A tall, bearded man, clad in what seemed to be a medieval monk's robe with a heavy cord tied around his waist, descended the stone steps and slowly opened the gate.

"YWCA" I shouted at this most un-YWCA-looking man.

Getting no response from his masklike face, I turned to the driver, who had already unloaded my suitcases and now shoved me through the gate.

Inside the building things were slightly better. There was a woman at the desk who, although she looked like a hysterical and cruel teacher in a reform school, somehow made the place seem a little safer. With a heavy accent, she told me in English that I was expected. At last I felt befriended and secure.

I spent my ten days in Paris sightseeing, usually with American tourists with whom I felt most at home. One unexpected discovery was the affectionate tone in which our French guides brought back the memories of Napoleon Bonaparte and Napoleon III. I had thought that all French people boasted more than anything else about their Revolution.

In every cathedral women of all ages were kneeling, either in prayer or supplication, with an expression almost of naïveté on their faces. Those were the same sad faces I had seen on Japanese peasant women, burning incense and murmuring prayers in front of temples and shrines. Where is that rational thinking of which the West is so proud and to which it claims exclusive ownership? I wondered. I wished that I could speak their language so that I could talk to them and ask the many questions which filled my mind.

33 ~

THE WORLD Christian Youth Conference which met in Amsterdam that summer was the first of its kind. Nearly a thousand young people, representing all denominations and many nationalities, assembled in this Dutch capital to discuss the problems of peace and the role of Christian youth in the world.

I joined the Japanese delegation of about a dozen young men and women, most of whom had come directly from Japan. They were extremely discreet and their apparent reluctance to talk freely even among themselves indicated more than the usual Japanese reserve and politeness.

"How is the unemployment problem at home these days?" I asked one of the girls.

"There is no such problem."

"Really? What has happened to the several millions who were jobless in the early thirties? Have they just melted away?"

"I don't know, but we are not supposed to talk about unemployment," she answered uncomfortably.

Perhaps growing heavy industries had absorbed a great deal of man power. But it was this girl's attitude toward the problem which astonished me and gave me a glimpse of the pressures which I had to expect upon my return home.

The sponsors of the conference treated the Japanese delegation as though it were something fragile. I think they were sincerely glad that the Japanese could attend the conference, but they also seemed keenly aware that we represented the most "unchristian" nation in the world at that time. As there were no official delegates from Germany and Italy, the spotlight fell upon us as the aggressor.

China sent many delegates—many more than Japan. Somehow this war-torn country always managed to send large delegations to the various international conferences. I felt that the Japanese students should engage in a frank discussion with the Chinese and proposed this to our delegation. I believed that even if we did nothing else, we should talk with the Chinese. But others were reluctant. It was at a carefully planned tea party that the two groups finally met officially. Behind the steam rising out of our teacups, we put on our Sunday smiles and exchanged friendly greetings. Sponsors were apparently relieved that there were no open clashes and embarrassment. Indeed it was a well-behaved party, but meaningless.

As I sat impatiently, exhibiting my best behavior, I recalled the World Youth Congress on the Vassar campus the year before. What a sharp contrast! It had been nerve-wracking then to be looked at with accusing eyes which said, "You alone are the enemy of human-

[105]

ity." But at the earlier meeting there was an electric enthusiasm, even though it failed to convince me as to the ultimate solution of the world problem.

Now in Amsterdam I was annoyed by the attitude: "You are wrong and I dislike you, but for the time being let's not talk about it." I asked myself: "Why can't we blow away this tea party steam between us and have a heart-to-heart talk? If Christians cannot talk frankly about the problems which separate them, and come to a decision without killing each other, who can?"

I wonder now where that frank discussion that I so firmly advocated would have led us. Very likely nowhere. But it might have taught the young Japanese Christians to look at themselves with brutal truthfulness. It might have strengthened—instead of shaken—my faith in Christianity.

On the last day of the session a communion service was held, and for the first time all the denominations represented assembled together to share the common experience. "This is truly an oecumenical movement," many said with joy. It is ironical to look back to that day, remembering what followed only a month later. Christians of the world hailed the Amsterdam Conference because it succeeded in holding one mass communion when the most inhumane war mankind has experienced was just around the corner. Many have said apologetically since, that a drop in the bucket was better than none at all. But how inconsequential that drop was! When it disappeared into the bucket, it immediately lost its identity.

While we were attending the YWCA conference which followed the Amsterdam gathering, a baby girl was born to the House of Orange. In villages near by the young and old, men and women, danced until late at night to celebrate the occasion. This apparently genuine and spontaneous show of affection by the Hollanders toward their sovereign struck me strangely. The Japanese did not have this feeling of intimate joy toward their Emperor. Our feeling was rather one of awe and reverence.

34 ~

FROM AMSTERDAM I went by train to Freiburg in southern Germany to visit my former teacher at Jiyu-Gakuen, Takahashi-*sensei*. She was one of the first women to be admitted to a university for men in Japan. There were only colleges for women. She was now studying philosophy at the University of Freiburg. Her intelligence, eagerness for knowledge, candor and honesty—a combination of qualities not often found in Japanese women—had always impressed me.

Takahashi-*sensei* was boarding in the home of a middle-aged German woman. A few hours before my arrival, the woman's husband had departed for the United States because he was a Jew. Owing to their non-Aryan blood, her two children also were away from Germany at school: a daughter in England and a son in Switzerland. Our landlady had seen neither of them for two years. I felt as though I were intruding by being a guest in her house at this inopportune moment.

From her blond hair and light complexion, I could tell that my hostess was a "pure-blooded" German. She carried herself with complete placidity and welcomed me in a cordial manner, as though nothing whatever had happened to upset the tranquillity of her household. Her manner reminded me of a well-trained samurai wife, who would even force a smile at the news of her husband's death in battle. This puzzled me because I had understood Westerners did not behave in this fashion.

My curiosity could not be restrained when the three of us—the Frau, Takahashi-*sensei* and I—took a walk in the rain in that quietly beautiful and serene town of Freiburg. I waited until we were away from houses and other pedestrians before I asked, "Why did you not leave the country with your husband?" Takahashi-*sensei* interpreted for me.

Without an expression of emotion, the woman answered, "I am a German. I must stay here."

Perhaps she did not have the money to go away. Perhaps there were regulations forbidding her to leave the country which she did not want to explain to a mere acquaintance. Or perhaps she had formed the habit of not giving honest answers to questions. I tried to catch her real meaning from her intonation, but could detect no shade of cynicism or indignation. This baffled me and then it made me sad. I did not know why.

I have thought about this woman often since then, trying to reason her calm acceptance of her situation. I think I know now why. It was not courage which made her calm; it must have been the loss of human feeling. That was why it was so sad. Apparently, she had lost the power to feel anger toward those who had killed what had made her life meaningful.

35 ~

SWITZERLAND SYMBOLIZED peace, as the home of the League of Nations and the country which kept its neutrality. Although I was not unaware of the League's weaknesses, I still had a dreamy attachment to that organization when I visited Geneva in August 1939.

There was not one Japanese in that beautiful international town when I arrived there. Even the Japanese Consulate had closed down. Japan had traversed into regions where Geneva could no longer follow, and I felt extremely lonely.

The white marble building of the League of Nations cast its shadow in the deep blue water of the Lake of Geneva. Standing on the steps trodden by so many who had aspirations to make this world better, I touched the cool column. What a tragic symbol for peace, I thought. The U. S. A. deserted it in the beginning, and now it is without Germany and Japan.

The Secretariat was still working busily in that otherwise deserted building. There were many visitors that day—mostly Americans— and we were taken on a tour by a guide who droned his well-memorized speech in such an uninteresting, businesslike manner that the most creative imagination could not have discovered a hint of the spirit with which the League was born. At the end of the tour we were led into a small auditorium where we were to be shown a film.

The silent motion picture began to unreel, and we were taken back to the day of Japan's withdrawal from the League in February 1933. Small Yosuke Matsuoka, the chief Japanese delegate, was making a speech in the center of the assembly room. His voice was not transmitted, but the text of his speech had been made well-known to the world. Japan and other members of the League held "different views," he said, as to the way to achieve peace in the Far East; therefore, the Japanese Government felt they had reached "the limit of their endeavors to cooperate with the League of Nations." As soon as Mr. Matsuoka finished, he took off his heavy-rimmed glasses and started to walk toward his seat. At this moment all the other Japanese in the room stood up. With the eyes of the whole world concentrated upon them, they walked out of the League of Nations in calm defiance.

My mind was still wandering through that day in 1933 when I heard the guide's voice droning on again. He was implying that Japan's withdrawal was solely responsible for the failure of the League machinery, a point of view I could not help but resent. Japan had perhaps given the League the last dramatic push, but the blame was not hers entirely.

I left the white marble building with a heavy heart, but still with a little hope that I might some day find myself in it again.

The old gray and uninspiring Disarmament Building was being used as a lecture hall. In its basement I found an exhibition of war photographs sponsored by the Chinese Government. The purpose of the display seemed obvious: to show the cruelty of Japanese "aggression" in China. It was not easy to look at these pictures of bombed cities and suffering people, but I was determined to see every one of them. One photograph halted me and it was to haunt me for many years afterward. It was a picture of a middle-aged Chinese woman dying on the street, apparently wounded by a Japanese bomb, and a child of about three, small and dirty, crying beside her. I could not take my eyes from the picture even after I had memorized every detail.

Bewildered and confused, I asked myself, Was this necessary? Could we not have avoided it?

Suddenly I saw a young Chinese approaching me. I remembered

his face. He had been one of the delegates to the Amsterdam Conference. With a conquering smile and in a voice so loud that everyone around could hear, he said, "Now you know what the Japanese are doing to the Chinese."

I stared at him with dignity, I hoped, and did not say a word. What was there to tell him? Whatever I might have said would have been taken either as a bad excuse or a timid apology, and what I had in my mind was neither. It would have been something like this: "Yes, it was unbearably brutal, but modern warfare is that. Moreover, the distinction between civilians and combatants no longer exists as it once did. I realize this does not excuse war itself. But it is the causes of war which we must study and cure."

I was back at the same place where I found myself after the World Youth Congress. I was still not convinced that Japan was entirely to blame for the disorder and chaos in the world.

I was staying in a small *pension* during my week in Geneva. There I was among students from the United States, Canada, England, Germany and Norway, most of whom were attending the Institute of Higher International Studies. Dinner time was gay and enjoyable, for we all ate together at a big round table.

The boys used to say half-jokingly: "The next meeting place will probably be on a battlefield."

It was indeed too gloomy a prospect, and yet they said it again and again and laughed. "Why must they mention it?" I wondered. They almost seemed to find pleasure in these words, and I could not understand. Perhaps they sensed that war could not be avoided, that it was coming within a frightfully short time, and there was nothing they could do to prevent it. Hating to admit that they were merely pawns in the world of power politics, they had come to Geneva to study in the hope of finding a solution. The flip remark was an expression of foreboding born of a wish to conceal their fears.

I have lost the names and addresses of these young men, although I can still see some of their faces. I wonder who else is alive to remember those delightful evenings at a Swiss *pension* only a little more than ten years ago?

36 ~

I SPENT the following week sightseeing from Venice to Rome, and from Rome to Naples, where I boarded a Japanese steamer. It happened that this was the last boat to leave Europe eastward, for Germany marched into the Polish Corridor just as our steamer slipped into the Red Sea, the bluest of blue seas I know. That was September 1, 1939. Two days later England declared war on Germany as she had promised.

Colombo, a port city under British jurisdiction, had a blackout when we arrived there a couple of days later, and German passengers were not permitted to leave the ship, a neutral territory. We were already feeling the impact of war in a small way.

I was appalled to discover in Colombo that all the Ceylonese working around the dock looked like Gandhi in physical stature, with their mosquitolike legs and arms and almost no stomachs. I wondered what and how much they ate.

Dozens of these mosquitolike men and boys swam around the boat, fighting to catch the coins thrown into the sea by the passengers. The sight made me ill, for I felt this to be the worst sort of exploitation of human dignity. At the loud laughter of a chubby Japanese businessman standing next to me, I burst out indignantly, "Don't you think this is an insult?"

The remark apparently surprised the man, but he answered calmly, "I don't see any difference between this and throwing coins to a beggar singer or an accordion player. Those men below need the money and if they want to get it this way, why not?" He gave me a sympathetic smile and turned away.

I was relieved not to have to reply to him. There was no plausible answer I could think of that would combat his logic, and yet his reasoning failed to subdue my indignation. Was I just an impulsive, emotional, inexperienced girl who did not know the hard facts of life? I walked away leaving loud and amused laughter behind me.

More bewilderment confronted me at Singapore. A Japanese newspaperman took me to a party given by a British customs officer. In a badly lighted small apartment, which looked as though it had not been swept or dusted for about a week, I found a dozen or so people of unidentifiable nationalities relaxing with liquor and cigarettes. A Chinese girl, an insipid beauty with cream-colored stockingless legs exposed by long slits on either side of a tightly fitted Chinese dress, was sitting on the lap of our host, who was fondling her like a pet dog.

I must have raised an eyebrow or dropped my jaw a couple of notches, for my Japanese friend whispered to me that the girl was the British officer's mistress. Even I did not need to be told that. I would have been more shocked if this were the behavior of a casual acquaintance. At first she repelled me, but as I continued to observe her she began to appear terribly pathetic. This was probably the easiest way for her—to be dressed in colorful silk dresses, to be fed well and sleep on a decent mattress. Now it became painful to look her straight in the eye.

The guests later decided to go to a cabaret. This was my first visit to such a place. Here the dancers were mostly Chinese; some Eurasian. They all wore Chinese dress, fitted like a bathing suit around the bust and waist, with a straight skirt slit up to their thighs to permit free movement of their legs. The men with whom they danced were a promiscuous assortment who looked either silly or stupid. I had never seen such a bold and shameless manner of existence and for the first time in my life I felt my middle-class puritan standards challenged. Was I superior simply because I did not have to make my living in such a manner?

Hong Kong was another British port. From Port Said to this Oriental-Occidental city, a distance which our steamer had taken three weeks to travel, every port at which we had stopped was under British jurisdiction. The immensity of the British Empire had become a living reality to me.

Father had told me about the beautiful hillside of the Hong Kong harbor. The white walls and colorful roofs of the well-built European style houses in this British section of the town gave it a meticulously clean appearance, particularly in contrast to the narrow, smelly streets and dirty dwellings of the Chinese section.

[112]

We had been warned before leaving the ship that we should pretend to be something other than Japanese because of a strong anti-Japanese sentiment in the city. The purser cautioned us not to ride in rickshaws for, "Not long ago a Japanese was thrown over by the rickshaw man." We were advised not to speak Japanese to each other on the streets and not to go about alone. Although it still seemed unreasonable that anyone should harm me because of something for which I was not directly responsible, I took all the necessary precautions. I went out with other Japanese girls to do some shopping in the center of the town and hurried back to the *Haruna-maru* while the sun was still high.

Compared with Singapore and Hong Kong, Shanghai was dirty, uncouth and confused. It was under Japanese military control when we arrived, but I soon discovered that that did not make it any more pleasant than the two previous port cities. An American missionary friend met me at the boat and took me in a car to show me the town. There was not much to see, however. A large part of what I did see had been crudely destroyed—no doubt by Japanese bombs. Perhaps that was what she wanted me to see. However, these scenes did not particularly arouse or distress me after the brutal war pictures displayed at the Disarmament Building in Geneva. What horrified me was the Japanese sentry standing in the middle of the bridge which connected the town and the pier.

This bridge was the only road leading to the pier, and we had to walk across it in a single line. The Japanese sentry was checking all passers-by going toward the pier. I observed that the Chinese had to show their identification cards as they reached him, but since I was a Japanese and did not have such a card, I assumed that I was expected only to follow the line of people and not deviate from it. I had been talking with my friend and kept on doing so as we came to this soldier.

All of a sudden he barked at me: "Stop!"

Thinking that he mistook me for a Chinese, I told him in Japanese, "I am a Japanese, you know."

This made him furious. I decided to show him my passport to convince him. He grabbed it, looked at it, and continued to hold it.

"Please give it back to me," I demanded, but he would not and looked at me with scorn.

Trying to suppress my indignation, I said as calmly as I could manage, "My boat leaves in a very short time. I need that passport. Please give it back to me."

"Don't you understand there is a war going on?" he shouted.

"What does that have to do with this?" I thought.

"Why talk to an American, you unpatriotic bitch!"

"She is a friend of mine. There is nothing wrong in talking to a friend, is there?" I snapped back, although I knew that was not what I should have done. What he wanted was humility and apology. But I was too proud.

I looked him straight in the eye, trying to conceal my indignation and fear, and demanded again, "Please give me back my passport." He barked some incomprehensible words and finally thrust it back into my hands.

As I joined my American friend, who had been standing helpless and frightened watching this spectacle, I tried to think what had made the Japanese soldier so angry in the first place. When I turned to have a last look at him, I saw a Japanese man approach him, take off his hat and make a deep bow. *"Gokurosama-desu,"* the man said —"Thank you" or "It's good of you to do this." Ah! so that was what I should have done! But why? Why thank and do honor to a soldier standing on a bridge to prevent "subversive" Chinese from going out on the pier?

However, after returning to the ship and having calmed down, I could see the situation in a slightly different light. Undoubtedly this soldier believed firmly in the "great mission" Japan was carrying on in China. In his eyes, I—Americanized in appearance and talking English to an American and paying no "proper respect" to the Emperor's representative—must have seemed to lack feeling for my country. He was probably a man of little education from a poor family, and the only way he knew to act big and "patriotic" was in that incomprehensible and barbaric manner.

I was still angry, but I felt that the root of the problem lay deeper. Wherever it was, the anticipation of having to face more of this was dreadful.

The miniature gardenlike landscape of Japan was beautiful as our boat approached the Inland Sea, and I could hardly wait to join my family again. But the feeling of joy and excitement had been considerably tempered by the events of the trip. It was with a mixed feeling of hope and apprehension that I ended my long journey home.

MANCHUKUO

37 ~

I FOUND my family busy with their affairs. Father was back with the *Mainichi* again, the newspaper on which he began his career as a journalist. Mother was active in women's organizations, writing and lecturing. Kwoko was finishing her junior year at the Tokyo Women's Medical College. Reiko was studying Japanese literature at the Tokyo Women's Christian College and belonged to their drama group.

Before I lost myself in this whirlpool, I wanted answers to the questions which had been troubling me. I had been seeing Japan from outside for seven crucial years. People of other countries by their criticisms and questions had put me on the defensive, and my natural reaction was to try to justify Japan's deeds, whether or not they might be so justifiable. But all along I had been aware of my dilemma. I had not been able to placate myself entirely by my reasoning.

Now I bombarded Father with all the unanswered questions: Why did Japan have to go into Manchuria? Was Manchukuo a puppet government as the rest of the world said? Was this sort of expansion the only possible way of solving Japan's population problem, since other nations, the United States and Australia in particular, had shut their doors to us? Could not Japan survive without the resources of Manchuria and North China?

Father's reply was pleasantly unexpected. "Why don't you take a trip to Manchuria and North China?" he asked. "You have seen America and parts of Europe. Now you should learn something about Asia." In order to make the trip as profitable as possible, he suggested that I get a letter of introduction from Mr. Yosuke Matsuoka, the former League delegate and at one time president of the South

Manchurian Railway Company. Father had known him years before when neither of them was married.

Accompanied by Father, I went to call on him. Yosuke Matsuoka was a short man—perhaps five foot three or four—with hair clipped even shorter than the "navy cut." His heavy black-rimmed glasses and black, bushy mustache almost covered his small, well-proportioned face. He was wearing a grayish-black silk kimono and *haori* (a coat which is worn on top of the kimono) with a *hakama* (a pleated skirt-like garment usually made of heavy silk, worn on top of the kimono but inside the *haori*). After greeting us, he sank into a large leather chair and proceeded to take over the conversation.

"What do you intend to do, Yoko-*san*?" he asked.

"I should like to go into journalism."

"That is indeed an interesting and important field. We lack good journalists, who are well acquainted with international affairs. I am hoping my eldest son will take up the profession." I gathered that journalism was one of many ambitions Mr. Matsuoka himself had held in his youth.

One lavender orchid plant, the only ornament on the mantelpiece in the Western-style living room, attracted my attention. Orchids were rarely used in Japanese flower arrangements, although they were relatively inexpensive. To me, accustomed to think of them according to the American sense of values, that one large orchid gave the finishing touch to the room's highly bourgeois atmosphere.

I mentioned this to Father when we had left the house. Looking slightly amused, he said in his usual casual manner, "That probably has been his dream of a living room ever since his student days in America while he washed dishes to finish his college education."

I was on my way to Manchuria early in November, only a month after my return to Tokyo. Thanks to the letter given me by Mr. Matsuoka and the courtesy of Mr. Ohmura, then president of the South Manchurian Railway Company, I had a first-class pass which permitted me to travel almost anywhere in Manchuria. Moreover, the company had offered to provide a guide, for safety's sake they said, when I visited a border town between the Soviet Union and Manchuria. This was indeed an exceptional courtesy to be shown a young female who held neither position nor influence. I don't believe

I was properly impressed by the power of the right "pull" in a society like ours.

Mukden, to which the headquarters of the South Manchurian Railway Company had been moved from Dairen, is the largest city in Manchuria. It was a full day's ride from Pusan, the port city in southern Korea where I landed. From this dirty industrial city of Mukden the railroads extended like the feet of an octopus—to Peking in the west, to Dairen in the south, to Peian in the north. Taking advantage of my privileges, I decided to travel as extensively as possible and see as much as I could. I was limited, of course, to the cities and towns on or close to the main railroad lines, for bandits—the most active groups were led by the Chinese and Korean Communists, I was told—were still active in other regions. Sometimes they even attacked the trains which were guarded by Japanese soldiers.

Although I had been told that there was not much to see at the northern border, I was curious for a glimpse of Japan's formidable and talked-about, but little-known neighbor. I wanted to say when I went home, "I have seen the Soviet Union." There was a choice of three border towns which I might visit—Manchouli in the west, Aigun in the north, or Hulin in the east. I chose Hulin because the train connections were better and it was rarely visited. Also, there was a concentration of Japanese settlements in northeastern Manchuria which I wanted to see.

On the way I passed through Tsitsihar, a junction where passengers enroute to the trans-Siberian Railway might change trains for Manchouli. Tsitsihar was a cold and dreary city. Apparently not many people were traveling to and from the Soviet Union. The Japanese population here seemed small, and the expressionless Manchus moved about as if they did not have very much to do. I could detect little enough life here, but Peian farther north, was still more lifeless. This town, which lies slightly above 48 degrees latitude, was bitterly cold in late November. Harsh winds pierced the fur coat which I had borrowed for the trip, and my feet, well covered by a pair of high fur-lined boots, were almost numb. Except for the area immediately around the station, there did not seem to be any inhabitants. With no vegetation in sight, it was a gray, barren village.

The train went southward to Harbin. Like Hong Kong and Singapore, Harbin was a combination of the Eastern and Western cultures, but the White Russians, unlike the British, created a sadly exotic atmosphere. There was none of the bubbling decadence of the two port cities. Here was simply a dying culture. But the incense-filled churches, shrunken and wrinkled Russian women selling odds and ends on the streets, beautiful blond Russian waitresses speaking perfect Japanese, dirty *yanchos* (the Chinese version of a horse and buggy) and the Japanese-operated hotels, cabarets and railroads made it a conglomerate and colorful city and a great tourist attraction.

Hulin was east of Harbin. Only those with special permission from the Japanese military authorities could visit it. There were few people left on the train when we arrived, all Japanese. I was the only woman, and I must have presented a puzzle. My general appearance was obviously Americanized and my face as obviously Japanese—but much too serious and plain to proclaim me an entertainer who might be visiting remote army outposts. The men passengers eyed me boldly from head to toe, apparently trying to size me up. For although the Japanese are noted for their politeness, the men can be most impolite toward Japanese women.

At Hulin the porter came through and pulled down all the shades. My guide, Kimura-*san*, who had joined me in Harbin, explained: "From here on it is a military zone. This town, Hulin, appears on the map as though it is the border town, but it's really not. Our destination, *Hutow*—the Tiger Head—is about a forty-minute ride from here."

Hutow was a village of probably a few hundred people. Although Kimura-*san* told me that some top officers had their families with them, I saw only military personnel. A major was good enough to take me to the border line, which was within walking distance from the center of the village. It was the river Ussuri, only a few yards wide at this particular point. The invisible line, I knew from my college seminar in international law, ran down the middle of the stream, which was quite frozen at this time of the year. On the other side was endless prairie, bare and cold, with not a soul in sight. This was the Soviet Union—so enigmatic and so ominous.

There were no bridges, but the frozen surface of the Ussuri was inviting. Yielding to a childish desire, I said half-jokingly to the major, "I could walk to the Soviet Union, couldn't I?"

"Oh! no," he replied in a voice of grave concern, apparently unable to decide whether a vicious intent was concealed behind my naïveté. "The Russians are watching carefully all the time, even though you don't see them. They will shoot you if you try to cross the river."

"Oh," I answered meekly.

Was he trying to scare me or was he telling me the truth? I could not see a single object on the other side of the river—only gray earth which melted into the gray sky above. I could have stood there for hours in the bitter cold, which froze my breath in front of me and made me aware of every crease in my face as I moved my mouth, just watching that lifeless expanse and pondering what it meant to the world. But I had seen what there was to see.

As we walked back to the station, I thought: If Russia does have ill intentions toward us, Japan is dangerously close—that is true. For any part of Japan is within five hundred or six hundred miles of Vladivostock. In that case a friendly Manchuria is essential for our security. Although military control by Japan is unfortunate, it seems inevitable that we protect Manchuria as well as ourselves because of her strategic position and her apparent inability to defend herself.

38 ~

LEAVING HULIN, within a few hours we came to the Japanese settlements. Even Westerners seldom refuted the argument that one reason for Japan's expansion overseas was her ever-increasing population. So it surprised me to find comparatively few Japanese immigrants in Manchuria even though they constituted 40 per cent of our overseas population. I was told that there were little more than 600,000 Japanese in Manchukuo and Kwantung Leased Territory, of whom only one per cent were farmer settlers brought there with the promise of a Government subsidy.

The oldest and best-known settlement was near Chamussu, a town northeast of Harbin. There, to my astonishment, I saw a small Japan—little wooden houses with *tatami* floors and women wearing cheap rayon kimonos. They looked cold and uncomfortable, and I could feel their suffering in this dry, windy, sub-zero weather.

"Why didn't they build houses more suitable to this climate?" I asked my guide. "Something like those the White Russians have. Just to have beds above the floor level would keep them warmer at night."

"The Japanese feel more comfortable sleeping on the floor," he said.

"Then why don't they adopt the Korean *ondoru*?" The *ondoru* is a stone construction beneath the floor made like a chimney, through which warm air is carried. Using this method, comparatively little fuel is needed to heat an entire floor.

"That is probably more sensible," he argued, "but the Japanese take their *tatami* anywhere they go, you know."

His apathy toward the problem shocked me. Population pressure was indeed real, and Manchuria with its vast uninhabited expanse had been widely hailed as a solution. Not only the Government, but the South Manchurian Railway Company, promoted emigration. To me it seemed a lack of ingenuity as well as responsibility not to see that the newcomers were assured the minimum of comfort.

My guide told me that each family owned its house and a piece of land, which was more than they had had in Japan proper. Farm implements were owned communally, and work was done on a cooperative basis. This was possible because the land was new and the fertility of all farms was equal, so that every farmer could hope for the same results as his neighbor, given the same expenditure of time and energy. Also the large size of the farms in contrast to the small ones in Japan proper almost necessitated using cooperative methods. It was an interesting experiment, for Japanese farmers like peasants the world over are confirmed individualists.

There was a common dining room in each settlement, for the purpose apparently of saving time and promoting communal spirit. After showing me one crude barracklike hall, Mr. Kimura said, "We have some trouble because different families have different likes and dislikes in food, and the women want to cook their own meals. You know the Japanese are very individualistic." Again his attitude toward the settlers seemed foreign and almost cynical. I could not tell whether he realized that he himself was one of those individualistic Japanese who had to carry his *tatami* everywhere he went.

I became almost angry when he added: "The women are completely unprepared for this sort of life. They insist on wearing their kimonos in this cold weather. They would be much better off if they adopted the thickly padded cotton trousers of the Manchu women. And hardly any of them know how to ride a horse, which is the only means of transportation around here."

Most Japanese women, particularly those in the rural areas, had not been brought up to think for themselves; they had been taught to conform to agelong traditions and customs. To ride a horse would be considered unwomanly in Japan except in a very few Westernized upper-class circles. Why blame these women for lack of ingenuity and skill? If any were to be blamed, it seemed to me it was the men, who wanted to keep their women submissive and doll-like. The officials of the Ministry of Overseas Affairs in Tokyo and those of the newly established Manchuria Colonial Development Company, who knew conditions in these desolate parts of Manchuria and had encouraged the undertaking, were really most at fault. These men were, I felt, both insincere and irresponsible, and I included my guide among them. But I did not dare argue back, for that would have been an impolite return for his courtesy.

So far as I could tell, the settlers stayed in this forbidding land only because they had been told that it was a patriotic undertaking. I think many would have preferred to return to Japan even if that meant becoming tenants again, but that would be losing face. Behind their tired, strained faces, the men wore a harsh, determined look, and the women showed almost complete apathy. In the eyes turned to me I read resentment and a slight antagonism. I was an uninvited visitor, who lived comfortably in Tokyo. I felt guilty. But what could I do?

39 ~

IN THIS troubled mood, I went on to Rashin, a port in northeastern Korea near the Soviet border, facing the Japan Sea.

Rashin was one of the most thriving ports on the entire eastern coast of Korea. A new railroad from the Manchurian border, connecting further inland with the Manchukuo State Railways, made it possible to transport from here to Japan the Manchurian exports which had formerly been shipped almost exclusively from Dairen in Kwantung Leased Territory. This railroad had been the scene of border clashes between Russia and Japan only a year before—in July and August of 1938. Peace and order were being maintained when I went through, however.

By going north through Kirin, I came to the capital of Manchukuo, Hsinking. Well planned, but half completed, this city gave the impression of a badly done crossword puzzle. Concrete government buildings of Western-style architecture were scattered over a large area and connected by wide paved roads. For the sake of beauty, I was told, there were no streetcar lines: only busses, but too few to be adequate, although they were newer, larger and more beautiful than those in Tokyo. This presented an awkward transportation problem, particularly for government officials who had to go from one department to another.

One Japanese official told me, "It was a noble idea to have a city planned in the beginning so that it would not grow incoherently like many Japanese cities. Someday we hope to make it into an ideal capital city, something we could not possibly realize in Tokyo. But, at this stage, buildings are too far apart for convenience. You simply cannot do business unless you have an automobile."

Although full of idealism, this official talked as though he owned the country. His attitude bothered me, for had not Japan proclaimed to the world that Manchukuo was an independent country? Then I began to notice a large number of Japanese in this capital city, particularly in the government offices. Although from the Emperor down, all the nominal department heads of Manchukuo bore Chinese names, the actual administrative work seemed to be carried on almost exclusively by Japanese.

I asked the same official what the population of the city was. He answered, "About three hundred thousand."

"And how many Japanese?"

"Nearly seventy thousand, most of whom are in government service," was his reply.

I wanted to ask, "Then it is really a puppet government, isn't it?"

But I lacked the courage, as the term "puppet government" connoted aggression on the part of Japan, which I hated to admit. Furthermore, I knew that he would not only make a denial but would think me subversive.

Highly disturbed by these discoveries, I sought justification for Japan's methods elsewhere. Since the literacy rate in Manchukuo is extremely low, perhaps there were not enough Chinese and Manchus of administrative competence to do the work, I reasoned. If Japan's intention is to benefit the people, as it is said—order had been restored compared to the days of the Manchu war lords and many industries had been started with Japanese capital—perhaps this overstaffing with Japanese officials is unavoidable. These Japanese call themselves immigrants. If their intention is to make Manchukuo their home, perhaps there is nothing wrong in their having so prominent a part in government.

The fact that there was practically no trace of Japanese assimilation, and the fact that many Japanese men had left their families in Japan, was cause for a little worry. But, after all, this was still a young country with an acute housing shortage, particularly in Hsinking and Mukden. It was not yet time to draw conclusions, I decided.

Truly independent and sovereign states are decreasing in number anyway, I told myself. Only a few powerful nations can maintain actual independence in their foreign as well as domestic policies. Military or political control of another country appears more crude than economic control, but can one say which is aggression and which altruism? So I argued myself into a position of realistic power politics. While I did not overlook the welfare of the subjugated Chinese and Manchus, or consider it insignificant, I found justification in the fact that the Japanese were accomplishing for them what they were unable to accomplish for themselves. It never occurred to me that the Chinese and Manchus might have felt different.

It was a relief, therefore, in Hsinking to find Sato-*san*, a young Japanese man who sincerely believed in the co-existence and co-prosperity of the five racial groups composing Manchukuo. He was working for the *Kyowakai*, a semipolitical organization whose purpose was to promote *minzoku-kyowa*, or cooperation and peace in cultural fields among the Hans (Chinese), Manchus, Mongols, Japanese and Koreans. (The Chinese constituted 80 per cent of the total population.) The five colored stripes of the Manchukuo flag were chosen to signify cooperative effort between these five groups.

Western critics would call the organization a Japanese propaganda agency, and no doubt it was, but I am convinced that the intentions and motives of some of the Japanese working there were truly sincere and noble. For example, Sato-*san* and others like him had learned the native tongue and did not insist that the Hans and the Manchus use the Japanese language. In their personal relations with people of other racial groups, they practiced equality. Sato-*san* said to me, "You know it is very strange, but we have more trouble with the Koreans than with any other group. They insist that they are superior to the Chinese and the Manchus because, they say, they are Japanese subjects."

Later I heard the same story in Peking. It certainly indicated that the majority of Japanese in Manchuria and North China acted as if they were superior to the other racial groups. In turn the Koreans claimed superiority either from an intention to embarrass the Japanese or from a need to take out their grievances on others.

Sata-*san* was clearly perplexed by this situation. Neither he nor I realized then that personal sincerity and good intentions operating within the framework of Japanese control could not overcome the evils which that framework itself produced. We took the position that Japan's method of expansion was perhaps unfortunate, but could not be helped if her security in Asia was to be maintained. Perhaps our attitude was fatalistic. Nevertheless, we would have been hurt and taken the defensive had anyone challenged us by saying, "The road to hell is paved with good intentions."

I met only one Manchu during my trip. Chen-*san*, a girl of about my age, had studied at my aunt's school, Jiyu-Gakuen, in Tokyo. Her father was a wealthy businessman. She invited me to lunch one day at her home in Mukden. In a large, bare Western-style dining room, she and I sat at one end of a long rectangular wooden table. We chatted about Manchuria as we ate with chopsticks the steaming hot *kaoliang*, which is the main staple of Manchuria—soft, slightly gluey and pale pink in color—and an assortment of vegetable dishes cooked more or less in a Chinese style but not so tasty.

She was extremely reluctant to express her opinions. Although she looked ill at ease and rather sad, I thought in my simplicity that she did not know enough to have her own ideas.

Having been educated in Japan, Chen-*san* was probably more pro-Japanese than many other Manchus but, being a Manchu, her acceptance of fate must have been mixed with other emotions. As for me, I was full of sincerity but incapable of understanding the feelings of the conquered because I wanted to rationalize the deeds of the conqueror of which I was a part. I probably would not have appreciated the delicate agony in which Chen-*san* found herself, even if she had been able to express herself candidly and with eloquence.

40 ~

COAL WAS the foremost mineral product of Manchuria, and the Fushun mine, only about an hour's ride from Mukden, was famous for its vast deposit and open cut. Escorted by a man from the South Manchuria Railway Company, which was operating this field, I visited Fushun. The open cut, which I was told was the largest in the world, was a miniature black Grand Canyon. I had never been so impressed with the abundance of the earth's resources as I was looking at the quantity of coal which spread before me. The salad-bowl-shaped pit was dug in many terraces, on each of which lay a level of the railroad track. The miners and the freight trains looked like toys, and the sky seemed ever so large and far away from the edge where I stood. This is the Ruhr of Asia, I thought, and felt how indispensable it was to Japan's industrialization.

The South Manchuria Railway Company, established in 1906, was an empire in itself. It boasted that it "has been and still is the carrier of the light of civilization into Manchuria." Not only did the company own and operate the railways and coal mines in Manchuria, but it controlled a number of joint-stock companies, industrial concerns, factories, experimental laboratories and farms. It also operated schools, libraries, research institutes, hospitals and hotels, and it administered the Railway Zone. The company provided residences for its Japanese employees and it had its own telephone system. Perhaps no other concern in Japan could equal this one in the diversity of its undertakings. Hence the president possessed tremendous power, unparalleled by any other individual in Manchuria.

Father had told me that Mr. Ohmura, the president, was the first railway technical expert to be appointed to this political job. His predecessors had all been men of political ambition and not purely railway experts. Mr. Ohmura happened to be the last president of the South Manchuria Railway Company, which was forced out of existence as a result of the war. I heard later that he died in a war prisoners' camp in Manchuria.

41 ~

I FOUND PEKING more colorful and picturesque than Kyoto, the old capital of Japan, whose beauty with its many old temples has been widely acclaimed not only by the Japanese but by many Westerners. The green, slanted roof and the snow-white wall of the Rockefeller-endowed Peiping Union Medical College, the gold roof and the lacquer-red wall of the Forbidden City, and other colorful Chinese architecture stood among an unusually large number of trees for a city of such size. The high stone walls, built by the Ming Emperor in the early fifteenth century, still surrounded this ancient capital, and seemed to absorb all the hustle and bustle of a modern metropolis of a million and a half people. Peking gave a warm and settled-down feeling, completely different from what I had experienced in Shanghai.

Aunt Hani had a school for Chinese girls here and this was where I stayed. The low-roofed gray Chinese structure made a small square compound behind a roofed gate and a tall wall, facing the street. There were a common dining room, kitchen and bathroom, and the rest of the building was divided into the students' sleeping quarters and study rooms. Nearly twenty teen-age girls, many of whom had come from low-class families, lived and studied with the Japanese graduates of Jiyu-Gakuen, who were selected by Aunt and Uncle

Hani as teachers. There were three or four of these permanent teachers, while my aunt, uncle, and cousin Keiko took turns in visiting this branch of their school.

After the Marco Polo Bridge Incident in July 1937, when the relationship between China and Japan was acutely strained, Aunt Hani felt that she must do something to help create mutual understanding between the two peoples. Being an unpolitical person with a firm belief that her way of living was the only road to a good society, she undoubtedly felt that cooperative living would make a beginning toward badly needed understanding between Japanese and Chinese. I feel sure that there was no ulterior design on her part, no wish to be on the right side of the Japanese military authorities through this project, as some have accused. She was genuinely sincere. However, she, too, was guilty of accepting the *fait accompli* as the basis for friendship between the Chinese and the Japanese. I am sure it did not occur to her—as it did not to me or to many good-intentioned Japanese—that this premise itself was the biggest barrier between the two nations. It was not surprising that some Western observers, and I feel sure most Chinese, charged that her school in Peking was a manifestation of Japanese cultural imperialism.

The Peking school was a small Jiyu-Gakuen. Cooperative living was rigidly scheduled. The girls rose early in the morning as the bell rang, prepared their own breakfasts, cleaned their rooms and studied. They were taught the Japanese language, sewing, weaving, cooking and other household chores. The Japanese staff members learned the Chinese language, and the school was conducted bilingually.

As the Chinese had various living habits and customs, the merits of these conflicting ways were discussed, and those considered most suitable by the majority were adopted. Keiko, who was in Peking then, told me, "We had quite a discussion about how many wash towels we must use. The Chinese girls insisted that it is more sanitary to use two towels—one exclusively for the face and the other for the rest of the body—as they apparently do. Although we in Japan are accustomed to using only one towel, we decided that in this particular case their sense of cleanliness was better than ours. Since then all of us have been using two wash towels." This explained the array of towels hanging in the bathroom.

[131]

I found how inconsistent the Chinese were in their habits, however, when I visited Peking's largest market place, the Eastern Peace Market. A large wooden building about the size of two tennis courts was filled with all sorts of commodities from meat to flower vases. The noise of bargaining echoed to the high ceiling, and the mixed odor of vegetables, fowls, meats, garlic and oil was thick in the air. Pigs' brains—pinkish, spongy, ball-like masses—sat on the wooden counter amongst dry goods and vegetables. There were no rules of sanitation that I could detect. Perhaps the Chinese would say that, since all ingredients are cooked thoroughly before being eaten, there was no need to put the meat inside clean glass cases. Nevertheless, it did seem strange that the same people should insist on two towels for sanitary reasons.

Another interesting difference in the attitudes of the Chinese and Japanese was pointed out to me by one of the Japanese officials. He said, "Formerly the streetcars in Peking had two classes—the first and second. We thought it better to abolish this distinction from the point of view of equality, and so we did. But, strangely, the complaints came not from those who used to ride first class, but from the second-class passengers. They argued that it is much better to have two classes because they could ride for a lower fare. We had thought the poor resented people who rode more comfortably."

Perhaps I should not have taken this story at its face value, as I did. Perhaps the motives of the Japanese officials were completely merce-nary: they might have reasoned that they would receive more revenue by having one class and setting the fare somewhere between the former first and second class fares; they might have used the idea of equality as a pretense. But I think this would be too harsh a criticism.

True, there were Japanese in North China as well as in Manchuria, who were entirely mercenary. They exploited their advantageous position, profiting as much as possible. Strange as it may seem to Westerners, however, the young Japanese officials as well as the army officers whom I met during this trip were genuinely idealistic—Asia for the Asiatics, prevention of the infiltration of communism, co-existence and co-prosperity for various racial groups, and peace for Asia. But their premise of Japanese leadership was not acceptable to the rest of the world, including other Asiatics, many of whom concurred with the ideals.

Wanting to feel that Japan, of which I was a part, was doing something good, I no longer questioned the validity of the premise. I believed that the motive justified the deeds. I did not know that idealism based on an unacceptable premise is just as dangerous as realism of a military kind or outright profiteering.

I returned to Tokyo feeling that there was no other course possible for either Japan or her neighbors. Time will prove that Japan is right after all, I decided.

JAPAN

42 ~

UPON MY return from Manchuria I was perplexed to see posted in public places the slogan: "Bear more children and increase the population." What a contradiction! I thought. One of the more convincing reasons for Japan's expansionist policy was her population pressure, and yet the government itself was encouraging an increase in population.

Although I had come to accept the position Japan had assumed in the international field, life in Japan, I soon found, was too uncomfortable to be accepted without question. I felt as though I were shut in a small cubicle where if I yawned I would bump the ceiling, and if I sneezed my nose would scratch the wall.

It was soon after my return to Tokyo that I discovered how low the ceiling of this cubicle was. Father came home one day, looking grave, and said to me: "Four of the books which you sent home from Swarthmore were confiscated by the customs office. It is bad to have such a record there as they report the names of those who own such 'subversive' literature to the Metropolitan Police Office. I asked one of our reporters, who has worked in the Yokohama area for some years and knows those officers personally, to have the customs office cancel the record and return the books to me."

He dumped the four books, carelessly wrapped in a piece of old newspaper, into my lap.

I was stunned. While in America I had been told that I should be careful about the books I shipped back to Japan. Some Japanese friends had warned me that anything which could be considered derogatory to the Emperor—such as caricatures of him—severe criticism of government policies, or Marxist writings would be confiscated. The only book I owned which it seemed to me could possibly come under this heading was Lenin's *State and Revolution*, included in a long list of required reading for the seminar on political theory at Swarthmore.

Despite this warning, I had shipped all my books to Tokyo, including the one by Lenin. Thinking I would find out for myself just how thoroughly the customs officers went through the baggage, I had put this one small booklet apart from the others, at the very bottom of my large trunk, and covered it with underwear, old stockings and all sorts of odds and ends which would be tedious to look through. If the customs men found and took it, I reasoned, my loss would be twenty cents, the price I had paid for it in a second-hand book store. It never occurred to me that if a book was confiscated the name of the owner would be recorded as someone to be watched.

I was chagrined that my curiosity and innocence should have caused trouble and concern to Father. Silently I opened the package: there before me was that old, dirty copy of Lenin; the June 1936 issue of *Fortune* magazine, devoted to Japan; and *Militarism in Japan*, by Dr. Kenneth Colegrove of Northwestern University. I have forgotten now what the fourth book was.

Bewildered, I asked myself, "What did I do that was so wrong? Could reading these books, some of which are critical of Japan's present policies, make me a subversive element? Could it make me disloyal? And what does confiscation accomplish? Can it stop ideas from flowing into Japan?"

My first words to Father were, however, "What shall I do with these books?" For a moment I thought that I should burn them. They seemed like hot potatoes in my hand. But at once I realized that burning them would be admitting guilt which did not exist at all.

Father had resumed his casual manner. "Oh! just put them somewhere where they won't be too noticeable."

I did so, but although I was convinced I had done no wrong, wherever I put them they appeared larger and more conspicuous than any of the hundreds of other books Father had on his shelves. I felt that I could find them blindfolded.

I felt apologetic toward Father, who had abused his privilege in order to protect me. But I did not apologize, for I knew he too disapproved of such government policies. He did not scold me for having brought the books from America, nor did he warn me to be more careful in the future. He just dropped the subject, and for this I was grateful.

After those first moments of dismay, I became angry. What nonsense, really, I thought. Half my indignation was toward the Government, the other half toward myself for letting the incident upset me so. I had lost the courage to take bold action. Why? Was it fear of the consequences which, at worst, would be imprisonment? No—at least then I thought I was not afraid. Neither did fear of exposing my family to this sort of "shame" worry me. Mother previously had assured me, "We would never be ashamed of the consequences of your action so long as it is what your conscience dictates."

This was at a time when I was being a little melodramatic. I had warned Mother that I would stand up for my principles, regardless of the cost. Then why did I lose my courage? Perhaps because of the caution which comes with so-called maturity. I had decided that it was childish to rub the authorities the wrong way unnecessarily; I was going to keep my head down lest I should bump the ceiling again.

I seemed to be scratching the wall, too. Mother told me that I bowed too high for a Japanese woman. Although she herself did not, like the orthodox women, spend several minutes bowing low in an exchange of greetings, she probably thought that I would be misunderstood—either as one who had never learned the proper etiquette or as one who was too conceited to bend my head down far.

Just as there is a hierarchical deference in our language, so is there also in the form of bowing. The lower your social position, the lower you should bow. The younger you are, the lower you should bow, unless your position is definitely higher than that of the older person to whom you are bowing. If you are a woman bowing to a man, you must bow lower than the man, except when you are of a higher social position. Therefore, the degree to which you lower your head is considered indicative of your attitude toward the other person. The only persons exempt from this form of greeting were policemen and soldiers in uniform. They saluted instead. Our policemen still do this —now like the American MP's.

43 ~

PERHAPS IT was to show me how orthodox Japan lived that Father invited me one evening to a *machiai*, commonly known in the West as a *geisha* house. He and Nitta-*san,* a university friend, were having a business talk there, and Father asked me to join him around nine o'clock on my way home from a dinner party.

I had read and heard about the *machiai* and had seen geisha on the streets, in department stores, at hot-springs resorts and in theaters, but this was my first visit to such a place. Shinbashi in downtown Tokyo had rows of *machiai*, and the geisha in this district were known as the Shinbashi geisha, who, with the Yanagibashi and the Akasaka geisha, were most admired in Tokyo.

The geisha are not prostitutes; they are primarily entertainers, who are trained from their teens to play Japanese musical instruments, to sing and to dance for men. Their foremost ambition, I understand, is to get married.

A *machiai* is an ordinary Japanese house—usually with two stories in prewar days—which has several *tatami* rooms. The whole building is surrounded by a rather high wooden fence. The stone or cement floor of the entrance is always cleaned with water like the deck of a battleship. On such national holidays as New Year's Day, when the front sliding doors are open, a bit of salt, shaped in the form of a pyramid and about an inch high, is placed in the middle of the railing as a symbol of cleanliness. There is a stone step in the entrance well below the wooden floor, where one takes off one's shoes before going inside.

The *machiai* which I visited was built in this way. Father and Nitta-*san* were waiting for me in a six-mat *tatami* room drinking *sake* when I opened the paper sliding door from the polished wooden hall. Two geisha—one must have been in her late thirties or early forties, the other in her middle twenties—were sitting beside the men, pouring *sake* and chatting. I noticed their polite but keen eyes taking in my not-well-powdered nose, my American-made gray suit and silk stockings. After sitting properly on the floor, I bowed to Nitta-*san*. Father then introduced me to the two geisha. I bowed again—this time not as low as before—and they bowed politely to me.

Their features were not particularly beautiful. I had known more beautiful girls even among my school acquaintances. What impressed me was their poise and understanding of the art of making themselves beautiful. Their well-pomaded black hair was immaculately arranged in the upswept style with carefully placed waves. The older geisha wore a black silk kimono with fine silver threads like spring rain. The younger one wore a kimono of sky-blue silk. The collars were carefully pulled out in the back—the characteristic geisha way of wearing a kimono—to show the back neckline. This line is considered the real test of feminine beauty in Japan. I imagine it is because Japanese women are so often in a sitting position, wearing a kimono which covers the entire body, that the back neckline—the only part of the body exposed—has come to represent beauty. The paintings of women in *ukiyoe* (old Japanese color prints) often show the back of the neck. Lowering the collar of the kimono in this fashion is comparable to a Westerner wearing décolleté—and this the ordinary Japanese woman would never do.

As is customary in any high-class restaurant, a steaming white hand-towel, like the one a barber uses after a shave, was brought to me in a small bamboo basket to wipe my hands. As I unfolded the towel, the odor of perfume curled upward with the jet of steam and pleasantly tickled my face.

The older geisha said lightly to me, "Your honorable father has been telling us that you have studied in America for seven years. Wasn't that nice."

Observing me carefully, but pretending to be casual, she then presented me with a little porcelain *sake* cup and poured the golden-colored *sake* into it.

"Thank you," I said rather stiffly and sipped the warm, mellowing liquid.

A pair of wooden chopsticks and a small dish of crimson salmon caviar, my favorite, were placed before me. I felt the eyes of the two geisha following my every movement as I ate. Apparently this was the first time they had ever served a feminine guest in the *machiai*.

[141]

They were not hostile toward me in any way. They were extremely curious to see and listen to the American-educated daughter of one of their male guests—a young woman who was not a bit shy in talking with the men.

I commented to Father after we came out into the chilly evening air a little later, "The *machiai* is not as bad as I had thought. It was rather pleasant, in fact, but I don't see why men should pay such fabulous sums of money for the *sake,* a few bits of delicacies and the company of geisha in order to have a business talk. Those geisha were charming, I must admit. And they knew how to talk with men. But I don't like this custom of men having parties alone outside their homes."

Father, who had had enough *sake* to feel happy, listened to me without comment.

44 ~

DURING THOSE first months after my return to Tokyo, I was often lonely because I had no friends of my own age. I had moved into regions completely apart from my former classmates at the Jiyu-Gakuen, who seemed to be clinging tightly to their "good living" and were not much concerned over what was happening outside their circle.

One afternoon I accepted an invitation to speak before a group of about a hundred Jiyu-Gakuen alumni and tell them of my experiences in Manchuria. In order to add a little color to my more serious comments, I recalled this anecdote:

"More than once in Manchuria I was mistaken for the daughter of Yosuke Matsuoka. At one place the station master came to welcome me as I descended from the train. He bowed deeply and escorted me to his office where he served me a cup of hot green tea. I was a little surprised at this unusual courtesy, but it did not occur to me that I was being mistaken for someone else. Then I was whisked off to a hotel owned by the South Manchurian Railway Company. There the proprietress rushed out to greet me and take me to an immaculately clean *tatami* room with Western-style veranda, apparently the best room in the hotel. When she bowed low and asked, 'How is your honorable father?' I knew that she and the station master supposed me to be the daughter of their former employer. But if I told her that I was not even a relative of Yosuke Matsuoka, she would be very embarrassed. I decided to avoid the issue. In that way her face would be saved and, as long as I did not lie, my conscience would be clear. So I replied, 'My father is fine, thank you.' Then she asked, 'How is your honorable brother?' Since I have no brother, I could not say he was fine. Instead I just mumbled and bowed very low."

My listeners did not even move their eyelashes as I told this story. Their faces were expressionless masks. Feeling let down and ill at ease, I finished my talk. Afterward I asked Mother, who had been in the audience, "Did you not think that was amusing?"

Mother smiled. "Yes, I thought so. But you should not expect these girls and women to have your kind of humor. Moreover, you must not say just 'Yosuke Matsuoka.' You must add an honorary title."

"Oh! but Mother," I protested, "I could hardly say 'Matsuoka-*san*.' That would sound too familiar. He does not have any military rank nor a title of nobility. Surely it is all right to say 'Yosuke Matsuoka' when a man is so famous."

But Mother insisted that this was not acceptable. "When you are talking of him," she went on to explain, "You can say 'Matsuoka-*shi*.' *Shi* is a masculine form of speech, but it is permissible for us to use it, too. But if you are talking *to* him—an elderly man whose social position is high—you should address him as '*sensei*.'"

45 ～

I HAD not discarded entirely the idea of becoming a newspaper-woman, but I believed with naïve conceit that I had a responsibility to work with some organization attempting to bridge the gap between Japan and other nations. Filled with idealism, but with little realization of the intricate problems involved, I set out to find a job which would in some way contribute to international understanding and world peace. I decided to consult Count Aisuke Kabayama, whom I had met two years earlier in New York. He was well known for his activities in the America-Japan Society and other international and cultural organizations.

Count Kabayama, a small, thin man who must have been in his late sixties, listened patiently as I talked, then said, "I think the International Cultural Association is the place for you." The Count was one of the directors of this organization. Prince Takamatsu, the second brother of the Emperor, was the honorary president and Prince Konoye, then the prime minister, was the president. The board of directors included many among the Japanese aristocracy.

The purpose of the Association was to introduce Japanese "culture" to people in other countries and to foreign visitors in Japan. I had known something of its work, but because of the group's highly dilettante air I had never been greatly attracted. In fact, I had no intention of working with the Association when I went to see Count Kabayama. But since I had no plans of my own and did not know how to say "No" to an elderly count, the decision was made before I was aware of it.

Count Kabayama went on speaking in his low voice. "Don't think that you can utilize what you have learned in college right away. You must begin at the bottom." I nodded to this good advice. Then he added, "Since you do not have to support your family or yourself, I should think that a salary which would cover your personal expenses would be enough."

This American-educated Japanese count could not possibly have subscribed to the Marxist dictum: "From each according to his ability; to each according to his need." I could only assume that this was a way to cut down the Association's budget. If it had been a philanthropic organization, I should have felt differently. But as I understood that the Association was heavily subsidized by the Japanese Foreign Office, it seemed reasonable that I should be paid according to my ability and not according to my need. Yet in spite of my dissatisfaction I remained silent.

A few days later I began working at the International Cultural

Association, which had its offices on the seventh floor of the Meiji Insurance Building, later to be used exclusively by the Occupation forces. This seven-story white marble building stands on one side of the front of the palace grounds, facing the *Nijubashi,* or Double Bridge, which is used exclusively by the Emperor. The Imperial Palace, the Emperor's home, is surrounded by a high stone wall which is in turn encircled by a moat. Besides *Babasakimon,* the main gate which leads directly to the *Nijubashi,* there are several lesser gates to the Palace, all guarded by policemen.

At the time I began to work for the International Cultural Association, in January 1940, it was the custom for all Japanese to bow every time we passed the Palace gates. Even while in streetcars, which circled the moat, the conductor would shout as we passed by a gate, *"Kyujo-mae!"*—In front of the Palace—and all the passengers promptly faced the Palace and bowed. The Tokyo streetcars were usually packed and the people nodding from all directions sometimes bumped into each other. It was absurd, but it seemed unavoidable. There was no law compelling one to bow in front of the palace, therefore the police could not arrest anyone who disregarded the custom. Still, social pressure was too great to be ignored.

I remember one day when Mother arrived home and reported angrily, "I was riding in a streetcar with an American friend. We were facing the opposite direction from the palace when we passed by the *Nijubashi.* I felt it would be silly to bow in that position, and I did not do it. Well, a man standing in front of us stared at me and called me unpatriotic. I stared right back at him. He didn't say any more, but it was indeed unpleasant."

The terms "patriotism," "loyalty," "unpatriotic" and "disloyal" had begun to be used indiscriminately, and refusing to bow when passing by the palace was considered defiance of the Emperor and the State. Although the Meiji Insurance Building was almost five hundred yards from the main gate, we were obliged to bow every time we crossed the street in front of it.

I tried to avoid crossing this street as much as possible, to relieve my conscience for doing something which I believed utterly absurd. Soon I discovered that I was not the only one who was avoiding these uncomfortable corners. I was walking one noon with Michiko-*san,* one of my colleagues at the Association, who was a graduate of a women's college in Tokyo. As we approached the Palace grounds, she interrupted me in the middle of a sentence to say, "Let's turn around now so that we won't have to bow."

"Yes, of course," I answered, happily surprised to find that she too felt as I did. Some men riding on bicycles tilted their caps as they passed by the *Nijubashi*. "Don't they look as though they were saying, 'Hi! Emperor'?" I asked Michiko-*san*.

No doubt it was thought that bowing would arouse a feeling of reverence toward the Emperor, but carried to idiotic extremes the custom was merely ridiculous. Though most of my acquaintances agreed with me about this, we did nothing and said nothing in public, reasoning: "This is indeed nonsensical, but it is a small matter. It would be foolish to bang our heads against a wall over such a trifle." We were not aware that even as we ducked the ceiling it became a little lower every time.

46 ～

AT FIRST my duties at the International Cultural Association consisted of typing odds and ends, addressing envelopes, sealing and stamping them. At parties given occasionally for foreign guests and "cultured" men and women of the Japanese upper class, I checked the names on a list as people arrived or helped to serve dainty sandwiches and cakes. For this I was paid a monthly salary of 60 *yen* (approximately $20 in American money)—10 yen higher than that received by girls who were graduates of Japanese women's colleges, but 10 yen less than the minimum salary for young men who were university graduates.

With 60 yen you could buy quite a few things at that time in Tokyo. A lunch which included a good-sized hamburger, two vegetables, bread and butter, coffee and Jello or pudding cost 60 *sen* or six-tenths of a yen. For less than one yen you could get a cup of clear soup and two large slices of broiled eels served on white steaming rice at a famous eel restaurant, Chikuyo-*tei*. The price of a bowl of *soba*,

Japanese noodles, was 15 sen—enough for a light lunch. A pair of good leather shoes could be purchased for about 15 yen, and for several yen you could buy a yard of excellent satin. A copy of any monthly magazine of the serious type cost 50 sen, and a daily newspaper 3 sen. A first-class ticket for the *kabuki* (classical Japanese theater) cost 7 yen, but the cheapest seat was somewhere around one and a half yen; admission to the movies was from 50 sen to one yen in downtown Tokyo. The streetcar fare in Tokyo was 10 sen; the postage stamp to carry a letter anywhere in Japan, including Korea and Formosa, was still less than 5 sen. A private lesson in a foreign language, taught by a foreigner, cost between 3 to 5 yen per hour.

My salary was ample to cover personal expenses. I even managed to save some money by taking my lunch from home as most of the girls at the office did. Many men were supporting themselves on less than 100 yen a month, and some even helped to support other members of their families.

Nonetheless, what Count Kabayama had said made me feel that I was receiving less than I was worth, and as a result I did not put much effort into my work. Moreover, I did not think the difference between the salaries of the men and the women in our office represented fairly the difference in our abilities. It was true that the academic standard of the men's universities was much higher than that of the women's colleges. Also, considering that the average wage of women workers in Japan was between one-third to one-half of the wage paid to men, the situation existing in our office was not unusual, and I realized this. Still I was resentful.

What I refused to accept was the men's treatment of us as inferior creatures. It didn't take long to discover that the girls were expected to arrive at the office a little earlier than the men in order to dust the desks and sometimes even to sweep the floor. We were also expected to serve tea to our male colleagues. Japanese office workers drink hot green tea when they arrive at the office in the morning, at least once again during the morning, at lunchtime, again in the afternoon, and whenever they have visitors. It seemed to me the girls accepted this as a customary practice and only a few complained. When they did it was only among themselves.

I should not have objected to dusting the men's desks or to pouring

[147]

tea for them, had they not taken the service for granted. But it annoyed me to have them act as though we existed only to perform such domestic tasks.

Although I had accepted the idea that I must work from the bottom up, I was not convinced that what I was doing had much bearing on the furtherance of international understanding. The work of the Association included more than tea parties and exhibitions of flower arrangements, during which I worked mostly as a translator. One department produced and edited cultural films about Japan. In another department representative works of Japanese literature were translated into English. There was also a staff which compiled material on Japanese history. The Association's library was said to be the largest collection of books on Japan written in English. A series of lectures in English about Japanese history was presented for foreign visitors.

No doubt many foreigners found the services of the Association useful. But to me its leisure-class atmosphere and its tourist-bureau-like presentation of Japanese culture seemed actually to bar rather than to promote understanding of Japan's course of action in the international field, which the rest of the world was condemning.

Had all the resources of the Association been made available to me, probably I should not have known how to utilize them in order to produce good will among nations. The conferences of my college days had left me disillusioned as to the efficacy of meetings in bringing about international peace. On a personal level, we who participated in them at least learned that people were people, whether they ate rice or bread; whether they shook hands, rubbed noses, or bowed to each other in greeting. It was something, but not enough to stop wars. I did not know what I or any group of Japanese could do at this time, but I was convinced that there must be something more worthwhile than what the International Cultural Association was doing. Perhaps my dissatisfaction was caused largely by the profoundly unexciting nature of my work. At any rate I was not content.

Many others on the staff felt as I did, but unlike me the men kept quiet. Perhaps this was because they could not get such "respectable" and easy jobs elsewhere. I could be vocal about my discontent because I had no fear of being out of work. Father was supporting me, and it would not matter seriously if I did not have my sixty yen for a few months. No doubt, I was considered an obstinate and strong-headed female. I had still to learn that one must be secure before one can speak one's mind freely. I believed conceitedly that I was courageous and the rest were cowardly.

One event which stands out in my memory of those days was the farewell luncheon given for Admiral Nomura by the American-Japan Society just before he assumed the ambassadorship. The American ambassador, Joseph Grew, and our foreign minister, Yosuke Matsuoka, were among the guests who attended this luncheon. When Admiral Nomura stood up to make his speech, in rather clumsy English, he was warmly applauded by hundreds of people who, like myself, were expressing their moral support of his mission.

"I am a sailor," he said, and if I remember the gist of his speech correctly, he went on to add that because he was a mere sailor he was not fit for such an important diplomatic post, yet he was going to do his best to serve his country. His thin hair was almost white, and I was particularly aware of his one glass eye, which did not move behind his heavy spectacles. This eye was injured by a bomb, thrown by a Korean in Shanghai in 1932, and I had been told by the Red Cross nurse who attended his operation how truly samurai-like he was then. Father was a good friend of the Admiral, and perhaps this • prejudiced me favorably toward him. I clapped my hands hard and long when the Admiral finished his brief and simple speech.

Yosuke Matsuoka had lost much weight in the interval since our meeting before my departure for Manchuria a year and a half before. This made his mustache and tortoise-rimmed glasses look ever so large on his thin, wrinkled face. Mr. Matsuoka was eloquent in the delivery of his speech, which was in English, but it did not move me as much as the one by Admiral Nomura.

Although I cannot now reproduce even a summary of Ambassador Grew's speech, I remember how highly I was impressed by his adroit use of the English language. This was the first time I understood that one could almost mean "To hell with you" when saying "Let's be friends." Even so, I believed that our Government was doing its utmost to achieve a peaceful solution of the differences between America and Japan.

[149]

As the days went on I continued to be dissatisfied with the work at the International Cultural Association. The general secretary did not discharge me for expressing my opinions, however. Perhaps he did not dare to do so since Count Kabayama was responsible for giving me the job. Instead he called me to his office one day after I had been working with the Association for a year, and said, "You would like to study, would you not?"

Not knowing what he was driving at, I answered noncommittally, "Yes, I would."

"I understand that you wrote a thesis on the subject of 'Japanese Ideas of Sovereignty' when you were in college. How would you like to study further on this subject?"

This was too tempting an offer, and he must have known that I would not refuse. Without looking at me, he continued: "I think it would be a good idea for you to study under a well-known scholar who has specialized in this subject."

Any well-known scholar at that time must, of course, have advocated extremely nationalistic views of the *Tenno* (or Emperor) system. Dr. Minobe's organ theory, which I had found the only plausible one when I wrote my thesis was not only refuted but was being attacked fiercely as disloyal. From the little that I had read and heard of the extreme nationalists, they appeared completely intolerant. Their hostility toward America was also well known. None of my friends or Father's friends belonged to this group and I hesitated even to associate with them, feeling that I could not be comfortable and honest at the same time. But after considering the matter carefully, I decided that I ought to know more about this viewpoint which millions of Japanese seemed to accept without question. I even became almost eager to discover the logic behind our national polity, which was said to differ from all other systems.

I accepted the general secretary's suggestion.

47 ~

BY THIS time I had acquired a new set of friends—men and women of my age—including some Americans, through the alumni meetings of the America-Japan Student Conference. All of us were concerned about the increasing tensions between the United States and Japan, and those of us working near by in downtown Tokyo sometimes met at lunchtime to discuss these matters.

I also attended monthly supper meetings held by those who had attended the Amsterdam Conference. This group was more interested in religious questions.

All the girls in these two groups were college graduates and most of them worked outside of their homes—many in the teaching profession, others doing research or translation.

One of them informed me that she had acquired a copy of Edgar Snow's *Red Star Over China*, then banned in Japan. Someone had bought it in Shanghai and had succeeded in smuggling it in. It was the secret pride of liberal intellectuals at that time to read as many banned books as possible. News was circulated usually by word of mouth as to which books had been banned and who had access to them. Although a novice, I was eager to claim the title of a liberal intellectual, and found much excitement and joy in this activity. It is a natural human tendency to want to satisfy one's curiosity, particularly when there is a "no trespass" sign. Had *Red Star Over China* not been banned, I probably would have felt no special urge to read it.

Carefully covered by newspaper, this book had been read by several others before it came to me. It was difficult for me to understand why such a book should have been forbidden. Was it not essential that we know as much as possible about our neighbor whom we were fighting? The book was also useful as a study of the growth of communism. However, once a policy of censorship is launched, the line between what is permissible and not permissible tends to become obscure. The inevitable result is absurdity, since everyone responsible is anxious to stay on the safe side. It seemed that we now were entering this last stage.

48 ~

THERE WAS ample reason for the general secretary of the International Cultural Association to want some tie with a nationalistic organization. This association—respectable as it was—was beginning to be criticized by the rightists. The weather was stormy in those days for any organization whose title included the word "international." It was almost as bad as the term "communism." Even the old League of Nations Association, which had come to be called "The International Association" after Japan's withdrawal from the League, had been renamed and was known as the "Diplomatic Association." Moreover, the International Cultural Association openly dealt with foreigners, including many Americans, some of whom were suspected of espionage work by the Metropolitan Police Office.

Later, in the fall of 1941, when I was questioned by the police concerning a correspondent for the *Wall Street Journal* whom I had come to know at the Association and whom I had invited once or twice to my house for supper, I realized how closely foreigners were being watched. And not only foreigners, but those of us who came in contact with them.

It was clever of the general secretary to think of sending me to a professor at the *Kokumin Seishin Kenkyusho*—the Research Institute of National Spirit.

Professor O., who had had his postgraduate work in Nazi Germany, was a large and handsome man, not a bit uncouth and military-like as I had expected. He did not wear his hair cut extremely short in the army style, which at that time many rightists insisted was the only true masculine way. He was even gracious when he welcomed me into a dark, dusty office full of books piled in a disorderly manner. His eyes were alert and sparkled with amusement, but they were not bold or harsh.

"The way to learn is to lose yourself in this atmosphere," were his first words.

I bowed politely and observed his untidy room with renewed interest. I could not imagine how on earth I could become lost in such surroundings.

The first assignment he gave me was to read a number of books and pamphlets which he himself had written. The professor was a prolific writer, who seized every opportunity to have his name in print. There was a good deal of repetition in what he wrote but in essence it was that the *Tenno* (Emperor) was *arahito-kami* or a "living god," and therefore, literally, sacred and inviolable as the Constitution stated. The *Tenno* was head of a hierarchy, the great family system of which we, his subjects, were humble members. It was our unique family system which distinguished our form of society from European totalitarianism and, according to the professor, made it superior.

Along with this theory, Professor O. valued the daily practice of bowing to the shrine and also *misogi*—a Shinto practice of standing under a waterfall to contemplate, although he himself did not adhere to this practice in wintertime as many ultranationalists were doing.

The professor had a little shrine in his small, untidy house. A shrine, whether large or small, is made of unpainted wood, without decoration. With its slanted roof and plain wooden body it looks serene and pure on a well-kept pebbled ground among twisted pines or tall, straight crytomeria. The miniature shrine, which belongs in a clean *tatami* room with hardly any furniture, is a familiar sight in a Japanese home just as a plaster statue of Mother Mary is a part of the White Russian household.

In the professor's home the light natural wood of the shrine stood out awkwardly on the *tokonoma* in the junky setting. The *tokonoma*, which is an alcove about the size of one mat of *tatami* raised slightly above the level of the floor, is the place to hang a painting or an example of calligraphy and to put a flower arrangement.

I could not decide whether the professor had the shrine in order to display his unswerving patriotism—he and others held that any loyal subject should have a Shinto shrine in his home—or whether

[153]

he really believed that it created an atmosphere indispensable to his theory of sovereignty.

One day he asked me to accompany him to the Kokugakuin, where he was teaching. It was a Shinto college in which young men were trained to be priests. After his regular class, we went up to one of the dormitory rooms where he conducted a small study group on the Japanese Constitution. Although well-swept, the *tatami* on the floor of this eight-mat dormitory room had been worn out and had turned dark yellow in color. Several serious-looking boys, all of whom wore their hair in the army style, were sitting on the floor with their legs folded in the proper manner. They bowed their heads low as we entered.

A small Shinto shrine about two feet high stood on the *tokonoma*. The place of honor in the room is directly in front of this alcove and the guest of honor is seated there.

Without a word, Professor O. went to this corner and seated himself facing the *tokonoma*. At this everyone turned toward the little Shinto shrine. There was a dead silence. Holding their heads high, with backs as straight as though they were in plaster casts and their faces solemn, the boys clapped their hands twice slowly, then bowed low toward the shrine three times. Sitting properly in the back of the room, I imitated them. Although new to me, this was a ritual just as valid, I supposed, as kneeling to pray or chanting a hymn. But I doubted that it was essential to my understanding of the Japanese Constitution, as the professor insisted.

49 ~

I READ more than Professor O.'s books. A large volume on the Japanese Constitution, written by Professor Sasaki, the chief opponent of Dr. Minobe, I read with care. While reading in Japanese I thought I followed the writer's logic, but as soon as I tried to translate into English, there was no logic.

"You see," I would explain to my foreign friends, "our idea is similar to that of the Divine Right of Kings in Europe."

Although in the West that idea was a thing of the past, at least the comparison made the Japanese concept less mystical and more intelligible. But of course, the Japanese theory of the *Tenno* had its point of difference. I went on to explain: "Our concept of gods is different from yours. There is no one God such as you have in Christianity. There are millions of gods and goddesses. In fact, all Japanese become gods or goddesses after their death according to the Shinto belief."

Inevitably the next question was: "How does the *Tenno* differ from anybody else and become a living god?"

To this I replied: "That is based upon our mythology, according to which our first Emperor Jimmu was given the imperial regalia of the mirror, sword and jewels. And our Imperial lineage has continued unbroken from the ancestral Sun Goddess to the present Emperor. The *Tenno* is a temporal as well as an ecclesiastical head."

Having said this, I still remained uncomfortably aware that my interpretation was distressingly inadequate and unscientific. Furthermore, I myself did not believe in the existence of so many gods and goddesses or in the fetishistic virtue of the regalia.

I would try to make clear the working of the family system: "The idea of rights and duties, the outgrowth of Western individualism, is not found in Japan because the relationship between the ruler and the ruled is not of a contractual nature. The *Tenno* is like a father to his subjects, therefore his way is synonymous with theirs."

"What if the *Tenno* happens to be tyrannical?"

"Well, he just wouldn't be," was my answer, and I was horrified at how unintelligent this sounded.

"Now really, how could anybody be sacred and inviolable?" my friends would persist.

In utter despair, I gave up. "I don't know, but millions of people believe this without question. Oh! there must be two systems of logic, don't you think? Otherwise, how can all this make sense to so many people, including intelligent people."

Many of us comforted ourselves with the belief that there were two systems of logic. To admit that the Japanese logic was not logic at all would have been too shocking.

The ambiguity in the thinking of the nationalist school I attributed to the Japanese language. I could not find any gray shades in the English vocabulary: all words were either black or white to me. "The Emperor is a living god; he is sacred and inviolable" in English made the existence of the *Tenno* completely above the earth. To most Japanese, however, the words "sacred and inviolable" did not connote anything holier than the position Catholics accord the pope, for example, but translated into English it sounded as holy as God himself.

I was oblivious to the fact that giving a legal basis to the *Tenno's* holy nature presented to those in power a weapon with which to seek more power. The Army, the Navy, and the Government were responsible only to the Emperor and not to the people. And since they alone, except for a few elder statesmen, had access to our *Tenno*, they could do anything they wished. Any opposition, any protest or criticism could be—and in many cases was—branded not only as disloyal and unpatriotic, but heretic.

The "two systems of logic" was a convenient way of accepting this status quo.

50 ~

BECAUSE MOTHER was known as a writer and was active in women's organizations, she was often asked to speak to women's groups throughout Japan. She complained that plain-clothes men came to the meetings where she spoke. "It has been bad ever since I returned from the Pan-Pacific Women's Conference. Those police-men do not say anything nor have they ever broken up the meetings, but knowing that they are there makes me very uncomfortable. It is particularly so in Kagoshima. [Kagoshima is a city on the southern tip of Kyushu Island where chauvinism was carried to extreme lengths.] The police there found a letter inside a comfort bag to be sent to soldiers at the front which read, 'Dear soldier, please do not die.' It was evident from the handwriting that the letter had been written by a child, but the fact that the comfort bag was prepared by church workers led the police to insist that it was subtle antiwar propaganda by the Christian Church. And the police made an issue of it. Ever since then the pressure has been particularly noticeable in that prefecture."

Mother reflected a moment. "At the time of the Russo-Japanese War, the feeling was quite different. A well-known poet, Akiko Yosano, gained her fame by that piece addressed to her brother in battle: 'O Thou! do not die.' To urge a soldier not to die was not subversive then."

What had brought about this change? It was more than just pressure upon the Church, for Christian churches in Japan were not strong enough to merit such attention. Perhaps because of the shift in the scales of war, the authorities picked on a minority group to demonstrate their determination to exact sacrifices from all. Like Mother, I felt that it was natural and right to ask a soldier at the front "not to die." But I did not attempt to think the problem through. My attitude was: There is nothing we can do to change the situation, is there?

Had I a brother or a close friend fighting in the war, I might have reacted with more indignation. But the issue of war and sacrifice for one's country was still an academic problem to me at this time. The situation was uncomfortable, but it had not become unbearable. It was easier to be silent and uncomfortable than to cry out and be crushed.

51 ~

KWOKO, THE older of my two sisters, was married soon after her graduation from the Tokyo Women's Medical College in April 1941. The proposal came unexpectedly from a family we had known closely for years—the Andos who used to live only a block from our little house in Tokyo before we moved to Osaka. It was Mrs. Ando's nephew, Tatsuo Fukuhara, who made the proposal, through Mrs. Ando, to my father.

We used to call Fukuhara-*san*, Yoichi-*san*, because he was the twenty-ninth descendant of a famous samurai, Nasuno Yoichi. Yoichi-*san* was a painter of Western style and "one cycle" older— that is, twelve years, since we count the years by twelve different animals—than Kwoko. As his parents had passed away long before, he lived with the Andos. And in any exchange of visits we three sisters treated him like an unexciting first cousin. Therefore, it was with surprise that we learned of the proposal. Father and Mother left the matter entirely up to Kwoko to decide.

Apparently Mrs. Ando was slightly apologetic because I was still unmarried. It is customary in Japan for the oldest to marry first unless there is a good reason for not doing so. This custom is not as strictly adhered to by boys as by girls, who normally marry in their early twenties. *Urenokori*—or "Leftover"—is the term used to refer to the older unmarried girls, and the usual reaction toward such girls is: "What is wrong with her?" I assured Kwoko—although I did not think she needed to be told—that she should feel free to marry any time she wished.

We did not discuss the proposal much. Kwoko was studying late every night for her final examinations, and I did not want to disturb her studies or influence her decision. She was not as surprised by the proposal as Reiko or I, and when she accepted it I thought that was what she wanted.

One of Kwoko's dreams ever since childhood had been to be married in a kimono. Mother agreed on condition that it would be an ordinary kimono and not an *uchikake*, which was a heavy white silk kimono over a scarlet silk kimono, to be worn only on the occasion of a wedding. It was to be a Shinto ceremony, since that was the religion of the Fukuharas.

The ceremony took place in an especially arranged room on the first floor of the restaurant where the wedding party was held afterward. The bride and groom sat on wooden chairs facing the small Shinto shrine at one end of the room. About two feet behind them sat the go-betweens. All the Fukuharas sat in a row on one side and all the Matsuokas sat in a row facing them on the opposite side. A priest clad in a stiff white costume like the wings of a cicada, and wearing a black hat which looked like a tea-kettle, stood in front of the couple. He mumbled a few words and waved a branch of *Eurya ochnacea* to clear away the evil spirits. A pair of teen-age priestesses in white kimono blouse and fiery red *hakama* (pleated skirt) appeared—one with a small red lacquer *sake* cup and the other with a red lacquer *sake* container. The first presented the cup to Yoichi-*san*, who received it with both hands. The second poured *sake* into the cup. Yoichi-*san* emptied it in three sips and returned the cup to the first priestess, who now presented it to Kwoko. Exactly as Yoichi-*san* had done, she took the cup in both hands, held it while the *sake* was poured, and swallowed the liquor in three sips. The first priestess then took away the small cup and brought a medium-size cup of red lacquer. She gave it to Yoichi-*san*, then to Kwoko, and the whole procedure was repeated. Finally, the priestess brought a third *sake* cup, still larger, and went through the ceremony again.

The marriage ceremony is often referred to as *san-san-kudo* or "three-three-nine times" because the bride and the groom take *sake* from three different cups in altogether nine sips.

When the *san-san-kudo* was over, the man go-between arose from his chair and read a pronouncement to *yaoyorozu-no-kami*—literally, eight million gods, or all the deities—signifying that the two were now properly married. At this point all the Fukuharas and the Matsuokas got up from their seats and bowed deeply to each other.

This was the first time I had attended a Shinto wedding. I found it solemn and simple, but I kept thinking what a peculiar and yet significant role ritual played in any society. Certainly none of us who attended the ceremony believed in the eight million gods or in the evils which were swept away by waving a branch of *Eurya ochnacea*. Still we accepted the ceremony as necessary to secure man and woman in the relationship of marriage.

Although rationing of rice, our main staple, had begun in large cities in April, that did not affect the party dinner that evening, which was mainly in Western style. The descendants of Fukuhara's subordinate samurais, who still called Yoichi-*san* "my lord," had brought the *sekihan*—literally, red rice, or sticky rice cooked with red beans, indispensable for happy occasions—from their village about a hundred miles from Tokyo.

It was only a little over three months after their marriage that Yoichi-*san* was called to the colors. He had already served some years in China as an army lieutenant, and as he was already thirty-six years of age this was indeed shocking news. All his relatives and many of his friends descended on him during the following few days. Yoichi-*san* and Kwoko were living with the Andos, and Kwoko spent her days greeting the guests, serving them *sake* and meals and washing dishes until late at night. From what I could observe she hardly had any time to talk with her husband. This made me indignant. I was angry at Yoichi-*san*'s relatives and friends for being so inconsiderate, and I felt impatient toward Kwoko and her husband for not being more selfish about themselves.

The only thing I could do was insist that Kwoko stay with me in a hotel after Yoichi-*san* left on a night train to join his regiment. At least she could escape from the demands of custom and convention for one night. Kwoko is the least sentimental of us three sisters; she is a practical person, full of common sense. As a child she never cried when scolded by Mother. But that hot and humid July night she cried lying on an iron bed inside a white mosquito net. I sat on my bed not knowing what to say and watched her until she went to sleep out of utter exhaustion. I was glad that she was going to have a baby and that she had a job—as interne in a hospital in Tokyo.

52 ~

IT WAS about this time that we heard that Japanese troops had moved into French Indo-China under an agreement with the Vichy Government. I wished very much that such a military necessity did not have to arise. Yet, I shared the indignation expressed in editorials in our daily newspapers when the United States retaliated against this Japanese action by freezing all assets of Japan in the United States and instituted an Anglo-American-Dutch embargo on the supply of oil and petroleum products to Japan. I was irritated because I felt that this American action squeezed those Japanese who were opposed to further military expansion and who wished to come to some kind of terms with the United States. However, I did not lose hope and I knew that both my parents and my immediate circle of friends felt the same way. Hence we were relieved when newspapers reported in August the proposal made by our prime minister, Prince Konoye, to meet President Roosevelt for a conference. Bitter disappointment ensued when the proposal was turned down by the American Government. Even so I never heard anyone express the fear of war between the United States and Japan, except a few who were known as ultranationalists.

Every Sunday morning during this period the Neighborhood Associations, which were formed to assist in the defense of the civilian population, were required to hold anti-air raid rehearsals. It was expected that each household would be represented by at least one individual, and women representatives were instructed to wear either a pair of slacks or *mompe* (a loosely fitted Japanese counterpart) during these drills. Many women were, however, too shy to appear in public in such a garment. They came dressed in everyday kimonos with long white aprons.

Yamatomura, the part of Tokyo in which we lived, was one of the better residential sections. There were about three hundred families living in this area, belonging to the upper middle class—professors, lawyers, doctors and business executives. Apparently the heads of these families felt that the situation did not necessitate lowering their dignity to the extent of attending air-raid rehearsals in costumes which would make them look like delivery men. Nor would the vanity of their wives permit them to come out on the street dressed like farm women. The result was that the drills were attended largely by servants sent to represent their households and by college and high-school students. In our family this was Reiko's chore.

One day that summer Aunt Hani's elder daughter, Setsuko, and her husband invited me to their house. In the course of our visit they asked whether I was at all interested in marriage. Apparently they were concerned about me because my twenty-fifth birthday had passed and Kwoko was already married.

"I would marry if I met someone I love," I replied.

"We know a nice young man," said my cousin, "and if you are interested in meeting him, we would be glad to arrange it."

"I could not possibly meet anyone on the assumption that I might marry him," I said emphatically, but added, "I would be interested in meeting any nice young men—to be friends."

Cousin Setsuko and her husband assured me that this would be the understanding. The young man, they went on to tell me, worked for the Domei News Agency, a semiofficial organization. Having been graduated with a major in history from Tokyo Imperial University, reputedly of the highest academic standing in Japan, he had served more than four years in the Army, as any healthy young man of his age was obliged to do. He had had combat experience in Manchuria and in Central China, and had come back to Tokyo, a lieutenant, only a few months previously. Apparently his career in journalism had just begun.

Being the youngest son in his family, Takashi Ishigami was free of any family responsibility. Neither of his parents was living, and all his brothers and sisters were married. He could, if we wanted, become a *yoshi*—literally an adopted child—which meant that he could take my family name upon marriage.

As my parents had only daughters, the only way we could continue our family line was for one of us to have a *yoshi*. And it was customary for the eldest girl to do so. If we wished, however, we could discontinue the family line. But we did not want or expect this to happen. I had assumed that I was the one to carry on the family name.

From all I could learn about him, Takashi Ishigami seemed to be an interesting young man. I agreed to meet him.

Cousin Setsuko and her husband invited me to their summer cottage in Karuizawa, a mountain resort, for a few days, and Ishigami-*san* came to spend the week end. I remember in detail our meeting. Although I insisted that I was not definite about marriage, I could not help but dress with particular care. I put on my favorite summer dress of turquoise silk with a square neckline and a well-fitted bodice with a full skirt—an old dress but a pretty one. Neither could I avoid thinking of my "date" as a possible husband rather than a friend of passing interest. And I hated myself for being so constantly self-conscious.

For a Japanese, Ishigami-*san* was tall—five foot eight or nine—and extremely well built with broad, square shoulders. His thick eyebrows and nicely shaped nose put him on the handsome side. He wore a gray suit and a bow tie. The brown leather boots he wore, because Cousin Setsuko's husband had invited him for horseback riding, made him look like a character in a movie.

My cousins, apparently wanting to make the occasion as casual as possible, had also invited two other young men—both unmarried —to luncheon the first day. Compared with them, Ishigami-*san* seemed ill at ease and did not talk much. Undoubtedly he was feeling just as self-conscious as I.

The Hani family, Ishigami-*san* and I took walks, rowed on the lake and ate together. And every time an opportunity presented itself, the Hanis either walked ahead or behind, or arranged to ride in a different boat to leave us alone. Although I appreciated the kindness of my cousins in giving me this opportunity, it was a rather distressing experience—both of us being so terribly aware of each other and yet trying to be unconcerned.

I came back to Tokyo filled with uncertainties. I was interested enough in the young man to want to see more of him, and yet it was horrifying to have the idea of marriage in the back of our minds every time we met. Ishigami-*san* and I met in inexpensive tea shops in downtown Tokyo or took walks together. Occasionally my family invited him to spend evenings with us. My parents were definitely curious but, as in the case of Kwoko, they left the matter entirely up to me.

After two months of courtship, I felt I knew a great deal about him, and I liked him. However, to me a lifelong partner had to be more than a sum of likable and admirable characteristics, as my American friends insisted. On the other hand, there were my relatives who advised me that love followed marriage, and that I need not worry about that, and this left me confused.

Meanwhile, my parents and relatives were waiting for an answer, and I had to decide soon. The pressure of the question added to my confusion, and made it more difficult for me to know him better.

My cousins felt that the time was ripe for us to be formally engaged. Wanting to be as unconventional as possible, I argued that an orthodox engagement ceremony would be superfluous, but Cousin Setsuko said that certain formalities and conventions should not be ignored.

53 ~

IT WAS while I was preoccupied with all these personal problems in the middle of October 1941, that General Tojo replaced Prince Konoye, accused generally of an "appeasement" policy toward the United States, and became the prime minister. Still I did not believe in the inevitability of war, nor did I hear any of my colleagues at the International Cultural Association or my Student Conference friends voice serious concern about this.

The newspaper headlines screamed and screeched about the obstacles raised by the American Government to prevent successful negotiations, culminating in a tremendous outcry when Secretary Hull's famous note of November 26 was published. The demands of this note—that Japan go back to her pre–July 7, 1937, position—were so obviously impossible to accept that the newspapers denounced it as an American ultimatum. Even then I did not believe war was possible. So I went ahead with plans for my marriage. This involved a good deal more than decisions made by the two of us. It meant that the families or "houses" were being linked together, so that the engagement was of first importance to the heads of the families. My parents were unfamiliar with these formalities since Kwoko and her husband had dispensed with the engagement ceremony. Cousin Setsuko directed us as to what should be done.

Following her instructions, I went to one of the department stores and purchased a small tray of plain natural wood made with four legs, and sheets of white rice paper especially designed for the exchange of betrothal presents. On the rice paper Father wrote with brush and India ink the names of all the members of the Matsuoka family and their relation to me. Father and I then took the tray and sheets of paper to Cousin Setsuko.

After examining them, she told Father, "We must take some money with this. I think a hundred yen would be enough since this is just a formality."

Father searched his pockets, but being completely unprepared for this sort of thing he could pull out only several creased ten-yen bills. While Cousin Setsuko was saying apologetically, "The Ishigamis will return you half this amount," I got out my purse and gave Father enough to make a hundred yen. Cousin Setsuko wrapped this carefully in a piece of white rice paper, and promised to deliver the present to the Ishigamis.

I was told that in case of a girl marrying into a boy's family, it was his family which initiated the exchange of gifts, and the girl's family then returned half the amount of money. But since the Matsuokas were welcoming Takashi Ishigami as their *yoshi*, we had to present the gift first. To take the presents back and forth was the duty of the go-between. Cousin Setsuko acted for us in this capacity.

Even after these formalities were completed, I was still not sure of myself. The date of the wedding was set and preparations were under way. Soon I found half of myself being lost in the excitement, dragging the other half, still full of uncertainties. I wanted my wedding ceremony to be as simple and unorthodox as possible. From pale pink satin I had a long but simple wedding dress made. The dress, a short pink veil and one lavender orchid to wear in my hair cost a little over fifty yen, and I was proud that I could manage to pay for it from my own savings.

Go-betweens are indispensable in a Japanese wedding, whether the ceremony is conducted according to the Shinto or Christian ritual. Usually they are an elderly couple, respected friends of both families. Their function is to witness the ceremony and to introduce the bride and the bridegroom to the guests at the wedding party, most of whom are friends and acquaintances of the heads of the families but not necessarily of the bride and the bridegroom. If after the marriage serious difficulties arise between the married couple, the go-betweens assume the onerous task of smoothing the relationship, and if they find the situation impossible to mend they talk to the two families concerned to negotiate a divorce, so that the families will not have to come into direct contact with each other. Presumably this minimizes ill feeling all around and consequently saves face for both families.

We asked the editor of Domei and his wife to act as our go-betweens at the wedding. The ceremony was semi-Western and took place in my father's club in the *Mainichi* building. Suzuki-*sensei,* my former music teacher at Jiyu-Gakuen and a well-known concert singer, and some of the girls who had attended the Amsterdam Conference with me in the summer of 1939 sang the wedding march for us. I walked to the front of the small room with Mrs. Matsumoto, my go-between. One of Mother's distant relatives, who had long been a professor of Hebrew and theology at the Aoyama Theological Seminary read the service. Then Mr. Matsumoto, who stood next to my husband, officially introduced the two families and relatives standing on either side of the room.

Since, by my marriage, the Matsuoka family was adopting an heir to carry on the line, it was an important occasion, to which nearly three hundred people were invited. As was customary, after the ceremony my husband and I sat at the center of the main table, sandwiched between Mr. and Mrs. Matsumoto. While Mr. Matsumoto introduced us to the guests, giving a brief resumé of our family histories, all four of us stood, stared at by all sorts of eyes—some curious, some critical, some friendly and others placid. The go-between's speech is usually like an obituary, except that you are right there to hear all of it. Most Japanese brides bend their heads down and do not lift their eyes while the speech is made, but I looked straight into the faces before me, trying not to miss anything.

Protocol is strictly observed in the seating arrangement at a wedding and the guests are seated according to their rank or title. The highest seat on my side of the table was occupied by Count Kabayama, next to Mrs. Matsumoto on my left, followed by the publisher of *Mainichi*. The highest seat on the bridegroom's side was assigned to the president of Domei, who spoke for Takashi after Mr. Matsumoto had finished. Then Count Kabayama gave a speech. The second speaker for Takashi was his section chief in Domei, and my second speaker was the publisher of *Mainichi*. He said something to the effect that I was unusual for a Japanese girl—frank and stubborn— and hoped that the bridegroom would be able to handle me. This was rather an unusual thing to say in a wedding speech, but everybody seemed to think it was a good joke and laughed, except my husband who kept a serious face.

According to the strictest etiquette the bride and bridegroom are supposed to stand through all the speeches, but our guests spared us this. Takashi and I could not eat, however, because that would have been impolite. The ice cream was melting, and the imported wines, which the chef at the Club had gone to Kobe to purchase, must by this time have become lukewarm. Dainty sandwiches and sweets looked delicious, too, but I was not able to touch them.

That evening Father gave a full-course Western-style dinner, including the chef's special dish of roast duck, at the Club for the immediate families. I was hungry and was able to enjoy every bit of it.

During the couple of hours between the tea party and the dinner, Mr. Matsumoto dashed back to his office because the serious international situation demanded his attention. We were aware that the times were difficult, but I did not for a moment suspect that a peaceful solution was impossible. After all Thelma, my only foreign guest at the wedding party, seemed just as friendly and cheerful, I thought. Thelma, an American girl, whom I had come to know through the America-Japan Student Conference, was working for the American Embassy in Tokyo.

Two weeks after the wedding Father took my husband, who was now Takashi Matsuoka, and me to Hachinohe, his home town, to report the marriage to his ancestors and to introduce the new heir to the members of his family living there. After Father's death, my husband would automatically become head of the Matsuoka family and inherit all the property. Thus it was important for him to acquaint himself with the living relatives as well as with the generations of Matsuokas peacefully buried in the moss-covered cemetery.

After this trip my husband resumed his newspaper work, and I went back to my study of the Japanese polity under Professor O.

[167]

54 ~

MONDAY MORNING, December 8, was like any other winter morning. It was brisk and chilly outside, but one room downstairs in our house was already warmed by a little coal stove which Mother had kindled. As usual, the day began with hot soup of fermented soya bean, in which delicate white bean curd and bits of scallion floated, a bowl of steaming rice, dark green seaweed, an assortment of pickles, and tea.

Takashi left home for his work around eight o'clock just as on other Monday mornings. I was still downstairs clearing the table when the telephone rang. As I lifted the receiver, I heard the excited voice of my husband, whom I had seen only about ten minutes before: "War has been declared! We have declared war on the United States."

"Oh, no! That cannot be," I said, unable to accept this. And then: "How did you find out?"

"Newspaper extras are posted on the walls of the station. The news must have broken early this morning. I will probably have to work until late tonight."

I felt as though the floor beneath me had sunk about a foot. In an effort to organize my thoughts, I sat down for a couple of minutes. Faces of my American friends whirled past my eyes—the Clarkes, the Pococks, Mano, Twitter, Lynne, Kat—the others at Shaker Heights and Swarthmore. My thought was: How incredible! Why did we start a war we cannot possibly win?

Father did not show much emotion when I told him the news. But I knew he had not anticipated it, for he hurriedly changed from his kimono to a Western business suit and left for his office. Mother was more excited than Father, but showed more control of herself than I. Soon she went about her household chores with her usual self-confidence. I tried to sit at my desk and concentrate on theories of sovereignty, but could not. I was like a nervous chimpanzee in a cage. I would walk aimlessly around the room, stare at a book on the Japanese Constitution and chew my nails, or give all my attention to listening for the ring of the newspaper boys' bells announcing more extras.

Later that day Father telephoned. It seemed that even he was excited. "Our Navy attacked Singapore, Manila and Hawaii. And we were successful."

The incredible had happened; I could hardly believe it, but it was true.

In retrospect it is easy to trace the steps—internationally and internally—which led Japan to her catastrophe. Father may have thought secretly that a showdown was inevitable, but certainly he did not expect it the way it came. Nor was my husband prepared any more than I. Pearl Harbor was just as jolting to the Japanese as it must have been to the Americans.

55 ~

AFTER RECOVERING from this first shock, those of us who would have said "No" loudly, had we been asked whether we were willing to fight America, reluctantly gave in to the situation and determined to make the best of it. There was, we told ourselves, nothing else to do. Westerners may describe this as the fatalistic attitude unique to Orientals. It may have been in part. That attitude has had too important a role in shaping our destiny as a nation, and it is to be hoped that in the future changes in our political and social structures will bring about a different and more positive way of thinking.

To put the responsibility on "fate" and sit back and sigh "Shikataganai"—What else is there to do!—was the easiest way out for those of us who were asked to make sacrifices for a cause we were not entirely convinced of. It is too agonizing to realize that the rope which one has helped to make may be used to hang one's self. A person sensitive enough to foresee danger ahead is often too sensitive to face his own mistakes. In order to compromise he must believe that what has happened could not have been helped or could have been worse.

There were many who sincerely believed that war at that time was the only way to emancipate Asia from "the yoke of white imperialism." I have a feeling that Father was one, although he was truly sorry for such a means; others welcomed it with enthusiasm and called it *seisen* or a holy war. To them it was a noble undertaking for which everybody should be willing to make the utmost sacrifice. Needless to say, these people became most vocal after December 8.

Our daily life did not radically change immediately. We continued to have anti-air raid drills every Sunday morning, but there was no noticeable change. Rice had already been rationed, but there was plenty to eat. Perhaps this was largely due to surprisingly swift victories within the first few months of the war.

The shortage which I felt more acutely the first winter was coal. This was the first time our family could not bathe every day. There was a choice of having one room in the house fairly comfortable, heated by a coal stove, and taking a bath every three days; or having a bath every day but leaving the entire house unheated. Against my feeble protests my family adopted the more sensible plan of having at least one room at a civilized temperature. There is nothing so exhilarating before going to bed on a chilly winter night as soaking leisurely in a steaming Japanese bath. To end the day this way had become such a cherished part of my routine that I felt my standard of living definitely lowered when deprived of it.

Early in 1942, I resigned from the International Cultural Association, after presenting a report of my studies with Professor O. A baby was due in September, but because of a tumor of some sort I had to expect either a Caesarian section or possibly an earlier operation. The doctor advised me to stay in Tokyo. So I decided to rid myself of all responsibilities other than those of a wife and mother.

To gather enough diapers for the baby became a problem of unexpected seriousness. Pure white cotton cloth could be purchased only on the black market, and at an exorbitant price. Even had I had the money, I should not have known the way to get it through such a channel. The cotton cloth available on the open market had so much staple fiber in it that my doctor sister, Kwoko, advised me against buying it. She said, "Any cloth with staple fiber is too cold for the baby." What most Japanese mothers were using was the old *yukata*, informal cotton kimono for summer, which Japanese also use to sleep in. The minimum for a baby's comfort would require at least four good *yukata*.

The only pure cotton *yukata* in our household belonged to Father, since the rest of us did not wear kimonos. As it did not seem fair to deprive Father of all his *yukata*, I told my relatives and close friends that I would prefer old cotton kimonos as presents for the baby to any other gifts—and not after the baby was born, but before. It took some persuading to convince several of them that this was what I really wanted, because most Japanese still considered it an insult to give anything that has been used even to a relative. And besides, diapers would not be considered appropriate as a present. By September, however, I had collected enough diapers of all sorts— some with large lavender peonies as a design on a white background, obviously once a young woman's kimono; others with small blue chrysanthemums on white, once an older woman's *yukata*; and still others with gray stripes on white cotton, once a man's *yukata*.

56 ~

APRIL 18, 1942, was an ideal spring day with a warm sun and soft breeze. If Father and my husband had not been so busy and if I had not had that tumor which might cause me trouble at any time, we would probably have gone to the Tama River on a picnic to celebrate Reiko's birthday. It would have been half a month too late for the cherry blossoms, but the peach blossons were just about ready to open their soft pink petals, and the fields were full of that yellowish green which means vigor and life. Pinkish-brown horsetail would be about three inches tall on the river bank, ready to be picked.

The horsetail is a small flowerless plant without branches or leaves of an ordinary kind. One soft straight stem stands erect on the ground like a forgotten chopstick with a cap shaped like a pyramid. To pick horsetails is a great sport, particularly for the city people. The plants are washed and cooked in *shoyu*, soya bean sauce. Their salty and slightly bitter taste brings that peculiarly earthy odor of spring to the dinner table, and the dish goes well with a bowl of rice.

But this particular spring day I stayed home with Mother and the maid. I was in the kitchen just before noon preparing the fried rice on a gas stove when I heard the roaring of an airplane, a sound which was unfamiliar to my ears. I opened the kitchen door and put my head outside to look. The plane was flying unusually low. On steady silvery wings, it sped out of sight toward the northwest. A few minutes later I heard a sound—heavy and dull—like the ominous sign of an earthquake. But the earth did not rock, and the sun continued to shine brightly. Neither Mother nor I thought much of the incident, and forgot about it almost completely until we saw the evening paper several hours later.

This was the first air raid on Japan proper by American airplanes. Later it came to be known as the Doolittle raid. Apparently the plane which I saw bombed factory areas in Oku, only a few miles from our house. Although newspapers did not report the casualties in full, stories of how the killed and injured looked—that a head was blown off a few feet from the body and that a body was scattered to bits—circulated fast and wide.

The Doolittle raid radically changed the casual attitude toward anti-air raid drills. The ladies were no longer shy about appearing in their *mompe*. Besides these ill-fitting trousers, we were asked to wear shoes instead of *geta* or *zori*, as Japanese footwear comes off too easily. Most women wore sneakers. A long-sleeved blouse, a pair of gloves, something to cover one's head, and a piece of white triangular cotton cloth (which would be needed in case of injury) completed the "anti-air raid costume." The men, who would have preferred to relax in their kimonos, sip hot tea and read the newspapers on Sunday mornings, were now seen more frequently at the drills. In our household, where these exercises had been more or less Reiko's job, the rest of us now began to take our turns.

Every Sunday morning around nine o'clock, the leader of the neighborhood Association, who served for a month in a system of rotation, would shout through his megaphone: "*Boku-enshu!*"— "Anti-air raid rehearsal!" From every house properly attired men and women would come out—each with an empty bucket—and line up in the middle of the street. The leader would then decide which house was supposed to be on fire. Swiftly the men and women would form two lines between the nearest house with a well and the house on fire. Someone would pump the well with all his might; the one standing next to him would start passing buckets of water, which at the end of the line would be splashed on the "burning" house. Empty buckets were returned to the well by the second line of people. This would go on for about fifteen minutes, until the leader decided the fire was properly squelched.

Besides a few buckets, each household was required to keep on hand at least one long ladder for climbing up to the roof, small sandbags, a long broomlike affair made of a bamboo pole and crude straw ropes, which when dipped in water could put out fires on the ceiling, and a tank about the size of a small Japanese bathtub filled with water. Blackout was strictly enforced, and the Association leader checked to make sure no streaks of light came through the windows.

First-aid groups were formed among the unmarried girls in Yamatomura, and Reiko became one of their leaders. Unmarried boys also organized themselves, and were used in all activities which needed strong hands. These boys and girls often worked together for greater effectiveness. Thus the ancient custom of separating young unmarried people, observed most rigidly by the upper and upper middle classes, was breaking down out of necessity.

57 ~

BY THE summer of 1942, Japan had occupied the Philippines, Malaya, the Dutch East Indies, Dutch and British New Guinea, French Indo-China and Burma. The only unoccupied country, Thailand, was Japan's ally in the war. Western colonial powers were ousted, and indigenous "independent" governments were to be established. The Japanese government decided to send civilian officials to the Philippines, Malaya, and Java to carry on the administrative work of the occupation. It also assigned these three areas to the three largest newspapers: The Philippines to the *Mainichi,* Malaya to the *Asahi* and Java to the *Yomiuri.* Each newspaper was asked to appoint representatives to start other papers in the occupied areas, the papers to be printed in the Japanese language as well as in the native tongues.

In late August, Father was chosen by the *Mainichi* to head the paper in Manila. He was over sixty-two then, but seemed happy that he could be useful in a constructive way. "This will probably be my last active service to the country," he said. Being true to the type of Japanese liberal born in the early Meiji era in a samurai family, Father undoubtedly believed that Asia must rid itself of colonial powers, however unfortunate and undesirable the method. As an Asiatic and a Japanese, he accepted this assignment as an honorable duty which he was happy to fulfill.

He was to leave by plane within a few days, and since nobody could assure his safe return in time of war, much had to be done. Mother made certain that she understood everything that had to do with his financial affairs. His unfinished manuscript on Japanese colonial policy was put in order and wrapped in one big *furoshiki.* There were people to be seen about business.

58 ~

IN THE midst of this hustle and bustle my baby girl was born on September 2. Moving to the hospital was no simple task. I had to take my own bedding, pajamas, toilet articles, the baby's bedding and clothing including the assortment of *yukata* diapers. In addition, I had to carry my own bag of rice, since this was rationed and it would have been too complicated to transfer my ration to the hospital. Several bags of cotton without staple fiber, which was rationed to pregnant women of over eight months, also had to be transferred for medical use.

My obstetrician sister Kwoko commented, "The Government is indeed stupid. They would not allocate cotton to women who have a miscarriage before eight months. Just as much cotton is needed for miscarriage as for a proper birth."

Kwoko also complained of the bandages made with staple fiber, the only kind available, because they came loose too easily. Soiled bandages were carefully washed and sterilized to be used again and again in all hospitals.

After I rushed to the hospital with a cab full of belongings, I had to wait quite a while before they had the operating room ready. Kwoko later explained to me, "It takes a lot of coal to heat the room and to sterilize all the instruments. Because of the terrific shortage of coal, they cannot afford to have the room ready all the time."

The Caesarian operation was performed by Dr. Higuchi, Kwoko's professor, and Kwoko was very proud to be the assistant. There was another girl who witnessed the operation—Pin-*chan*, a daughter of Wang Ching-Wei, the president of the Nanking Government of China. Pin-*chan* was studying in a Japanese women's medical college and staying with the family of one of my friends. She was taking special courses with Dr. Higuchi and was very anxious to see a Caesarian performed. Tall and big for an Oriental girl, with a broad square face, Pin-*chan* looked very like her father. Stuttering in her accented Japanese, she said: "My blood type is O, and in case you need a transfusion, I will be glad to give it to you."

Under local anesthesia, I could hear what was going on—the clattering of the instruments and occasional brief remarks. I heard Dr. Higuchi say: "The baby's head is too big. Let's open five more centimeters." It was an agonizing hour and a half, but when Pin-*chan* whispered after the baby's first cry, "It is a girl, Yoko-*san*," I was gripped by a tremendous sense of relief and accomplishment.

When I was taken upstairs to my bed in a ten-mat *tatami* room, the best in this small private hospital, the baby was already sleeping in her small padded silk *futon*, breathing the dusty air of Tokyo for the first time. A small pinkish creased face reminded me strangely of that pig brain on the counter of the Eastern Peace Market in Peking. The ten little fingers on her clenched hands could be stretched open like the soft delicate petals of a plum blossom.

"How astonishing," I thought, "that this tiny creature will someday learn to speak, to think, to have a mind of its own!"

[175]

Looking at the squashed pink face again, I thought it resembled strikingly the wrinkled face of Aunt Hani. "Oh! dear," I said to my husband, who had been anxiously waiting outside the operating room, "I had hoped that our child would be an improvement, at least in looks, over the two generations of Matsuokas, but it doesn't seem that way, does it?"

He did not answer me. Instead he said, "I am glad you are feeling all right."

Father was scheduled to fly early next morning for Manila, but he took time to visit me and the baby in the afternoon. While his secretary bowed on the *tatami* and muttered words of congratulations to me, Father just stood beside the *futon* with his eyes fixed on his second grandchild. Kwoko's son had been born eight months earlier. As I thanked the secretary politely for the visit, I wondered what was on Father's mind. He must be saying to himself, "This may be my last farewell," I thought. The two did not even have time to sip the tea prepared by Hasegawa-*san*, my private nurse. The secretary again bowed. And before I could finish saying, "Thank you, Father. Go well," he slipped through the heavy paper sliding door, or *fusuma*, which separated my room from the hall.

My husband and I named the baby *Seiko*—meaning "to go forward." We chose this particular Chinese character in commemoration of Father's trip to the Philippines. After Seiko was properly registered as a new member of the Matsuoka family, a ration card was issued to her. She was now entitled to milk—either fresh or powdered—a little sugar, and 120 grams of rice per day, slightly more than one-third of the ordinary adult ration.

Japanese doctors have always encouraged mothers to breast-feed their babies. Particularly with the shortage of milk and fuel, and lack of good refrigeration, this was the best possible way. I had more than enough for Seiko. A warm and irrationally happy sensation went through my body when I first held her to be fed. As she clung tightly to my breast, I was overwhelmed by a sense of importance and responsibility beyond anything I had experienced. Here was a new life, which I more than anyone else was to shape in growth.

59 ~

DUE TO complications which developed, my stay in the hospital extended to forty days. My husband visited us almost every day. He seemed to take pride and delight in photographing Seiko and started an album and a diary for her. Being much more meticulous and orderly than I, Takashi kept the diary for quite a while.

After we returned home, life revolved around Seiko. When she was asleep, everybody tiptoed; when she cried we all dashed to see whether her diapers were wet or a safety pin was hanging open; when it was time for her to take a bath, we surrounded her small bathtub, and were joined by any relatives and friends who might be visiting at that time. Although the second winter since Pearl Harbor had brought more shortages of coal, charcoal and wood, we managed to give Seiko a bath every day and to keep one room in the house at a fairly comfortable temperature. The rest of us took fewer baths than a year before.

Father wrote us regularly from Manila. I don't believe the ordinary mail service between the Philippines and Japan was as safe as the air service which the *Mainichi* was privileged to use. Not even a postage stamp was necessary for our mail. Father addressed his letters in care of his secretary in the Tokyo office, who upon the arrival of mail would telephone to let us know. We, in turn, took our letters to this secretary, who would put them in a *Mainichi* bag to be sent to Manila. Even small packages could be sent this way. Father's letters told us little about what was going on there—only hurried notes assuring us that he was well.

When Seiko was five months old and could be left with Mother and the maid for a few hours, I began to work part time for the America Research Institute. Extreme nationalists had already been vociferous in their disapproval of anything American, and one could not even open a book written in English in a streetcar or any public place without being stared at accusingly. Except for intelligence work undertaken by the Government and the Army, only a small group of civilians openly indulged an interest in American government, politics, economics or literature. The Japanese branch of the Institute of Pacific Relations had closed down, and the International Cultural Association was carrying on its work on a smaller scale than ever before. My first assignment at the Institute was to study the public opinion trends in the United States during the preceding few years.

60 ~

AS THE summer of 1943 approached, our newspapers reported the establishment of "independent" governments in the occupied areas. Such names as Ba Maw of Burma, Laurel of the Philippines, Soekarno of Indonesia made headlines. I remember the visit of Laurel and his entourage to Tokyo that summer. As the *Mainichi* had a special connection with the Philippines, Mr. Laurel and his party were invited to its main office in downtown Tokyo one afternoon. Because of my father, I was included among the guests.

Short and bespectacled, Mr. Laurel seemed deceptively polite. Although he spoke very few words, his sharp eyes appeared to observe all that was going on. I followed the group when they were taken on a tour of the five-story *Mainichi* building—through the editorial room, the printing department, past rolls of newsprint and the press room with its high-speed rotary press, of which the *Mainichi* was very proud. I felt sure that behind the heavy-rimmed glasses Mr. Laurel's eyes were saying, I am not a bit impressed by all this. Our civilization, which is more Western than yours, is far superior to what you can show. It seemed rather ironical that the Japanese should display machines of the West in order to impress these Asiatic leaders, who at the same time were being encouraged by the Japanese Government to establish Asia for the Asiatics.

About this time, all unmarried girls who were not working outside of their homes were recruited to work in factories. It was no longer patriotic to marry young and bear many children. The old slogans disappeared from sight, and women were exhorted now to produce "more airplanes." Kwoko commented cynically, "It would take twenty years before a human being could be useful as a soldier. Apparently the Government decided they couldn't wait that long. And pregnant women are not very useful in factories."

This was a disquieting development for the upper middle-class families of Yamatomura. Many of their daughters had been brought up to believe that it was shameful for girls to work after finishing school. The only occupations approved as ladylike, until they were safely married, were the arts of flower arrangement, tea service, cooking, and perhaps Japanese dancing. Speeches made by the so-called feminist leaders had done little to change this. It took the war or "the national emergency" to blow traditional ideas into unrecognizable bits. The militarists, formerly the stanchest supporters of "women in the home," now became the strongest advocates of "women in the factories."

Many of Reiko's friends decided it was preferable to work in a place which was more "respectable" and safer than a munitions factory. Some of them, in order to avoid being drafted, took jobs in offices where their fathers were employed. The mothers of others frantically searched for eligible men who might not be conscripted.

The three-year university course for men was shortened to about half that time, and young men who were healthy and had sufficient education were rapidly turned into army and navy officers. Many of the *kamikaze* pilots—the suicide attackers—were recruited from university graduates. The term *kamikaze*, which means literally "God's wind," had been used to refer to the particular typhoon which swept the invading ships of Kublai Khan into the sea off the shores of Japan in the thirteenth century. I do not know who first applied this word to pilots whose mission was virtually a one-way trip. Perhaps it was thought that young men so designated would feel themselves elevated to the level of God, empowered to drive back the invading forces as the great "God's wind" of seven hundred years ago had done.

After the war ended I asked one of the surviving kamikaze pilots, a brilliant young man and a graduate of the Tokyo Imperial University, why he had joined the suicide squadron. "The immediate reason, I think, was social pressure," he replied. "However, it was completely voluntary. The commanding officer interviewed us separately and asked whether or not we were willing to volunteer. He did not exert any pressure. I could have refused to join if I had wanted to. But one felt it would be cowardice to say 'No.' You just couldn't refuse when your friends went one by one. You may call it vanity, but that is what it was."

He added: "After I joined the kamikaze squadron, I tried to justify my action by saying it would protect my family, particularly my mother, who was living in Tokyo and endangered by the enemy bombings. To die for the Emperor never entered my mind. I think that idea was largely invented by newspaper writers."

High-school students also—both boys and girls—gave up part of their school hours to work in munitions factories. It became the task of the teachers not only to teach but to supervise the conduct and work of their students in the factories. At Jiyu-Gakuen the beautiful green lawn was converted into a vegetable garden and the girls seemed to spend more time farming or working in a near-by airplane factory than in actual study. I saw boys being rigorously drilled by an army officer in front of the school building. Aunt Hani was wearing her ordinary kimono when I visited her at school— which was seldom since I was working and it took almost two hours from our house by streetcar. Her *Fujin-no-tomo* was one of the few women's magazines permitted by the authorities to be published throughout the war.

6 I ~

IN DECEMBER Father returned home rather unexpectedly. He had had a slight cerebral hemorrhage and was flown back from Manila. Although he did not tell us much of what was actually happening in the Philippines or in the surrounding areas, I sensed that the war was not going as well as the newspapers insisted. The only thing Father said was, "I had wanted to die in the Philippines at my post." Being a samurai, and probably realizing that the Japanese there sooner or later would have to face a bitter battle, he no doubt felt cowardly at leaving his post and his subordinates.

He was particularly concerned over one young reporter, recently married, at whose wedding Father and Mother had acted as go-betweens. "Not that I think one person's life can be spared more readily than another's," I heard him say to Mother, "but he is the kind of person who could endure less under physical strain than any other man in the office. If I had had any say in the matter, I would not have sent him to Manila. I hope his wife will realize that."

Father was right about this reporter. He never returned.

The doctor ordered complete rest for Father, physically and mentally. After the tropical climate of Manila, the damp and unheated house in Tokyo that winter would have been hard on anyone. We persuaded Father and Mother to leave Tokyo for a warmer and more restful place. Although reluctant, they finally agreed to rent a room near Atami, a hot-spring resort. To settle them there involved even more work than moving me to the hospital the year before. They not only had to take their own bedding and clothes, but to supply their ration of rice, *miso* (fermented soya bean), *shoyu* (soya bean sauce), salt, sugar and charcoal. Either Reiko or I made week-end trips to Atami to deliver these supplies.

The war news was becoming increasingly unfavorable to Japan. Although the military spokesman for General Headquarters never said that our Army was defeated in a battle, or retreating, it began to be reported that the Japanese forces were abandoning or withdrawing from certain points for "better strategic purposes." But we knew what was happening. Our victories were blasted in large headlines; our losses in small type. It seemed that since the battle of the Coral Sea and the retreat from Guadalcanal in May 1942, we had been steadily suffering losses.

We heard stories of enemy atrocities. One which received wide circulation was that Japanese prisoners in some South Sea island were rolled under a tank. Another was that a lamp shade was made of a Japanese prisoner's skin. We also heard that Japanese Red Cross ships had been torpedoed—a violation of international law.

It was about this time that someone drew a large stars-and-stripes flag on the busiest street in downtown Tokyo—Ginza—and made pedestrians step on it. Most of my acquaintances dismissed the incident with the thought: How foolish can people get!

As the Allied forces approached nearer and nearer to Japan proper, the large, congested cities adopted what was known as *kyosei sokai* or forced evacuation. The Government designated areas which were to be evacuated, in order to stop fires from spreading in case of incendiary bombardment. Families living in these areas were ordered to move out and their houses were pulled down. Property owners were compensated for their losses, but certainly not enough to rebuild comparable houses. In peacetime the Government would have faced the strongest resistance if it had taken even an inch of anybody's property for public welfare. But in this time of crisis, the people obeyed.

62 ~

IT WAS in the middle of March 1944 that my husband received his *akagami* or draft notice. *Akagami* means "the red paper," which was the color of the paper on which the draft notice was printed. Apparently the four and a half years of army life which Takashi had had in Manchuria and China did not exempt him from further service. Some newspapermen avoided the draft by becoming war correspondents, on the theory that they were apt to be stationed in relatively safe places. Takashi and I had talked about this, and we both felt that it was not fair to take such an advantage unless the editor of the Domei sought his services. I don't think either of us was being heroic or self-righteous.

Father and Mother came back from Atami, and a hectic week of preparation and farewell parties followed. It was customary to present to one called to the colors a silk Japanese flag scribbled with the signatures of friends in black India ink, and a piece of white cotton cloth one meter long with one thousand stitches in scarlet thread. It was said that the prayers of one thousand people, each of whom sewed one stitch, would make the cloth bullet-proof. The soldier wore this cloth around his waist. After the Pacific War began, one could not cross a busy street of Tokyo without bumping into some woman holding a piece of cloth to be stitched. I had disliked intensely being asked to add my stitch. The custom seemed nonsensical to me and I decided to dispense with the cloth for my husband.

Takashi and I also felt that a flag covered with black signatures was distasteful. Instead we bought a scroll of heavy rice paper and asked our relatives and friends to write a few words and autograph it with a brush and ink. After the others had finished, it was my turn. What could I say? The best I could do was: "Let us fight side by side and live together."

I wanted him to live and return to me. The chances were slim, and we both knew it. The fact that the odds were against us stirred my emotions. Although I had been confused about the role of love in our marriage, Takashi had become very much a part of my life. I had borne him a child, whom both of us loved dearly. The thought that I was going to be without him after the following morning left a vague and uncomfortable feeling of emptiness. In all sincerity I whispered, "I want you to come back."

Before he left, Takashi insisted that I get out of Tokyo and take Seiko to a safer place. I did not feel right in leaving Father, Mother and Reiko, but they pressed me to do as he wished. So I resigned from the America Research Institute and took Seiko with me to a small town in the Iwate prefecture, the northern part of Honshu Island, where Mother's elder sister was living.

The country life was restful but uninteresting. To feed and care for Seiko and myself in an eight-mat room which I rented did not take much time. Fuel and food were relatively abundant if one was not too choosy about what one ate. I could even buy fresh milk every day if I was willing to walk three miles. But after a few weeks, I became restless and slightly ashamed of idling away my time reading de Tocqueville's *Democracy in America* and Tolstoy's *War and Peace* in the peaceful atmosphere of Hanamaki while others were busy with war activities.

It seems curious that though I hated war and believed the Japanese leaders fatally wrong in attacking Pearl Harbor, once we were in it I could not sit back and watch as from a gallery. It was not through fear that I would be accused of being unpatriotic. Rather, it was because of the irrational emotional attachment one has to one's own country and people. As much as I hated the militarists and

[183]

what they were doing, still I was unable to reason that their down-fall would be accelerated by my fighting on the Allied side, or sabo-taging Japan's efforts from within. Perhaps that was the measure of my intellectual limitations. It was easier to collapse with the whole framework than to be unscrupulously rational.

At any rate, when Cousin Setsuko wrote me in May that a position was available in a girls' junior college in Tokyo, I returned.

63 ~

THE KOKUMIN-SEIKATSU-GAKUIN was financed by the editor of *Chuokoron*, the only liberal magazine which had survived the restrictions put upon freedom of speech in the thirties. The magazine had compromised in order to continue, but it was still comparatively liberal. The school, which had been founded in 1941 as a liberal arts college for girls, was now training its fifty-some students to be dieticians and practical nurses. At that time there was no other excuse for this sort of school to exist. Girls were permitted to learn practical skills for immediate use, but nothing in the field of the arts alone.

"I could not possibly teach dietetics and nursing," I told Mr. Shimanaka, the editor of *Chuokoron*, in bewilderment. "The only thing I can teach is elementary English, which probably would not be acceptable. I suppose I can teach a simple introductory course in political science, but my American training would hardly be approved by the authorities."

Mr. Shimanaka assured me that since it was a private school I would not have to worry much about the Ministry of Education. He said, "We have three men professors and one young woman who does secretarial work on our full-time staff. What we need is a woman who can look after the girls and help to give them a general education. Why don't you come to the school next Monday and give a lecture on America?"

Apparently he wanted to test me before committing himself. A lecture on America was a big order, but I accepted. Mr. Shimanaka and Professor N., an up-and-coming economist of rightest tendency, who was the senior member of the school staff, were to be in the audience. I could say many things about America, but I had to say something which would be understandable to girls slightly over high-school age, intelligible and acceptable to both Mr. Shimanaka and Professor N., and at the same time would not deny my own honest convictions. After pondering the problem, I decided to talk about de Tocqueville's analysis of American democracy, which was still fresh in my mind.

After listening to me for an hour on de Tocqueville, Mr. Shimanaka and the professor found me qualified—to do exactly what, I was still not sure. But I was happy to receive a monthly salary of 150 yen, quite an improvement over anything I had received so far, even with a slight rise in the general price level. I was also glad to be doing something useful. Tokyo still looked safe enough for Seiko and me, and we moved back to the house in Yamatomura to join the rest of the family.

The Kokumin-Seikatsu-Gakuin was located in one of the suburbs of Tokyo. The two Western-type houses evidently had been built and lived in by foreign missionaries. The grounds were about the size of three tennis courts. On one side were these school buildings, on the other side a small church. The curriculum was planned and had been in operation since the beginning of the school year in April. So I was not required to do much teaching except when outside lecturers were unable to attend at the last minute.

Professor N. appeared to be the nominal head of the school, since Mr. Shimanaka's first responsibility was to the magazine. But this professor, like European professors who existed only to teach, could not be bothered with administrative chores. He seemed to have many other more important ambitions to fulfill. Sasaki-*sensei*, the second in command, might have been a teacher of morals in a small-town boys' school. He was thin and bald-headed, with an under-nourished look, and beneath a scant mustache his gold-filled teeth were visible. His trousers were too narrow and too short, and he walked totteringly in high black shoes with his back slightly bent.

Sasaki-*sensei* was prompt as a clock and was always on a small platform in one corner of the grounds ready to make a bow toward the Palace at eight in the morning. Since the start of the war in the

Pacific, it had been customary before any gathering to hold a ceremony at which everyone bowed at an angle of forty-five degrees in the direction of the Imperial Palace and gave a silent prayer for the war dead. The head of the school would ordinarily conduct this simple service to begin the day, but since Professor N. was never available so early in the morning it became one of Sasaki-*sensei*'s more important tasks.

The third and youngest professor was Tanaka-*san*, a pale and earnest young man who was unlikely to be drafted as he had had a bad case of tuberculosis. I addressed him with *san* instead of *sensei* because he was about my age. Except for a small concrete pool of water on the grounds, the school was hardly prepared for air raids. Sasaki-*sensei* and Tanaka-*san* and I decided that we should have shelters, and since no male labor was available we had to dig them ourselves. Tanaka-*san* did not look strong enough for this labor but he insisted that he was quite able. As he was the only young man at the school, we relied on him for much of the planning and execution.

Very little summer vacation was allowed the students, and all of us spent most of July digging holes. We were told that bombs would explode at an angle of about thirty degrees, and it was safer to be inside a hole than outside it. We were also informed that holes in the ground would protect us from machine-gunning from the air. If an enemy plane approached from the west and started gunning, one was to squeeze his body against the western wall of the hole, and if the bullets came from the east, one was to press his body against the eastern wall.

64 ~

THE B-29's appeared infrequently, high up in the sky, although they did not bomb. Each time the air-raid siren blew, we dismissed the school. Warnings were issued whenever the radar, located in some island south of Honshu Island, detected the coming of enemy planes. Thus there was always at least half an hour before the planes reached Japan proper. After the students left, I hurried home—always to find Father waiting for me at the gate. Unlike his earlier self, he had become nervous and could not be calmed until I had Seiko in my arms, all bundled up in her padded air-raid costume.

Only two blocks from our house in Yamatomura was a large science laboratory with a cyclotron. We feared that it might be a target for bombardment. Since Father could not be persuaded to move outside of Tokyo, we decided to rent a house on the outskirts within commuting distance. After some difficulty, we were lucky to find a small, dirty place without running water. From there it would take me slightly more than an hour to go to my school and Reiko almost two hours to reach her place of work. But we felt safer in that location, and safety was most important.

Father was able to hire two trucks from the *Mainichi* for the moving, but Reiko and I did the packing and cleaning. Any outside help was expected to be fed in addition to the pay. Since the truck drivers were doing a special favor for Father, we sacrificed our bowls of rice to give them salted rice balls with pickles and tea when they arrived at our house in Yamatomura and after they unloaded our furniture in the house in Seijo. We could not possibly take all our belongings, but we were able to move the essentials. Our house in Yamatomura was rented to a doctor and his family, who had lived in downtown Tokyo and apparently regarded a residential section as safer.

There was no air-raid shelter in the small garden of the Seijo house, which had not been inhabited for some time. As Father's health was failing rapidly and since no male help was available, Reiko and I decided to dig a shelter. We chose the spot farthest from the house—only a few yards away at that—under a big pine tree. Somehow we felt that the long branches of pine, which shut out the sight of the airplanes, would afford protection. We planned a trench a little deeper and longer than a regular foxhole. Soft black earth was not difficult to work in, and both Reiko and I were proud that we were capable of doing a man's job. Finally an oblong hole five feet deep and long and two feet wide was completed. We climbed in to observe the world outside. The pine branches looked bewilderingly feeble with the strong summer sun shining through the dark green needles.

[187]

"Do you suppose this would protect us?" Reiko asked rather dubiously.

"No, I don't think it would. Let's put a top on," I answered.

We crawled out and laid an old wooden door across the narrow ditch.

"Don't you think we should camouflage it?" I suggested. This we did by covering the door with some of the earth we had dug up and sprinkling some old pine needles on top. Two narrow sloping entrances were added in a U shape to the ends of the ditch, so that even Mother could walk in and out of it.

Reiko and I then reported blithely that we were now safe. I have shuddered to think how unscientific we were under tension and fear. It should have been obvious to any twelve-year-old that the damp earth would gradually rot the wooden door, and with that much weight on it the top might have collapsed at any moment. However, this danger did not occur to me or to anybody in the family until after the war had ended. Luckily that roof of earth never collapsed on us. The famous Japanese saying "*Atama kakushite shiri kakusazu*" —To hide the head and expose the rear—fitted the situation perfectly. When I recall how much safer I felt inside that damp and dark ditch than out on the ground, I do not even have the power to laugh at my own stupidity.

Yet we scoffed at reports that in some towns in Kanagawa prefecture civilians were being trained with bamboo spears to prepare for possible invasion by the enemy forces. I remember commenting to Reiko, "Hmmn. What stupidity next! Do they believe they can fight the B-29's and tanks with bamboo spears?" I was so sure that my own intelligence could never sink so low.

65 ~

ON OCTOBER 15 Father insisted on going to the Philippine Embassy in downtown Tokyo to attend the first anniversary of the Philippine Independence Day, despite the fact that his health was not equal to a ride of an hour and a half on a crowded streetcar. I accompanied him and attended the brief ceremony and celebration which followed. When I put him on the streetcar which would take him homeward, he looked relieved and happy. It was the first time in weeks that his face had glowed with peace. He said, "Thank you, Yoko," before I dashed off to my school.

Those words were to be his last to me. When I returned home that evening, I found Father partly paralyzed. Mother was struggling to put him to bed. There is nothing so sad as to see a man who has been active and mentally alert fail in his coordination. His eyes had lost their intelligent, penetrating look. His mouth no longer showed that twist of humor, a great part of Father. Only incoherent sounds echoed hollowly in the air.

We tried many doctors. They would not commit themselves, but from their grave looks I knew Father was not going to live long. Kwoko came to stay with us, and told us on the morning of October 28 that the end was very near. Father had not gained consciousness since the evening of his attack.

Kwoko's hands trembled and her eyes were filled with tears when she gave Father the last hypodermic injection. Yoichi-*san*, her husband, was in the room. He had been sent back to Japan after his submarine was torpedoed in the middle of the Pacific. Between our sobs he said quietly with a bow, "Thank you, Father."

This was the appropriate thing for children trained in the traditional Japanese way to say at the death of their parents, but it sounded artificial and out of place. There is really nothing one can say when one's deepest emotions are stirred.

Much had to be done—the doctor's certificate of death to be obtained, a white silk kimono to be made for Father, and the funeral to be arranged. I learned that a coffin at the official price was made of such bad quality wood that the bottom might fall off, and that it was not easy to have the body cremated immediately due to the shortage of coal. I was also told that handsome tips to the proper persons would oil the way. There were three classes of cremation. I was not clear as to the differences, and the result in any case would be the same, I thought. But Kwoko, who was more familiar with such matters, convinced me that arranging for the first-class cremation was the only way to get good service. She said, "You cannot have the body lying around for days. The only way to get it moved is to pay the price. People say that one cannot even go to heaven without tips."

After Father was properly dressed in a white silk kimono and a pair of white *tabi*, he was placed in a plain, unfinished casket. A small ceremony was performed by the immediate relatives when the lid was sealed on. (No metal is used on a Japanese coffin. The wood is cut in such a fashion that the whole casket can be put together without nails or hammer.) When the top was lifted into place, the relatives took turns pounding the corners with a piece of stone. This was the first time that Seiko—then two—realized that something extraordinary had happened to her grandfather. Holding the stone in her chubby hand, she turned and asked, "Is Grandpa asleep?"

The crematorium was a bare place. On one side of the grounds there was a row of about six furnaces labeled according to class. After having seen that the casket was placed in the proper furnace, we three sisters and one of Father's friends retired to a *tatami* room across the grounds where we were served hot tea. Mother stayed at home to receive the guests. We waited what seemed like the whole afternoon until we were informed that the bones were ready to be picked.

Putting on our shoes, we followed the man in charge to a cement hall which led to the furnaces. In the middle of the hall stood a high table, on which were four pairs of long wooden chopsticks. Presently another man appeared with a large tin plate full of bones and placed it on top of the table. The bones remain solid but in small particles. Dead human bones are called *hakkotsu* or "white bone" in Japanese, but those bones, which were once Father's, were smoky gray—some almost black.

I asked the man why they were not white. Wiping his forehead with a gloved hand, he answered, "The coal shortage makes it impossible to cremate bodies with electricity. So we have to use lumber, and the temperature does not rise high enough to bleach the bones white."

To pick the bones with a pair of chopsticks and place them inside an urn is part of the Japanese funeral. Whatever its significance, it was a gruesome experience. And I was glad that Mother did not come with us.

From the beginning I had advocated a simple secular service. Now,

[190]

assuming the authority of the eldest daughter, upon whom the family responsibility had fallen in the absence of my husband, I said to the relatives who had come to the house, "Father often told us to throw his ashes into the Pacific Ocean from that rock in Hachinohe. Obviously this cannot be done. Although he was baptized, Father had a distaste for the Church and particularly for preachers. I am sure he would not like a long Christian ceremony. For that matter, he would not like any elaborate religious ceremony. He never believed in that kind of thing."

There was a silence which Uncle Hani was the first to break. He said, "But from a practical point of view, it is much easier to follow some standard formalities—whether they be Christian, Shinto or Buddhist. It's too difficult to explain to hundreds of people something utterly unfamiliar."

Mother agreed, and added, "Since the Matsuoka family had been Shinto for generations, would it not be best to have a simple Shinto ceremony?"

Aunt Hani nodded, and so the matter was settled.

The funeral was held on the last day of October in one of the larger Shinto funeral parlors in Tokyo. In the center of a plain rectangular hall, large enough to hold at least three hundred people, was the altar, where all sorts of seasonal vegetables, fruits, bits of rice, and *sake* were placed beneath a black-framed photograph of Father. Four Shinto priests, clad in stiff white robes with black caps and black lacquered wooden shoes, sat on either side of the altar on chairs facing each other—each with a bamboo flute. While they played an unfamiliar theme of high minor chords, the chief priest officiated in a ritual with a branch of *Eurya ochnacea*.

As my husband was away, I headed the procession with Seiko, the next in line. Then came Reiko, and third Mother. According to the family structure recognized under the old civil code, the wife of the deceased held a position just below that of the youngest unmarried female child. The life of the wife was considered ended with the death of her husband, and she was expected to obey her son-in-law, the sole heir and new head of the family. Unless so willed by the husband, the widow—which in Japanese means "not-yet-dead person"—was not even entitled to a portion of the property. Although Mother conformed to the customs in ceremonial occasions, she remained as the pillar in the family matters.

After Mother came Kwoko and her husband. Since Kwoko had married into another family, she was no longer a Matsuoka and, therefore, came at the end of the procession. Father's younger brother followed her, then Uncle and Aunt Hani—and so on down the line of immediate relatives.

It was not until much later that we were able to take the urn of ashes to the Matsuoka ancestral cemetery in Hachinohe.

66 ~

THE DAY after Father's funeral Tokyo experienced the first bombing since the Doolittle raid. From then until the war ended, air raids became a part of our daily life. We were indeed grateful that Father had passed away before all this took place.

The B-29's followed a certain pattern in raiding Tokyo. They came either from the east or from the west, but followed the same route. When they invaded from the west, they apparently flew directly to Mount Fuji and turned east to Tokyo. When they entered from the east, they came through Chiba prefecture. The Kokumin-Seikatsu-Gakuin was directly under this route. In those late autumn days we grew very familiar with the sight of glittering silver wings against clear blue sky. Antiaircraft guns were used at first, but soon we no longer heard them. There was a rumor that more casualties were caused by our own shrapnel than by the enemy bombs. How true this was we had no way of knowing, but we began to see Japanese fighter planes go up to make suicide attacks whenever B-29's visited the sky above Tokyo. The fighter planes looked small and insecure beside the B-29's, and when one of them flew toward an enemy bomber it looked as though it were exerting all possible energy to attempt something beyond its power. I saw many of them miss their targets by the flash of a second.

I remember one of our planes coming down like a falling leaf— so quickly to death. It made me sick to my stomach. Another day we saw a B-29 blowing fire at the tail end, the first time we observed one of them in trouble. The whole school stood in the yard to watch. Compared with the Japanese fighter plane, which whirled itself straight to the ground, this heavy-bodied bomber did not lose its balance. It came down gradually, breaking formation, and it was fully fifteen minutes before it disappeared completely out of sight. We all clapped when that B-29 finally nosed itself toward Tokyo Bay. Somehow it did not occur to me to wonder what might happen to the men on that plane, as I did when our own pilots were endangered. I had no feeling of hatred toward the American pilots, but I did experience a kind of joy—similar to the sensation one has when an opponent misses his punch.

One day in December downtown Tokyo was bombed. Mother and I worried about Reiko because her place of work was in the center of the city. Reiko returned safely that evening, however, and excitedly reported her first experience in seeing casualties of a bombing. She said, "A friend and I were standing in line to get some *zosui* at the Toho dining room. You know their *zosui* is still the best. Chopsticks still can stand in the bowl. (*Zosui* is rice diluted with water, with some soya bean and bits of radish greens added—the only rice dish available on the open market. It was common to test the substance of it by putting a pair of chopsticks into it. The chopsticks would not stand if it was too soupy.)

"While we were waiting in line, a dozen or so army officers were having a party at the Sansuiro (a famous Chinese restaurant only a block away). People around us were saying in a sort of accusing tone that the army officers had access to food not available in the open market. It was then that a bomb dropped right through the Sansuiro. It blasted the whole place! Soon the military police arrived and took all of the injured away on stretchers. None of us felt in the least sorry for those officers."

Reiko told her story breathlessly and did not appear alarmed. On the contrary, she glowed with pride at being able to give a first-hand report of something extraordinary and exciting.

Mother was shocked to learn that Reiko had been so near the scene of bombardment. "I wish you could change your place of work," she said.

[193]

From January on the raids became so frequent that Mother, Reiko and I did not dare change to our pajamas at night when we slept. We would put our overcoat, shoes, gloves, thickly padded headwear (which covered the head and shoulders), and a knapsack beside our *futon* when we went to bed. The knapsack contained one set of underwear, a sweater, a day's ration of rice, some biscuits, bandages and other first-aid material, a flashlight, a box of matches, a few toilet articles and some cash.

When the sirens sounded, during those freezing nights of January and February, Mother was always the first to get up. Armed with the necessary clothing and equipment, she would turn on the radio to discover the whereabouts of the invading bombers and then would open the door of our veranda which led to the garden. Reiko followed her. I was usually the last one to get up. After only a couple of hours of sleep, my body felt as though it were floating in a warm bath with all the bones comfortably disjointed. Even the imminence of bombardment could not bring me to face the sharp night air which would penetrate my bones and make my feet numb. Still half-dreaming, I would think, It would be much more comfortable to die in bed than to survive in that damp, cold shelter. There was the story of Harold Laski, who was reported to have been blown through the second-story window of his London house while he was asleep, and didn't wake until he and his bed had landed safely on the ground. . . . Perhaps fate will be as good to me. Then the reality of Seiko, whose quiet and regular breathing I could hear beside me, would penetrate and make me jump to my feet. Quickly I would bundle her up in a blanket and go outside to crawl into our crude and dangerous shelter.

67 ~

THESE SLEEPLESS nights were followed by strenuous days at school. The students took turns in working at an airplane factory. They were no longer permitted to devote themselves to school work alone. Professor N. and Sasaki-*sensei* had resigned and gone back to their country homes. Although we now welcomed another male, a writer-professor, as head of the school, more responsibility was placed upon me. The factory where the girls worked became one of the constant targets for B-29's. Even though I commuted back and forth between the school and the factory, I felt guilty because the girls were exposed to more danger than I.

Physical and mental strain was telling upon all of us, and in March I decided to take Seiko away from Tokyo again. Mother, Reiko and I studied the map of Japan carefully to find the safest place. The more closely we looked, the narrower and smaller the island of Honshu appeared. All the large cities and the coastline towns were out of the question. Yet, it had to be a place with relative abundance of food and a locality where we knew someone, so that we could acquire a room. After much deliberation we decided on Hanamaki, the small town where Seiko and I had stayed before.

I asked Mother to go and take Seiko with her. She refused, saying flatly, "After all, you are her mother. You go with her."

"How can I?" I argued. "I have fifty girls to take care of. I cannot give up my responsibility at the school."

"Well, we shall just have to ask Reiko to take Seiko," Mother said, and added, "I am old and I won't live long. If anything should happen to you, I should not be able to take care of Seiko until she is old enough to take care of herself."

Reiko agreed to go in my stead. When I again tried to persuade Mother to leave Tokyo with them, she said determinedly, "No. I am going to stay in Tokyo as long as you stay."

Early in the morning of March 10 Reiko and I started for the Ueno station with heavy knapsacks on our backs. I went ahead carrying Seiko. The previous night there had been a heavy raid, but neither Reiko nor I realized how serious it was until we reached the station. There we saw a moving mass of hopeless, dirty, bewildered people. Some had lost their shoes and were walking aimlessly in bare feet. Their faces were black with smoke, and many could not open their eyes, as if they had trachoma. Apparently the heat and the smoke of fire had blinded them.

We asked one man what had happened. He said, "Incendiary bombs were dropped in a big circle and they started fire in all directions. At first we tried to fight it back with buckets of water as we had been told to do. But it just could not be done. Many who tried until the last minute were surrounded by fire and lost their chance to escape. We were lucky to have survived." This man and his family of three had not decided where they were going; they just wanted to get away from Tokyo as quickly as possible.

This was the first mass raid on Tokyo. Although the newspapers did not report the number of casualties, I heard later from one of the Red Cross doctors that there were nearly 200,000.

The train was packed with survivors, and it was impossible for us to move for the next fourteen hours. The people around us had lost their knapsacks in the course of trying to escape from the fire. We shared our rice balls with them at lunchtime. The only way to get out of the train when it stopped was through the window. I was glad to find that I had not lost my athletic ability and could climb in and out without much difficulty.

Returning from Hanamaki, I resumed my work at the school, determined to stay in Tokyo. There was much talk of a possible invasion of Honshu Island. Nobody seemed to know what was likely to happen next or what to do except to wait until we were bombed out. Mother and others of the family insisted that my first responsibility was to Seiko. I argued that I could not leave the school, but at the same time I was aware that there was another reason why I was so obstinately set against leaving Tokyo.

I knew that my responsibility toward the school could not be more important than my responsibility toward my child. Then why did I want to stay? It was mainly because I did not wish to be thought irresponsible and cowardly for not sticking to my job. The desire to survive the war with Seiko was motivated by selfishness. But after all, is not mother's love for her child essentially selfish? I let myself be persuaded to leave Tokyo consoling myself that I would have acted differently had it not been for Seiko.

Mother and I left Tokyo for Hanamaki in early April, but as it turned out I took one-third of my students with me. It was becoming increasingly difficult to carry on any kind of study in Tokyo, and I worked out an arrangement under which the students would be able to get credits toward their degree by working in health centers in Iwate prefecture.

Reiko, who started to work for a local newspaper, and I took turns going back and forth to Tokyo to report to school and get what belongings we needed. It was during Reiko's first return to the city that the second mass raid occurred on the night of April 13, 1945. Almost all of Yamatomura burned that night, including our house which we had rented to the doctor. Reiko brought back that vase which Father had cherished from Yamatomura, informing us that it alone had survived the fire.

When I returned in late May, a large part of Tokyo had been flattened out except for a few chimneys belonging to public bath-houses, which stood awkwardly alone. I went to see the remains of our house in Yamatomura. Our hundreds of books had turned into a large pile of snow-white ash. Mother's once highly prized cut-glassware had melted, and the ribbons of twisted glass made surrealistic patterns on the ground. The iron coal stove was standing in the middle of the debris all by itself. Our persimmon tree was now only half as tall as it used to be, with black burns as though it had been struck by lightning.

As I stood there and gazed about, there was no feeling of revenge toward the Americans, nor sorrow at losing our house and belongings. Uppermost in my mind was the thought that we were all alive. I thought of the family of four who used to live across the street and had been burned to death in that raid. I thought of millions of people—soldiers and civilians, men, women and children—who were now known simply as casualties, a ghastly impersonal word. What is this for? Must it continue? I wondered helplessly. As I turned to go, the fresh green leaves of the bush clover, Father's favorite plant, almost hurt my eyes. This had survived the bombing and the fire. It looked infinitely powerful and beautiful.

Even Hanamaki, the small town to which we had evacuated, which had no military or industrial significance of any sort, was bombed and burned in the latter part of July. Only a few incendiary bombs were dropped, but the frightened people would not fight the fire. Within a couple of hours half the town of about a thousand homes vanished into ashes.

On August 7 the morning newspaper reported that an unusually powerful bomb had melted almost all of Hiroshima the day before. The nature of this new bomb and what it actually did to that city was not disclosed until after the war ended, however.

On the eighth we learned of Russia's entry into the war. This was a blow, particularly as there was a neutrality pact between Russia and Japan and it was understood that a note of Japan's desire to end the war had been sent to the Allies through the Soviet Government.

A few days later Reiko came home and reported, "This is still a secret, but our office heard today that the Emperor is to broadcast on the fifteenth."

"That must mean that the war is going to end!" I exclaimed.

Air raids continued, however, until the morning of the fifteenth. The radio announced several times that morning that there was to be an important broadcast at noon. Mother, Reiko and I waited nervously, with mixed fear and hope, for noon to arrive.

68 ~

THE NEAREST radio was in our farmer neighbor's house. Mother, Reiko and I, with Seiko in my arms, still clad in our anti-air raid costumes of trousers and long-sleeved blouses, hurried there as the clock was striking twelve. Our neighbor, a sturdy-looking, bald-headed man of forty or so, was standing erect with his head slightly bent in a prayerlike attitude.

We heard the Emperor saying: "We have ordered our Government to communicate to the Governments of the United States, Great Britain, China and the Soviet Union that our Empire accepts the provisions of their joint declaration."

The voice was high-pitched, almost shrieky—not at all beautiful by any standard. So this was the *gyokuon*—the sound of the jewel—the special term used to refer only to the Emperor's voice! It had been believed by those in power that since the *Tenno* was sacred and inviolable, the *gyokuon* should not be transmitted by a man-made device. For the first time, the Emperor was speaking to his people over the radio, an unprecedented event.

Although I had never believed in the divinity of the Emperor, the solemn and oppressively quiet atmosphere created by his voice made it impossible for me to sit casually on the floor. Like the farmer, I too stood with my head bent to hear the announcement of Japan's surrender, also unprecedented in our history. Mother and Reiko did likewise.

The Emperor did not say that Japan was defeated. He merely said, ". . . the war situation has developed not necessarily to Japan's advantage" and because of the use of "a new and most cruel bomb . . . should we continue to fight, it would not only result in the ultimate collapse and obliteration of the Japanese nation, but also it would lead to the total extinction of human civilization."

Some Westerners have observed that many Japanese did not understand the true meaning of the Emperor's broadcast because the words he used were different from the ordinary written or spoken language of the people. It is true that the Emperor used words and style peculiarly his own, and he did not say that Japan had lost the war. Yet I cannot believe that any Japanese misunderstood this speech which could only mean that Japan, as a nation, was going to experience a defeat.

Tears rolled down my cheeks as I heard the Emperor say: "We are keenly aware of the innermost feelings of all of you, our subjects. However, it is according to the dictates of time and fate that we have resolved to pave the way for a grand peace for all the generations to come by enduring the unavoidable and suffering what is insufferable . . . " It was not humiliation, nor sorrow, that made me cry. It was complete physical exhaustion and emotional letdown—like a full-strung bow suddenly unstrung without having accomplished its purpose. I had neither the strength nor the vanity to want to wipe the stream of tears from my face. I just stood there, feeling as though all my bones had become disjointed.

Our neighbor broke the heavy silence. "Would it be unpatriotic if we continue fighting against the will of the *Tenno*?"

The thought of continuing the war now repelled me. I had lost all power to face the constant threat of bombardment. My body painfully yearned for a good night's sleep in pajamas instead of the heavy anti–air raid costume which I had worn for eight long months. I replied without hesitation, "Yes, I think it would be unpatriotic to go against the will of the Emperor." It seemed the simplest way of convincing him.

As he turned away, looking perplexed, I realized with horror what I had said. The reasoning I had employed was exactly that which had been used by leaders "hiding behind the Emperor's sleeves" for the past eighty years to make us as a nation resigned to our fate. This was probably the first time my neighbor had seriously questioned the authority which had ruled his life. Yet I had appealed to his traditional submissiveness.

Just as the Emperor did not mention Japan's surrender, so all the official announcements referred to "the termination of war" but did not use the word "defeat." Nor has the Army of Occupation been called officially the "Occupation forces" or *Senryogun*. Instead, it has been known as the "Advancing Army" or *Shinchugun*. Inouye-*san*, a newspaper man, called this a good face-saving device.

It is a matter of record that some army officers, believing that the Emperor had been forced by the officials close to him to accept defeat, broke into the Palace grounds late at night on August 14 in an attempt to destroy the recording of his rescript. Fortunately they were unable to locate it and the attempt ended abortively.

69 ~

I DECIDED to go to Tokyo as soon as possible to find out what was happening in the capital and to make arrangements for the family to return there. Furthermore, I was anxious to see if I could learn anything about my husband, from whom I had received no word for several months. He had gone to Singapore and been assigned to the Japanese Army headquarters.

On August 17 I made the trip. In spite of rumors of insurrection contemplated by the army officers, and all the confusion and un- certainties following the surrender, the train to Tokyo was packed to the full. I seated myself in one corner on a crude bench in the third class, and listened to voices around me humming with speculation as to what the American forces would do when they landed— "Will they harm us?" "What will they do to the Emperor and high government officials?" "Do you think women will be safe?"

A Japanese Army captain in uniform came into our car, obviously expecting someone to offer him a seat, as would have happened in the past. Most of the passengers paid no attention to him; some looked at him boldly, as he tried to make his way along the narrow aisle filled with people.

Finding his way blocked, the captain became angry and shouted, "Get up, you . . . "

I was amazed that no one stood up to make room for him. With scorn in their eyes, the passengers, who, judging by their appearance and language belonged to the lower middle class, watched him indifferently.

A man in the back of the car shouted, "Don't be superior. You lost the war, didn't you?"

The captain was now outraged. He put his right hand on his sword and drew it. What he met at the point of his shining blade was not fear and obedience, but hatred, scorn and defiance. He looked shocked and then helplessly perplexed. Without a word, he put his sword back and struggled out of the car.

During the long silence which followed his departure, I wondered at the swift turn of the tide. The almighty Japanese Army was being challenged by common ordinary people for the first time in decades —with force, although in a crude manner—and it was as if the people were astounded to discover a power they had not known they possessed.

When I reached Tokyo, the city seemed ominously quiet. The downtown streets near Tokyo Station had the appearance of an early Sunday morning around Grand Central Station in New York City. In these deserted streets the gutters were cluttered with paper and dust; there was none of the hustle and bustle peculiar to the railroad terminal of a modern metropolis. With my knapsack on my back, I walked aimlessly around to breathe in the air. It was menacingly like the oppressive atmosphere before a typhoon.

From there I went to visit friends near the Atsugi airfield, the large naval air base where two weeks later General MacArthur was to land to take over the command of the Allied occupation forces. I was told that there had been a huge bonfire at the base after the Emperor's broadcast, in which documents and even some furniture were destroyed.

The Army and the Navy in Japan proper were swiftly disarmed after the surrender announcement. Many stories circulated about looting by former officers and soldiers. Our farmer neighbor told us that a soldier, the son of a poor farmer, who was given a large army truck, blithely drove the gift home only to find that there was not even parking space for it in his front yard.

Having been assured that an insurrection was not likely to occur, I went back to Hanamaki to arrange to move my family again to the house in Seijo.

70 ∽

DURING THE latter half of August the whole nation buzzed with talk of the surrender, some expressing hope and some fear of what would happen when the Occupation forces arrived. This was to be in early September, the newspapers reported.

Mr. T, a lecturer at the Kokumin-Seikatsu-Gakuin, expressed the ideas held by one group of liberals when he said with confidence: "This defeat was expected from the beginning, of course. You undoubtedly have read the Potsdam Declaration, which commands the Japanese Government to remove 'all obstacles to the revival and strengthening of democratic tendencies among the Japanese people.' From now on we shall enjoy all sorts of freedoms."

Those who agreed with him asserted that this was "the only way Japan could have democracy," and they were jubilant. Their smiles seemed to say, See, I told you so.

I wanted to ask in annoyance: "If you knew better, why did you not more vehemently oppose the militarists so as to prevent their rise to power?"

"The history of any nation is marked with at least one defeat, and such experience makes a nation mature," Mr. T asserted. "It's like growing pains, you know."

How can you be so objective and happy about a defeat? was my thought. Even though it might lead to something better, it had been brought about with so much sacrifice and devastation.

There were others who advocated "One Hundred Million in Repentance." Foremost among them was the Reverend Toyohiko Kagawa, the noted Christian leader, who became an adviser to the Higashikuni Cabinet, formed at the time of Japan's surrender. The idea, as implied in the slogan, was that everybody was responsible for the war and, therefore, all should repent. I remember Reiko saying to me: "I don't deny my share in the war effort, but don't you think the difference between us and General Tojo, for example, is so vast that it merits a distinction?"

"Of course, it does," I agreed emphatically. "We who had no voice in policy-making should not be lumped with those, particularly the leaders, who deliberately chose the path to war. This movement has the look of face-saving for the leaders."

Almost all of us were confused—some like my farmer neighbor, who had not known the war was going so badly and felt that Japan still could fight with a chance of winning; others because they believed sincerely in the ideal of "co-prosperity for Asiatics" and "Asia for Asiatics," and now that ideal was lost.

One of my former students from Kokumin-Seikatsu-Gakuin wrote to me: "Although I would never want to go through another war, we had a purpose for living then. For this purpose—that is, for our victory—we were willing to sacrifice everything. That willingness to sacrifice for a cause is a beautiful thought. Now that purpose is gone."

I think that is the way many of us felt during those first few weeks. We were silent now because a new purpose in life had not yet been found to replace the old.

71 ~

IT WAS soon after I had returned from Tokyo to Hanamaki that the police chief of this small town came to call on me. I was puzzled and a little frightened when I went to the door. He bowed very low—unusual behavior for a policeman, particularly toward a woman. It was also unusual that he addressed me with something like shyness.

"I understand you were educated in America. It seems that you are the only one in this town who can speak English. The Advancing Army is to arrive here soon. Will you act as my interpreter when the Americans come?"

I was relieved, but at the same time flabbergasted. For more than four years I had not spoken English and I was not confident that the words would flow easily. But this did not seem a good enough reason for a refusal, considering the predicament the chief was in. So after consulting Mother, I told him that we were getting ready to leave for Tokyo, but I would be glad to be of service until our departure. He promised to find another interpreter by that time, and bent his heavy body to make another bow.

One morning in early September I dressed carefully in an old woolen skirt, a short-sleeved cotton blouse, a pair of Father's socks (since I did not have any silk stockings or cotton socks of my own) and low-heeled shoes. I did not have any lipstick or rouge, since I had not used them during the war. I was nervous, but I soon discovered that the police chief was even more disturbed. Probably he had never seen an American in his life and, having been a policeman for many years in a small Japanese town, exposed only to Government propaganda, he undoubtedly dreaded having to face these unwelcome guests.

The police station was a large wooden building with the chief's office in the back. The room was crude and bare except for a wooden desk, a precarious round table, and a few creaky chairs. It had been carefully swept and well dusted. Just before the designated time the chief and I went to the front steps to give our most polite greetings to the men of the Advancing Army.

Soon a jeep arrived, raising clouds of dust off the dirt road. As three young officers jumped out of the car, the chief bent his fat body nervously to bow. The Americans approached and stood in awkward silence. I hastily said in English, "I am the interpreter." Obvious surprise crossed their grave young faces. Without a word they followed us inside to the chief's room.

As is customary, hot green tea had been prepared and was served, but the guests did not touch it. The captain was a well-built young man with beautiful blond hair. One lieutenant, obviously Jewish, was more talkative than the others. His friendly grin put me at ease. The last was a tall and handsome second lieutenant who had that innocent shyness characteristic of a boy born into a good middle-class family.

As they spoke, I translated for the police chief. Soldiers were to be brought to this area and they wanted to make arrangements for a billet. As Hanamaki is well known for its hot springs, several good inns were available and the chief offered one for their use. This settled, we all climbed into the jeep and went to inspect the quarters.

The management of the hotel had been informed of our coming and was ready to receive us. At the entrance of the inn, I told the men that it was our custom to take off our shoes upon entering a house. They obliged and removed their army boots. Then we inspected the well-cleaned *tatami* rooms and a huge kitchen, where they were to do their own cooking. The Americans seemed satisfied.

Lunchtime arrived. The three officers dismissed the police chief, asked for some hot water and cups from the inn, and gave me a box of K ration to eat with them. After years of rice, soya bean soup, fish and a few vegetables, the hard biscuits, cheese and Nescafé with sugar melted on my tongue. I carefully slipped two pieces of caramel into my bag for Seiko, hoping that nobody would notice.

The captain remained aloof and did not talk much, which I assumed was his way of maintaining his dignity before an enemy interpreter. The Jewish lieutenant asked where I had learned my English. I told him that I was graduated from Swarthmore College. "Oh! Swarthmore," he exclaimed as though that word had touched a forgotten memory. "That is a very good college." He had studied at New York University, and the other lieutenant was a graduate of Brown University. I learned that these officers were a part of the 11th Airborne, parachute troopers, from the Philippines. Not long before they had been fighting bitterly against the Japanese in Leyte. Although it was obvious that I held no hatred or prejudice against these particular men, I still belonged to the people who had been their enemy for the past four years. Yet the fact that I had gone to an American college seemed to melt the barrier between us. The Americans were almost friendly, and treated me with the respect they would have shown one of their own women.

The GI's arrived the following day. The first lieutenant assembled them in the kitchen and instructed them how to behave and what their schedules would be. It was a long speech, but I still remember one thing he said: "Our interpreter is a graduate of Swarthmore College. You must respect her."

Most of them probably did not know where Swarthmore was, but their curious eyes never became bold. They behaved extraordinarily well.

A few days after they were settled, this lieutenant and the army doctor told me they wanted to talk to the police chief. The lieutenant appeared embarrassed and hesitated. Then taking courage, he said, "Tell the chief the boys want women and ask him where he can get them."

When I translated this, the chief blushed and said, "I am sorry. During the war we abandoned those houses in this town."

He thought for a moment, then said that he knew of five who were doing business privately not too far away. The women were brought to be examined, but it was found that all of them were diseased.

The chief was asked where he could find others. He mopped his head. "Sorry," he said.

The men were horribly embarrassed to have to carry on this conversation through a woman interpreter. But somehow I was not. Neither was I repelled. War and its aftermath had created a situation which brought out human weaknesses at their worst. Yet I felt relieved when I resigned from this job a few days later in order to return to Tokyo.

[206]

72 ~

WITH MOTHER, Reiko and Seiko, I came back to Tokyo at the end of September. Things had already begun to move with extraordinary speed. One of the first things I noticed was that the same people who had catered to the Japanese military authorities during the war now seemed to be seeking the favor of the Occupation authorities. Those who eagerly had obeyed the rulers in the past, now cursed them as though they had been their bitterest enemies throughout their lives. Tanaka-*san*, my colleague at the Kokumin-Seikatsu-Gakuin, called this group "people of geisha-like existence"— flirting to suit the fancy of the master.

The newspapers which had glorified Japan's war aims, had made little gods out of kamikaze pilots, and day after day had printed photographs of General Tojo, now changed their appearance overnight. They were all for "democracy." " 'One must not be late for the bus,' you know," Mr. S., one of Father's colleagues at the *Mainichi,* said—using the popular phrase to refer to those who tried to get on the bandwagon.

Another change was that a number of foreign plays were presented in Tokyo. They were mostly American, English and French. John Drinkwater's *Abraham Lincoln* was played by the Zenshinza troupe, most of whose actors had been trained in the classical Japanese theater. A few years later the members of this troupe joined the Communist Party.

During those days it was not safe to go out at night because robbery was quite common after dark. Mr. S. was stripped of his clothes at gunpoint around eight o'clock in downtown Tokyo in the early winter of 1946. Scarcity of electric bulbs made the streets extremely dark, and whenever new bulbs were put in they were stolen within a few days.

73 ~

AFTER MY father's death I had become the main breadwinner in the family, but I did not realize what this meant until after the war ended. The insurance on the house, burned during the war, had not been paid in full, and much of our savings, which was in bonds, could not be cashed. Moreover, the value of money was declining rapidly and savings no longer had the same purchasing power.

The Kokumin-Seikatsu-Gakuin had been reduced to a single room because the air raids had completely destroyed all its buildings. With the war over, there was a shift of emphasis from vocational training to liberal arts. I could not fully agree with the new program and was not very happy.

Then one day in late November 1945 when I was visiting Radio Tokyo, I happened to meet Dennis McEvoy. He had come to Tokyo to establish the Japanese edition of the *Reader's Digest*, and asked me to work for him. To introduce American writings to the Japanese, who had been shut off from the outside world for several years, seemed fascinating and worthwhile to me and I agreed.

There were many foreign correspondents in Tokyo by this time —mostly Americans, who seemed to spend most of their time at the Correspondents' Club in downtown Tokyo, at Radio Tokyo where SCAP's Public Relations Office was located, or at the Dai-ichi Building, General MacArthur's headquarters. The Japanese they were meeting were largely people of fame or position such as high government officials, newspaper editors or business executives, and a few colorful figures such as gamblers and ex-spies. Foreigners seemed to accept the opinions of those Japanese who spoke English fluently and whose manners were polished according to Western standards. This limited them to the upper class, the mission-educated, the Eurasians and American-born Japanese.

Perhaps this could not be helped; most foreign correspondents did not know the Japanese language. But I wanted the Americans I knew to meet other Japanese—housewives, working girls, farmers, laborers and those of the non–English speaking intelligentsia. These people made up the majority of the nation and, after all, was it not the pattern of the majority which would determine the course of democracy in Japan? I decided that my knowledge of English could best serve the "new Japan" by interpreting their thoughts, rather than working for the *Reader's Digest*, particularly since only through the writings of these correspondents could we reach the outside world. With this in mind, I resigned from the *Digest*.

Among the correspondents, Edgar Snow of the *Saturday Evening Post* and Darrell Berrigan of the New York *Post*, I thought, would be interested in such a view of Japanese life. I reasoned that the author of *Red Star Over China* would want to know more than he could observe through the windows of the comfortably warm Correspondents' Club in Shimbun Alley. And "Berry" I had been unable to forget because of an incident following the Emperor's first trip to downtown Tokyo.

"Ah! so. Ah! so," Berry had shrieked in high-pitched mimicry, stretching his neck and opening his mouth wide. "That is all the guy says." At this other correspondents joined in hearty laughter. I was both hurt and angry, to have fun made of something which was a part of me. But underneath the mimicry I sensed an impatient inquiry, "Why do you believe in such a myth? Why do you want to perpetuate such an institution?" I wanted to know Berry better.

It was in March that I invited Ed and Berry to visit my brother-in-law's country home, where his ancestors had been feudal lords for twenty-eight generations. The sun was warm, but the wind was still harsh as we sped through the rice paddies in an open jeep. It was late in the evening when we finally arrived at the small but fairly well built house.

Yoichi-*san*, sister Kwoko and the Andos were waiting for us in their formal silk kimonos adorned with the family crest. No doubt this was a great occasion for them to have two "distinguished American correspondents" as their guests, but I found their welcome a little too elaborate. I had come wearing my father's old trousers, which fitted me with big and small wrinkles, but I was anticipating an unheated house and it was the only sensible attire.

To my surprise, a charcoal fire glowed in a deep blue pottery brazier and was reflected warmly in the *shoji*, the white-paper sliding doors of their *tatami* guest room. I knew that fuel was extremely scarce, even in country places where it was possible to buy it on the black market. The casually liberal way in which my sister was putting charcoal in the brazier worried me. I called Yoichi-*san* and said, "If you are using all this charcoal for Snow-*san* and Berrigan-*san*, don't do it. It is true that they are accustomed to well-heated rooms, but they came here to see how we live. It is not necessary to go out of your way to entertain them."

He replied unconcernedly, "Don't worry. We received a special ration of charcoal and *sake* (which was also on ration) from the village council office for this occasion."

I could not tell whether he was saying this to put me at ease or whether it was really true. Yoichi-*san* had been brought up in the traditional samurai fashion and could always conceal his thoughts. As the old saying goes, "The samurai uses his toothpicks even when his belly is empty." Perhaps he did receive special rations. As the descendant of the local feudal lord, he still might be enjoying special privileges. I decided not to worry.

The following night we invited some of the villagers—a Buddhist priest, a schoolteacher, several farmers—both men and women, old and young. They formed a circle two rows deep sitting on the *tatami* floor around Berry and Ed, who asked questions which I interpreted.

The conversation turned on the subject of the Emperor. "Don't you think that this is an expensive system?" Ed asked.

Even to me this was a shocking question then. I had not heard anyone discuss the problem in this way before. Many Japanese would have answered as the schoolteacher and the priest did that evening, with pride, "Only 'materialistic' Westerners could think of the *Tenno* in that light."

To those who believed literally that the Emperor was sacred and inviolable—and I judged many who were there did—the question was sacrilegious. To others, who considered the *Tenno* an inseparable part of Japanese polity, it would not be possible to attempt to evaluate him in such a way.

During this visit Berry and Ed became interested in a group of about twenty young men who were putting up a small building across from Yoichi-*san*'s house.

Berry asked them what they were building.

[210]

"A place where we can meet together," one of the boys answered, taking his cap off. Questioned further, he added, "All of us were either in the Army or worked in munitions factories during the war. When we returned to the farms we felt that it was not right to go back to the old way of life. Yet we didn't know what to do. So we talked it over and decided to build a hall where we can meet and study together."

"How are you financing it?" asked Ed.

"We told our fathers and other men of the village of our plans," another young man answered. "It wasn't easy to convince them at first, but they finally said they'd contribute the material and the village loaned us this piece of land. After we finish the day's work in the field, we meet here to work on the house."

Berry nodded enthusiastically.

Then one of the boys asked a question, knowing that Ed and Berry had traveled extensively in the Far East, "What do you think is the difference between the youth of other Asiatic nations and the youth of Japan?"

Ed thought a minute. "I think the biggest difference is that the youth of other Asiatic nations protest, whereas you don't." From the expressions on the boys' faces as I translated, I knew that these words were to remain in their minds as they have in mine.

To Ed and Berry this project, though small, was in effect an expression of protest against traditions. Berry particularly wanted to encourage them and showed his interest in the group for many months by writing to the members, visiting them and sending them books which they wanted but were unable to buy.

74 ~

IN THE New Year Message to the people that year, the Emperor renounced his divinity.

"This is the way it should be," remarked Mother, who I think was relieved that the pronouncement would prevent the ultranationalists from deifying him again.

"Undoubtedly this will save a great deal of trouble for the GHQ [meaning the Occupation authorities]," Mr. S. said.

It was still undecided whether or not the *Tenno* was to keep his traditional status, and the question was widely discussed by people of all classes. The Communists were the only group openly advocating the abolition of the *Tenno* system. This is said to have been the main cause for their unpopularity at the first postwar election held in April 1946.

In talking with a physicist friend, I said, "As the *Tenno* has such overwhelming popular support, isn't it unwise to abolish the throne completely? I don't see any harm in keeping him so long as he remains a titular head."

"But that's what he has been," my friend replied impatiently.

"Yes, I know. What I meant was that we must see to it that undemocratic elements will not have a chance to use him as in the past. It might be done by making the legislature the supreme organ of the State."

My friend shook his head. "Even if the *Tenno* is stripped of all political powers, it would be dangerous for the growth of a democracy to keep him as head of the State. He still represents inviolable authority to many. The very fact that he had to declare he was not a god shows that that myth still exists."

I was curious to find out for myself how much myth still existed in regard to our Emperor. So when the Imperial Household Ministry announced that the *Tenno* was to make a series of trips to various parts of Japan, I asked to accompany one of my American correspondent friends as his interpreter. This was arranged for the Emperor's second trip, which was to Saitama prefecture, a couple of hours by train from Tokyo.

As a measure of safety, a special train preceded the Imperial carriage by fifteen minutes, and I rode in that with the foreign press corps. When we reached our destination, these foreign press correspondents, having little appreciation of our feeling toward the *Tenno* and taking advantage of their superior status in occupied Japan, located themselves boldly on the platform of the station to await the Emperor, and it was obvious that the Japanese officials and police were afraid to say anything to these foreigners. I was curious enough to take full advantage of the situation and hide behind them.

The Emperor arrived. For the first time in my life I saw him at close range—only a few feet separated us. His face was pale as though he lacked the proper vitamins, and his legs shook nervously as he came down the steps. With his old brown hat and suit which needed pressing, he could have passed for any nondescript gentleman in his middle forties. The mayor and other officials, stiffly dressed in their morning coats, bowed deeply in the traditional fashion, standing at a respectful distance, as if utterly awed by this extraordinary honor. Mobs of people who had gathered around the station cheered at the sight of their sovereign, and the police found it difficult to push them back from the Imperial procession—an unprecedented event. Cries of *"Banzai"*—long live the Emperor—continued for several minutes and seemed genuine and spontaneous.

The first stop was the roof of a five-story concrete building, apparently the tallest building left unbombed in this town. There the mayor, in the most polite language, reported to the Emperor the city's population, its industries, and how much of it had been destroyed during the war. The Emperor was whisked away from one place to another with groups of officials, foreign correspondents, photographers, the people of the town and near-by villages following.

Occasional "Ah! so's" were almost the only remarks the Emperor made. This is a common Japanese exclamation which means almost the same as the words do in English. "Ah! is that so!" But what else could he say? Secluded entirely in a revered atmosphere, almost like a living god, he was undoubtedly lost in the new role of a popular sovereign who was expected to be as human as the rest of us. I felt truly sorry for him.

Later he was escorted to the countryside. There the village elders, clad in their black formal kimonos, sat on thin mats on the ground, the only way in the old days in which people were permitted to "worship the Son of Heaven." From their wrinkles and bent backs I judged most of these men and women to be in their seventies. As the Emperor approached, tipping his hat and nodding, they seemed speechless and bowed their heads almost to the ground while tears rolled down their cheeks.

Their genuine humility overwhelmed me. These people must

have believed that the *Tenno* was more than man, and undoubtedly there were many others like them. A myth had become reality, and it was not the myth but the reality which had to be faced.

Perhaps my physicist friend was right, I thought. Perhaps Japan's fault does not lie entirely at the door of its military and chauvinistic leaders who hid behind the Emperor's sleeves.

75 ~

IT WAS during this first spring after Japan's surrender that all samurai swords were ordered confiscated as a measure of SCAP's demilitarization policy. Unless the swords could be proved to possess definite artistic value, they were to be presented to the nearest Japanese police station.

Because of our samurai ancestry, we owned several swords which I had carefully kept in a fireproof storage vault in Hanamaki during the war. Father had always been very proud of them, particularly two very old ones which had been handed down from generation to generation. I, too, had a deep attachment for them and felt their confiscation wholly unnecessary. True, the sword was a symbol of the samurai, a warrior, but possession of that did not make me a warmonger. And from a practical standpoint this ancient weapon, in whatever numbers, surely could not possibly constitute a danger to the Occupation forces.

I did not want to give them up, and I knew Mother felt the same way. It would be parting with something very dear to my heart. Yet I realized that this attachment was irrational. I no longer believed in war as a solution to problems; I had never felt the superiority of the samurai class. Then why did I want to keep such a symbol? Why could I not discard the swords like a piece of old rug which was no longer useful? I suppose it was the same sort of feeling you would have about old love letters, or grandmother's wedding dress. It was sentiment—a great human emotion. It was irrational. But who can be entirely rational?

I said to Mother, "I hear many people are hiding their swords.

Kwoko told me that one of her friends had wrapped them in strips of rubber, apparently to thwart police rumored to be detecting them with the aid of radar. Couldn't we do something like that?"

"I would not want to do anything illegal," she answered, and added slowly, "Perhaps it would do us good to rid ourselves of the remnants of the past. Why not give the swords to your American friends? At least they would be appreciated and not tossed with thousands of others in a police station as a legacy of Japanese militarism."

We gave our two ancestral swords to Ed and Berry as a token of friendship. An indescribable feeling of insecurity and loneliness came over me as I parted with this part of my tradition, Japan's past. It must have been even harder for Mother, but she uttered no words of complaint or regret, then or afterward.

Demilitarization and democratization, the primary ends sought by the Occupation, meant to the Japanese peeling off sentiments and attachments which had been ingrained for centuries. Had the Allied Powers not been so filled with the enthusiasm of "total victory," they, too, might have felt that confiscating the swords was unnecessary for their stated objectives of demilitarization. What this confiscation did, however, was to force us to realize the scope and depth of reforms implemented by the Occupation. Moreover, its peculiarly personal and innocuous nature shook us out of our complacency, making those among us who had not become revengeful or cynical re-evaluate and re-examine all phases and expressions of our thinking. It was a painful process. Perhaps this was what was known as "maturity."

76 ~

GENERAL MacARTHUR'S announcement that Japanese women were to be given the suffrage meant not only that we could vote for the first time, but we were privileged to run for office in the election scheduled for April 1946. The new Constitution had not yet been written and we found ourselves in the strange position of possessing political rights although our legal, social and economic status was far inferior to that of the men.

Under the old Civil Code, a Japanese mother did not have the right of parenthood over her own children except in the absence of the father or when he was found to be incapable of such responsibility; a wife could not divorce her husband on the same grounds employed by him to divorce her; a divorced woman could not remarry for at least six months, although a divorced man could remarry immediately.

Socially, women were still considered an instrument to perpetuate the institution of family. Girls were educated to the end that they should be good wives and wise mothers—the terms "good" and "wise" being synonymous with "obedient." As a result, academic standards for girls were much lower than for boys and the boys studied an entirely different set of textbooks. There was no co-education above the grammar school level, except in a couple of private schools.

Economically women were not assured equal pay for equal work, nor the same rate of promotion as their male colleagues. A woman could earn on the average somewhere around half the wages paid to a man.

This inferior position of women led many people—particularly men—to insinuate (since they might not openly oppose or criticise Occupation policies) that Japanese women were not ready for political equality. In a way I think they were right. But as I look back upon that experience and many others which have followed, I am of the opinion that the quickest way to mature is to make mistakes and then realize that they were mistakes before the impact of the errors becomes too big to defeat you. The only way we could learn to vote intelligently was to go to the polls and vote. The consequences of mistakes—once they are made—are often overwhelming. But the virtue of a democratic system—so we believe—is that the people are given a chance to correct such mistakes in time.

April 10 was an exquisitely sunny spring day, when the weather alone could warm even a cynical heart. The school building which was the polling place in our district was about a twenty-five-minute walk from our house. There was no means of transportation available. Mother, Reiko and I walked, thinking our separate thoughts of the imprint we were going to make in the history of Japan. The night before we had discussed at length the merits and demerits of some eighty candidates from whom we were to select three. However, none of us asked the others how she was going to vote, for somehow that would seem to be a violation of the secret ballot.

We took Seiko along with us, partly because it was easier than to leave her at home, but also because I wanted her to remember this day. Ever since then I have made a point of taking her with me each time I have voted.

A large number of men and women already circled the school building in an orderly, though irregular, line when we arrived shortly before nine o'clock. It took almost an hour before we finally reached the school entrance, but people waiting in line were well-behaved and quiet. Perhaps it was the magnificent weather which kept them patient. Or perhaps it was the excitement of voting for the first time.

At the entrance we handed in our identification cards, which had been sent to us by the local Government office. An official handed us each a ballot, a piece of white paper on which we were to write with a pencil the names of the candidates of our choice. The booths were made of crude wooden boards and partitioned like library desks. I wrote my choice carefully in *kanji* or Chinese characters (*kana*, a simpler Japanese phonetic writing, was also permissible). Then, folding the ballot, I put it through a slit in a large wooden box.

Altogether 257 parties, many of which were the so-called "one-man parties," had nominated candidates in this election. Of these, 32 were successful in sending their representatives to the Lower House. The main parties were: Liberal, Progressive (later known as the Democratic Party), People's Cooperative, Social Democrat and Communist—from right to left in order as they have developed.

There were 89 women candidates and 39 were elected, constituting over 8 per cent of the total seats in the House. This was hailed as real progress toward democracy by some Western observers.

[217]

I, too, shared responsibility for electing some of these women—which called from Ed Snow the quizzical comment, "You are a feminist, aren't you?"

Shortly after the election it was suggested that we should honor the newly elected Diet women, representing all major parties except the Communist, by presenting them with bouquets of flowers. Heated discussion ensued among women active in Tokyo. One faction argued: "Political and social issues cannot be divided according to sex. There is no reason to congratulate these women who have been elected just because they are women." Another objected: "But this is the first time in Japan's history that women have been elected, and they deserve to be congratulated."

I do not now remember what was decided about this, but I do know that the Diet Women's Club could not accomplish anything of importance. It soon became apparent, as the lines between political parties became sharply drawn from right to left, that there was no such thing as "the women's point of view" in politics. They differed as widely as the men. However, because the discrepancy between the standings of men and women had been so great, and women had been denied rights for so long, it was easier to blame men for all the wrongs. Hence democratization often took the form of a battle between the sexes.

An example was the establishment of separate women's sections in labor unions. When I asked one woman labor leader why this was necessary, she replied: "For two reasons: First, because not only management but also our male colleagues support discrimination. They think they are protecting themselves by having their wage level higher than ours. As men came back from war, we were the ones to be discharged. Then, many girls are still too shy to speak up in front of men. So we hold separate meetings where we talk and make decisions and a few of us, who are more courageous, present these in general meetings."

Although discrimination against women existed to a large extent even after the new Constitution purported to give us complete legal, political and economic equality; at times the benefits worked in our favor, since the progress of women was regarded by some

Westerners as an important criterion of democracy. I heard the one time Speaker of the House remark, when forming a committee in the Diet: "Let's put a lady in. That would please GHQ."

77 ~

LAURA LOU BROOKMAN, managing editor of the *Ladies' Home Journal,* joined the corps of correspondents in Tokyo that spring, the first representative of a foreign women's magazine. When Ed Snow suggested that I might do some interpreting for her, I agreed with reluctance. I expected her to be suave, sophisticated, and interested only in meeting women of position, in seeing exotic and quaint things like kimonos, pearls, ivory chopsticks, and paper sliding doors. Instead, I found her warm and unassuming; well-dressed, but not a bit ostentatious, and eager to learn how common, ordinary people lived in Japan. I was happy to do anything I could to help her.

One day when I was visiting Ed and Berry at the "Press Nest," where they lived with a few other correspondents, Ed told me that Laura Lou and Berry were going to "liberate" a Japanese prostitute. Before I could hear his answer to my exclamation, "But why?" he dashed away with them in a jeep. These Americans! I said irritably to myself. They seem to have unlimited curiosity to satisfy. But what do they propose to do with such a girl?

I had never seen a prostitute—or if I had, I was not aware of the fact—and I waited, partly with curiosity and partly with anxiety, to find out what Laura Lou and Berry had in mind.

When the group returned, I could not look the girl straight in the face. That would have been impolite and unkind. Yet I did not want to appear as though I paid no attention. That would be unnatural. On the other hand, I did not want to bend backward, either, to be friendly and protective. I just wanted to act like myself. But the more I tried, the more my middle-class background got in my way.

Tomiko, the liberated prostitute, was a tiny girl who did not look any older than sixteen. Her hair was stringy and her complexion dull. She wore a pair of old shabby *mompe* and a dirty, creased blouse. But it was her eyes which startled me. They were sneaky, uncertain, frightened, and glowed like the eyes of a hungry stray cat wanting to steal a fish head out of your kitchen.

Berry's face lighted up with enthusiasm as he said, "A few days ago when I was showing Laura Lou the red-light district in Asakusa —the one controlled by the gambler boss Sekine—we happened to see this girl in one of the windows. Prostitution does exist, you know, although General MacArthur has abolished it. This girl was different from the rest—unpainted and in shabby clothes. So we stopped to talk with her."

When they found that she wanted to be free but could not pay 2,000 yen, which she owed the house for room, board and clothing, they decided to put up the money for her. Berry proudly showed me the receipt signed by the boss Sekine with a brush and stamped by his chop (a seal to formalize a document) on a piece of rice paper. "Mind you, only a hundred and thirty dollars in American money," he said, raising his voice as if to impress upon me the atrocious side of Japanese life.

"But, Berry," I had to protest, "the reason many of those girls take to prostitution is because they are assured of certain security. At least they don't have to worry about the next meal if they take in more than four customers a night—so I understand. It's the same reason laborers cling to their gangster bosses even when they know that they are being sucked. It works something like a social security system."

"Ah! that's your feudalism," he said in disgust.

"I know that, and I'm not defending the system."

I wanted to add that it was a complicated problem which could not be solved by either abolition or liberation. But I did not have the heart when Berry and Laura Lou seemed so genuinely sincere in what they had done. Instead, I asked Berry, "What are you going to do with her?"

He was going to educate and reform her. "After all she is only twenty years old," he added.

Such infinite faith in humanity impressed me, but I was still skeptical. Have they done this to satisfy themselves that they have made a noble gesture, I wondered, or are they really prepared to carry through the project, which will entail tremendous effort and responsibility?

Tomiko was dirty. She had to be cleaned up. I was amazed when Laura Lou took her to the bathroom, rolled up her sleeves and began to wash her hair. I could not even touch Tomiko. Although theoretically I had considered her my equal, it was obvious that I had put up barriers of prejudice against her—the prejudice bred in me against a group of people who indulged in a "lowly profession." If I could have detected benevolence or a desire to show off in Laura Lou, I would have felt differently. But she was nonchalant, not a bit affected. Thoroughly ashamed, I too rolled up my sleeves in a hurry.

After Laura Lou returned to America, Tomiko came under Berry's sole sponsorship. Mother said to me one day:

"It is wrong to put all the responsibility upon Berrigan-*san*'s shoulders. It is the communal responsibility of all Japanese women. Tomiko should be put in a school or a dormitory sponsored by those who know how to deal with such girls. Once a girl becomes a prostitute, it is not easy for her to go back to a respectable business. We had a maid once, when you were small, who had been sold to a house of prostitution by her parents, who needed money. We paid the debt and kept her in our home for a while, but she soon went back."

I inquired about several institutions where Tomiko might be placed, but none was quite suitable. The acute housing and food shortage added to the difficulties.

"You should send her to a vocational school rather than to a regular high school," I suggested to Berry. "She seems to be clever with her hands. If she learns to use the sewing machine, she could work in a factory."

"But Yoko, those are sweatshops," he contended in exasperation. "First of all, she needs to feel like a human being, and for this she should be sent to an ordinary school."

So we set out to find such a school. The only place which would take her in was a private coeducational school, considered progressive in an extreme *laissez-faire* style.

A month passed and I wrote to Laura Lou:

Really Tomiko is looking more like a schoolgirl every day. Nobody could suspect that she was ever a prostitute. But I don't believe she fully appreciates the meaning of her present position, although she now understands that Berry did not "liberate" her to be his mistress.

Last Sunday she brought four school friends to the Press Nest as though she owned the house. Berry was extremely nice about it and let the girls use his study for a while. Afterwards he lectured her and said that when she wanted to bring her friends, she must ask him first. He added that she was not a daughter of a rich man.

Tomiko acts like a Cinderella and a bad one because she is not aware that the clock is going to strike twelve sometime—when Berry leaves.

Berry had stubborn faith that kindness and patience, rather than harsh words and suffering, would make anyone—even Tomiko—see the true light sometime. Although I felt that much of this was wishful thinking, when the time came for him to leave Japan several months later, I promised that I would take care of her. I could not turn down without a trial the faith and idealism which I wished to share.

One day Tomiko reported to me proudly, "*Sensei* [she addressed me with this form of respect], I learned in school today that Columbus discovered America in 1894." A few days later I visited the dean of women at her school and inquired about her. "She is a very sociable girl," the dean said, "but I cannot say that she is taking her studies seriously."

Despite Berry's wish, I decided that it was more practicable for Tomiko to learn a vocation. As she wanted to learn typing, I transferred her to a business school, but she showed no progress there, even after several months.

Since I no longer had patience or means to look after her, we had a long talk, and she decided to return to her grandmother in Hokkaido. I did not hear from her for several months. Then a letter arrived from her sister, asking Tomiko's whereabouts, and I gathered that she had disappeared.

One day in the early fall of 1948—almost two years after she had left Tokyo—Tomiko burst into my office in downtown Tokyo. "Where have you been?" I asked, noting her American-made cheap

[222]

pink rayon suit and green socks. She was much thinner than she used to be.

"I have been in Osaka. I came to Tokyo with my GI friend, who will take me to America. I am not a bad girl any more," she said with pride, and added, "Will you see him, *Sensei?* He is waiting outside."

I was flabbergasted, but nodded and straightened myself in my chair to appear dignified. The GI, who could not have been much older than twenty, had an undistinguished face difficult to remember and a pair of tired, dreamy eyes. I invited him to sit in a big chair facing me and said in English, "I understand you intend to marry Tomiko."

"No, I ain't promised anything like that. I'm going home in three months," he answered without interest.

"What do you intend to do with her?"

At this he shrugged as if to say, "Don't ask such a stupid question."

I felt utterly silly. It had been obvious to him from the beginning that Tomiko was not a typical girl, that he owed her no responsibility. And who was I to say what he should or should not do? But I continued: "Apparently Tomiko wishes to make her living by legitimate means. Since you have gotten her into this, I hope you will provide her living expenses and send her to a business school to take some more typing lessons until you leave. This would cost very little in American money."

He agreed unenthusiastically.

Then I turned to Tomiko and said firmly in Japanese, "He has no intention of marrying you. But I asked him to support you until he returns to America. In three months you can learn to type, if you try hard enough. Making a living is not easy for anybody, Tomiko, particularly for women. But you must try."

She nodded as though she did not fully understand. "*Sensei,* will you give my regards to Brookman-*san* and Berrigan-*san?*" she said as she left with her GI friend.

I sank back into my chair.

Nothing has been heard from her since.

78 ~

THE REFORMATION of Tomiko was still in its early, experimental stages in June, 1946, when a telegram arrived informing me of the return of my husband to Japan. I had not received any word from him for more than a year. He was still in Singapore when the war ended and was taken prisoner by the British, a humiliation not easy for Japanese men to accept. The swift and radical changes which had taken place since he left Japan in 1944 must have been perplexing to him; these changes had affected me deeply and it was not easy to pick the thread up exactly where we had left it.

I do not now wish to uncover the wound which both of us experienced with pain, for we finally decided, in 1948, to be separated. Each of us has started a new life apart.

Since ours was a divorce by consent, the formalities were simple. We had to fill in a form witnessed by two persons, and send it to a local government office. There was no need to appear in court since we had both agreed that I was to take the sole responsibility of supporting Seiko and there was no problem about the division of property. Takashi, who had been head of the Matsuoka house, resumed his own family name.

The merits of this simple "consensual divorce" were widely discussed, particularly among women when the bill for a new civil code was presented in the Diet in 1947. Some women lawyers contended that since in the past men had used this means to free themselves of wives who were ignorant of the law, all divorce cases should be decided by the court. Others disagreed, arguing that if the freedom of marriage is recognized, the same freedom should also apply to divorce. The revised Civil Code of Japan provides for both consensual and court divorce, given on the same grounds for women as for men.

79 ~

IN THE spring of 1946 I began to make my living by writing articles for newspapers and magazines and also speaking to women's organizations, trade unions and cultural groups. During the years following the surrender, people were anxious to know how peoples of other countries lived, and my experiences in America became useful.

I obtained an office next to the New York *Herald Tribune* in the *Mainichi* building in downtown Tokyo. Commuting there from our home in the suburbs was a torturous two-hour trip each morning. Streetcars were so crowded that passengers had to stand on the seats in order not to be crushed. A surgeon friend told me that every day patients were brought into the hospital to be treated for broken ribs. He added in a matter-of-fact way: "Since we don't have any good adhesive tape, the only thing we can do is have the patients lie absolutely still until the bones heal." He warned, "Don't ever put your arms up when you push into a car, although that is the easiest way to get in. It leaves your ribs unprotected."

Women and children suffered so much from this crowding that finally the elevated trains in Tokyo made a rule reserving to them half the compartment next to the "Advancing Army Only" car. This helped to alleviate the danger. But some men unashamedly would ride in the women's car because it was usually less crowded than the others.

On many such occasions I wanted to tell the men to get out, but somehow I could never gather enough courage to do so. It was always the *pon pon*, or street girls, and black-marketeers who dared to protest openly and vehemently against these men. The rest of us could only stare at them reproachfully. Why could I not protest? It hurt my pride that street girls and black-marketeers would stand up for their rights when ordinary women could not. It seemed that there must be something more than the unscrupulous nature of their professions which made these women strong. Although crude and ugly, they were independent, equal and free. Here was a tormented picture of emancipated women in postwar Japan.

One American correspondent commented on the behavior of the Japanese in streetcars and railroad stations: "These damned Japanese. They don't know how to behave." This remark suddenly and uncomfortably brought back memories of my two years in Seoul, Korea. "We weren't this way before," I said resentfully. There were many things uncommon in prewar days, which had now become everyday affairs. Pickpockets and burglars were as common now in Tokyo as they had been in Seoul. A picture of Tokyo now would have to include war orphans picking up cigarette butts around the Occupation buildings, paupers leisurely stirring the garbage cans outside of Occupation billets, street girls speaking pidgin English loudly in public places, and rickshaw boys cheating GI's. I used to say so proudly, "The Japanese would never do that."

80 ~

IT WAS a hot July afternoon that same summer that I visited the International Military Tribunal. Many of the seats in the small visitors' gallery had been taken by the families of the twenty-eight Class A criminal suspects and it was not easy to obtain a ticket to one of the sessions.

Humidity and heat melted the asphalt pavements in Tokyo, and the mildly sloping hill leading to the Tribunal building felt like discarded chewing gum beneath my heels. I had climbed this hill four years before when Takashi was a Domei reporter assigned to the headquarters of the Japanese General Staff, which occupied this same building. Then Ichigaya Hill was the symbol of the Japanese Imperial Army, the nerve center of Japanese "aggression." As my shoes made marks on this hill, now representing "International Justice," I recalled a Chinese saying: "Even though the nation is defeated, mountains and rivers remain the same." The Tribunal, which set out to try Japan's top "war criminals," was for the purpose of proving to the Japanese that Japan was guilty of "the oldest of all crimes"—mass murder—and to prevent "the scourge of aggressive war" in the future.

Japanese spectators were waiting in a line in front of one entrance, where we were to present our admission cards for examination by an American military policeman. Each of us was then searched individually—the women privately by a woman MP upstairs in a small room. The spectators' gallery was divided into two sections—one for the Japanese and the other for the Allied personnel. The latter space was filled mostly by GI's.

Eleven flags representing the nations of the eleven judges were displayed on the left wall of the immense hall. Beneath the flags was the judges' bench, slightly elevated from the floor. Nearby at a round table in the center I recognized the square red face of Mr. Keenan, the chief prosecutor, among others. They were obviously the prosecution staff. Another group around a table near the accused included both Allied (to my knowledge all Americans) and Japanese lawyers. These were as clearly the defense attorneys.

Watching them, I wondered about the state of mind of the Americans at that table. Even though it was the business of attorneys to defend known criminals, what a strange sensation to have to defend a group of men who until recently were their enemies. Lawyers must have a separate compartment in their minds for their own convictions and beliefs.

A hush swept the hall when twenty-six of the accused were brought in, escorted by MP's from the entrance on the right. (Yosuke Matsuoka was in the hospital with tuberculosis, and Shumei Okawa was in a mental hospital as a result of striking Tojo in the head at an earlier session.) These were all familiar faces.

Some of the men turned to the spectators' gallery as they entered, as if looking for their families. A timid smile spread slowly over the face of Admiral Oshima, our last ambassador to Germany. He must have found his family in the gallery. I recognized Mr. Hirota's daughters, sitting a few rows in front of me, but our onetime foreign minister did not look up at them or smile. His face seemed clouded with heavy thoughts. General Minami appeared to be at least fifteen years older than when I had last seen him in Seoul, in December 1939, when he was the governor general of Korea. His face appeared al-

[227]

most childlike, as if he could not comprehend the meaning of all this, and it was difficult to believe that this tottering man had once symbolized the tyranny of Japanese colonial rule.

General Tojo, the one most hated by his enemies and also by his once-obedient followers, kept his dignity and importance. The Occupation doctors must have taken good care of him following his attempted suicide just before his arrest the previous October, for he was looking extremely well.

Mr. Shigemitsu, Japan's foreign minister at the time of the surrender, had to be assisted by an MP when he seated himself. He had one wooden leg and walked awkwardly with a cane, as a result of the bomb thrown in Shanghai in 1932, at the same time Admiral Nomura's eyes were injured. As I watched his irritable face, I remembered how his wife's sister, one of Kwoko's classmates at Jiyu-Gakuen, had taken on an air of importance because her sister had married a promising diplomat. I could only too well imagine her humiliation now.

Then I looked at the insignificant-appearing Mr. Shiratori, who was said to be the strongest proponent of the Axis Alliance in the Foreign Office during the war, and Kingoro Hashimoto, instigator of the *Panay* incident and the author of many fascistic publications.

It was not easy to believe that men such as those arrayed in front of me had controlled the fate of eighty million people. I felt indignant. I felt like slapping Tojo and all the rest, who sat there so placidly and knowingly. Then suddenly I could see myself slapped with the same hand. If they were guilty of "planning of war" and taking leadership in aggression, we too must be guilty of following or not being able to prevent them from taking that leadership. Leaders cannot start a major war without the active or passive support of the people. Painful though it was, I had to admit that I was a part of that wrong.

This awareness was different from that called forth by the slogan "One Hundred Million in Repentance." Whether or not Japan again pursued the same path depended not on repentance but on the actions of people like me who had the responsibility of saying yes or no to every issue which crossed our path.

I recalled the suicide of Prince Konoye in December of the year before, when he discovered that he was on the list of war criminal suspects. The Prince considered himself a liberal. It was true that he did try to negotiate peace between the United States and Japan. Whether he was bluffing or truly sincere could only have been known if he had lived to take his stand in this hall—a test which he refused to face. When his efforts failed, he resigned from the premiership.

To many Japanese like myself, his arrest seemed a little unfair. Yet I had to admit that, as the prosecution contended, the policies which Japan had been following since the Manchurian Incident in 1931 had crystalized rather than been thwarted during his premiership. By the most kindly judgment, he had been a tool of the militarists.

It was logical to ask, What could Konoye and other liberals have done to prevent the catastrophe? Had they resigned from their posts earlier, would not that have hastened the crisis and allowed the Army and ultranationalists to run wild?

It came to me as a shock that this was the identical reasoning which liberal collaborators were using to justify their deeds during the war. Those who suggested conscription of students to work in munitions factories had said: "That is the only way to minimize their sacrifice." Those who served on the *Genron Hokoku Kai* (the association to serve the country through speech and press) had excused themselves: "This is the only way to minimize the amount of censorship." I wondered what Father would have said about his appointment in the Philippines had he lived. For he, too, would have been put in the general category of war criminals. I felt sure that he would not have tried to justify himself in order to be cleared. Nevertheless, I was truly glad that he had not lived to see this day.

Yet those who were now coming forward insisting, "Our record is clear," were not necessarily the ones who had opposed Japan's *ancien régime*. Many of them simply had not happened to hold responsible positions during the war years. On the other hand, those who had most vehemently opposed what the prosecution at the Tribunal called "a criminal, militaristic clique" seemed to be the Communists, who were freed from long imprisonment the autumn before by a directive from General MacArthur. Sanzo Nozaka, a famous Communist leader who had been exiled for sixteen years, received a hero's welcome when he returned to Japan in January 1946. He had fought the war on the Allied side, the "right" side.

We were told that Japan had committed a wrong, and it was on this premise that the Allied Powers justified their "democratization" program. Were the Communists then the only people in Japan who were not guilty of Japan's aggression?

Such thoughts led only to confusion, from which I was roused by the pounding of the gavel. I stood up with the rest to watch eleven judges in black robes march in to take their seats in front of the eleven flags.

During the session General Tojo took notes diligently, as he was reported to have done since the beginning of the Tribunal. I did not understand why he did this for, of all the war criminal suspects, he was certainly most sure to receive a death sentence.

When the two-hour session ended, and after the judges had retired, the accused were led away by the MP's. Tojo, who sat in the front row, gave a snappy little bow before he turned and disappeared. It was the kind of bow Japanese men and children would make when entering or leaving the room of their superiors. I was taught to make such a bow whenever I went into the teachers' room in the Great South Gate School in Seoul. Tojo obviously did not think the judges and prosecutors superior to him in the sense that teachers were superior to school children. I decided that he was showing his respect for the "fair trial" given a defeated general.

On my way home that day I was able to get a ride with an American correspondent and his newly arrived wife in their jeep. He asked his wife, "How did you like the show, dear?" And the wife replied that she had been duly impressed by the "spectacular drama."

It was months later, in December, 1946, that the prosecution began to detail Japanese atrocities in China, the Philippines, Malaya and other areas. This was the first time most Japanese had heard about these events in full. When I had read about "enemy atrocities" during the war, I did not believe, as the newspapers sometimes implied, that atrocities were an enemy monopoly. And now that it was made to appear that atrocities were peculiar only to Nazism, Fascism and the Japanese form of militarism, I was reluctant to accept that idea at its face value. I said to an American friend, "In the light of all the evidence, I don't deny that atrocities took place, but it must be the abnormal condition of war which is responsible."

"If that is the case," he argued, "there ought to be atrocities on both sides. Why is it that only German and Japanese atrocities are so notorious?" And he went on to say that such inhumane actions were products of a political system which disregarded fundamental human rights. The obvious implication was that they could not be committed by people brought up in a democracy.

To this I could only reply, "I know many of us are incapable of doing things like that, and we too are products of the same system. There must be some other reason."

Yet, as the Tribunal unveiled more of Japan's past in its naked reality, I began to be more receptive to the idea that aggressiveness was inherent in our political, economic and social system. To accept this completely would compel admission that the entire basis of our life was a fallacy. The set of values we had nurtured would have to be discarded. As we asked again and again, "Wasn't there anything good in what we lived for? Wasn't there any truth in what we believed?"—it was as if an earthquake were tearing at our roots.

General MacArthur had described this metamorphosis in his statement on September 2, 1946, the first anniversary of the surrender on the *Missouri*. He said ". . . it was the collapse of a faith—it was the disintegration of everything they (the Japanese) had believed in and lived by and thought for. It left a complete vacuum morally, mentally and physically. And into this vacuum flowed the democratic way of life. . . . A spiritual revolution ensued almost overnight, tore asunder a theory and practice of life built upon two thousand years of history and tradition and legend. . . . "

This change was not so simple, smooth and complete as these dramatic words portrayed, however. It was a slow and painful process. When I asked Tanaka-*san*, my former colleague at the Kokumin-Seikatsu-Gakuin, why he was not actively participating in our democratization, he remarked with some strain, "I have to find my criterion first. I cannot have a set of values which would crumble to pieces in another thirty or forty years. I want something more absolute to live by, and I want to find that for myself."

81 ~

THOSE OF us who were trying to find a new criterion came upon part of our answer in the new Constitution. The day the House of Representatives was to vote on the pending Constitution bill, I went to witness the session.

The main entrance in the center of the white marble Diet Building is reserved for the Emperor, and the driveway leading to it is usually roped off on both sides. The Lower House is situated to the left of the center dome and the Upper House to the right as you face the building. The front entrance to each wing is used solely by Diet members, who can be distinguished by the fact that they wear a small purple chrysanthemum badge, and this privilege is jealously guarded by several uniformed officials, seated behind a long rectangular desk inside the door.

I carefully followed the arrow pointing to the visitors' entrance, through a semi-basement door at the back of the building. Many guards were stationed here, too—some behind a barred window to issue entrance-permit cards to visitors, and others in hallways to prevent any illegitimate entrances.

"Aren't we supposed to have democracy?" a young man, who looked like a trade union leader, was arguing indignantly with one of the guards. "Why can't we just walk into the Diet Building without this nonsense?"

"Rules are rules," answered the guard indifferently.

Given a permit card, I went inside. The red carpet on the long corridor and stairs was worn out in spots and the whole building—now without any central heating system, because it was removed during the war years for use as scrap metal—looked as though it needed better care. I passed uniformed guards at every corner in the hallway before I reached the spectators' gallery, which was filled mostly with young men whose tense earnestness was very different from the curiosity of tourists.

The Chamber is fashioned more like the American Congress than the English Parliament. The first speech from the floor that afternoon was made by a member of the Liberal Party, the majority party (which is the most conservative). After quoting Abraham Lincoln, the speaker said, "The new Constitution contains profound philosophies of both West and East—democracy of the Occident and the 'way' of the Orient. It is an embodiment of the spirit of the 'way' in modern terminology."

To me this pronouncement sounded shockingly anachronistic. The new Constitution explicitly places sovereignty in the people for the first time in Japan's history. It guarantees to them all sorts of rights familiar in the Western democracies, and the Emperor is declared to be no longer the source of authority, but a mere symbol of national unity. Moreover, our Constitution was the first in history to renounce war "forever . . . and the threat or use of force as means of settling international disputes."

I felt that its adoption would not only encourage those who so far had refused to return to the old order, but would also condition the thinking of others, like the Liberal Party representative, who were trying to turn the clock backward. It was immaterial to me that the document was initiated by external forces rather than internal pressure.

The Emperor was to promulgate the new Constitution on November 3, 1946. I was surprised to receive an invitation to the ceremony in the Diet Building and the reception afterwards at the Akasaka Palace. For the occasion I borrowed Mother's heavy black woolen dress, since I did not own a semiformal kimono and it seemed to me that trousers would be inappropriate.

Only a handful of women had been invited to sit in the gallery that day. Among the male guests, most of whom wore morning coats and striped trousers, were the editors of important newspapers and news agencies, several professors from Tokyo University and other civic leaders. The Diet members filled the Chamber and the Cabinet members aligned themselves on the platform. Young Princess Mikasa, who stood next to her husband, the youngest brother of the Emperor, was the only woman on the platform. Her light-colored "Palace gown," a silk kimono blouse and matching *hakama* (a long pleated skirt down to her ankles), appeared strangely refreshing.

[233]

After everyone was properly placed, the Emperor entered, also wearing morning coat and striped trousers, and ascended to the chair adorned with the sixteen-petal chrysanthemum crest in the center of the platform. All sounds were blanketed by the red carpet except the clicking of cameras and flash bulbs. Of course, we were all standing at attention, but I cannot remember anyone bowing at ninety degrees as would certainly have happened before the end of the war.

The Emperor read his rescript, written on a scroll. "*Banzai!*" shouted the Speaker of the House, throwing both arms upward, and "*Banzai!*" we echoed, also with arms raised. "*Banzai!*" the speaker shouted again since it is traditional that this cheer (literally meaning "long life") be repeated three times. I noticed Princess Mikasa's small black purse moving up and down as she joined in the *Banzais*.

The Akasaka Palace, copied after Buckingham Palace in England, is only a few minutes' ride from the Diet Building by automobile. It had been used by the Imperial Family for entertaining in prewar days, and this was probably the first time commoners like myself had been invited to enter its massive iron gate. Weeds covered the spacious grounds and it was obvious that the whole establishment was badly in need of care. A magnificent chandelier in the hallway was only a sad reminder of the past. It had been decided to house the Diet Library in this building, since the Imperial Family had to economize.

Rectangular tables with white tablecloths had been set about in several rooms on the second floor, and we were permitted to enter any room we wished. Following more *Banzais,* we toasted the new Japan with *sake* and chewed pieces of dried squid, traditionally served on all happy occasions.

Unfortunately, my thoughts turned to the scarcity of fuel which allowed my family a bath only once a week, to the inadequate rationing of food which restricted us to diluted rice in the morning and a cold lunch at noon. I thought, too, of wounded soldiers begging on the streets, uncared-for war orphans running loose, and a judge who had died of malnutrition because he refused to buy on the black market.

The ideals and principles set forth in the new Constitution seemed very far away.

82 ~

DESPITE GENERAL MacArthur's statement about the "spiritual revolution" of the Japanese, there were foreign observers who were extremely skeptical of our "moral demilitarization." Lady Rama Rau, wife of the first head of the Indian Mission in Tokyo, said to me, "The world does not trust Japan yet. We cannot expect anybody to change so fast."

This was the first time I had heard such a critical view of us expressed so candidly, and it was a surprise to me. Japanese newspapers had been reporting only the friendly attitude of other nations. I discovered later that, among the Allied Powers, it was the United States alone who no longer saw any danger in her former enemy. Others, particularly those which had suffered military defeats from the Japanese Army, were still reluctant to voice their approval.

I wanted to say to Lady Rama Rau: "Some of us have really changed during the last two years. I have; so have Mother and Tanaka-*san*. In normal times I don't suppose people do change so rapidly. But when the very fundamentals of your life are questioned and the status quo reversed as it has been in Japan, you are compelled to change. Of course, there are some who gave in when their assumed faith collapsed. Others have turned cynical. But we have really struggled to find a new source of strength. We had to. It was impossible to go on living without any belief or standards."

I did not say all this, however, for the occasion was a cocktail party where such conversations seemed inappropriate. Moreover, as the only Japanese present, I felt shy about speaking up.

Even then I knew there was real basis for her suspicions. Many of those whose old faith had not crumbled became suddenly more vocal when the split between the "two worlds" began to be more apparent, when the emphasis of the Occupation policies was shifted from the demilitarization and democratization of Japan to the maintenance of American security in the struggle against communism. When General Tojo stood in the witness stand in the Military Tribunal in late December 1947 and defended himself with high-sounding oratory on the grounds that Japan was forced into war for self-defense, I was appalled to hear murmurs in the streets and tea shops of downtown Tokyo: "It takes Tojo to say it, doesn't it?" These same people had booed at pictures of Tojo in early 1946. Now he was becoming a hero among people who were not convinced that Japan had committed a wrong.

These murmurs and whispers became an open inquiry by the spring of 1948. When I went to give a talk on "Japan's Democratization" in a middle-sized town in Yamanashi prefecture, a young, intelligent-looking man stood up and asked, "Whatever you say, might is always right, is it not?" This was the first time I had heard such a bold question in a public meeting, expressing doubts about the moral rightness of the Allies.

I had just presented a case for Japan's democratization on the grounds that we had pursued a wrong course. The renunciation of war, I pointed out, was a prerequisite to the establishment of a peaceful and democratic Japan. Without denying the importance of historical and other factors intricately tied up with her foreign policies, I was contending that the internal political, economic and social structure was largely responsible for Japan's past aggression. My first thought following the young man's question was: If might is right, there is no moral basis for Japan's democracy. In that case, there are no morals at all. To me there had to be right and wrong; just and unjust; good and bad.

I was uncomfortably aware of the silence which fell upon the audience when I answered that I believed there was more than power politics in the world. The young man was polite and did not push me further in public, but he came to me afterward and said, "Don't you really think that morals exist to justify the deeds of the powerful?"

Then I recalled what Mr. Keenan had said in his opening statement at the Military Tribunal: "We now come to the point where we shall show the facts of Japan to be among the most treacherous and perfidious of all time. In 1904, Japan opened the Russo-Japanese War with an attack on the Russian Fleet at Port Arthur without notice or warning. The civilized nations of the world recognized that a continuance of this practice would be intolerable."

I remembered how I had fought Mr. Keenan's contention. The

world had not accused Japan of treacherous acts at the time. Father had told me that public sympathy in the United States was for Japan, the underdog. Moreover, the world had accepted the results of the Russo-Japanese war for nearly half a century.

83 ~

AFTER THREE years the Tribunal was finally ready to give verdicts in the trial of the twenty-five Class A war criminal suspects. Two of the original twenty-eight had died. I attended the funeral of Yosuke Matsuoka, who died of tuberculosis, feeling it was a strange irony that the service for this most dramatic supporter of the Axis Alliance should be held in a Catholic Church, to which faith Mr. Matsuoka had been converted during his student days in America. A third suspect, Shumei Okawa, was still in the mental hospital.

It was almost impossible to obtain tickets to visit the Tribunal on this last day in November 1948. Interest had dwindled during the three years, partly due to passage of time and partly due to changes taking place in world politics. Suddenly it revived during the last week. Speculation as to which suspects would receive death penalties and which would not was the topic of discussion everywhere.

I was in my office in the *Mainichi* building that afternoon with my secretary, Tsuji-*san*. All the large newspaper offices in Tokyo have loud-speakers facing the streets, which transmit radio programs of general interest, such as election news, baseball games, and wrestling matches. On such occasions, a large sheet of paper is posted on the outside wall of the building, where summarized reports are written down with a brush and ink as they are received. Usually a large crowd gathers in front of press buildings to read these bulletins.

Tsuji-*san* and I went to our fifth-floor window from where we could see the twenty-five names of the war criminal suspects written on the wall across the street. There was a crowd beneath us despite the chilly November air. Men with their collars turned up and women with scarves covering half their faces were listening intently and in silence.

The man with the brush and ink wrote the verdict in the blank space below each of the twenty-five names as it was broadcast from the Ichigaya Tribunal. The sentences were given in the alphabetical order of the prisoners' names.

General Araki was first. I remembered him as the Minister of Education in the Konoye Cabinet. He received a life sentence. . . . "Death sentence by hanging" was written beneath the name of Doihara. This had been expected, as his name was synonymous with the Kwantung Army in Manchuria. But when the same sentence was announced for Koki Hirota, the only civilian among the seven who were later hanged, there was a little stir among the crowd below us.

I said to Tsuji-san, "I don't understand why his sentence should be heavier than Kingoro Hashimoto's, for example. No doubt, Hirota's Cabinet post under Konoye and Tojo was important, but this does seem too severe." She nodded in agreement. Then I added, "Perhaps I am prejudiced against militarists."

I later read that Koki Hirota was the only one among the accused who did not join in the *Banzais* at the last rites given by a Buddhist priest just before the seven men were hanged. It seemed that only those who could justify their deeds could shout *Banzai* at their death.

When the death sentence was written below Matsui's name, it was Tsuji-san's turn to say, "My father knew him well." I did not ask questions, for I knew what she must be thinking. Her father, a major general and at one time under General Matsui's command, had survived the demilitarization with only a "purge," which prohibited him from holding public office or a teaching position. Almost two hundred thousand had been so purged by General MacArthur since the beginning of 1946, but Tsuji-san's father was one of the unfortunate ones, too old to find a suitable position elsewhere and with very little income.

A few days later Tsuji-san received a postal card from her father, who was now supporting himself and his wife by fishing and farming in the country, urging her to pay a visit to "His Excellency, General Matsui" at the Sugamo Prison to extend deepest sympathy.

With an embarrassed smile, Tsuji-san said, "It is difficult for Father to realize that times have changed. Even if I were permitted to see General Matsui, what could I really say? I suppose it is harder for older people to adjust to a new situation than for us."

The death penalty for Tojo was expected.

When the broadcast was over and we had watched the crowd disperse quietly Tsuji-*san* and I returned to our desks and just sat. All I could say was, "Well, at last it's all over."

I did not feel shocked by the sentences, nor did I feel upset for those whose lives must end or whose future must be spent behind prison bars. There had to be some logic to this long-drawn-out drama, despite the fact that political factors in the world have radically changed since the Tribunal was established, I told myself. Aloud, I added, "Yes, there must be right and wrong."

Japan seemed to have journeyed far from the time when these men were indispensable at the helm. Yet the way they, particularly Tojo, were played up in the press, apparently without annoying the SCAP authorities, once so acutely sensitive to signs of recrudescent militarism, made me painfully conscious that Japan, too, was in the "cold war," and that the wrongs of yesterday had assumed a different proportion in the changing context of history.

84 ~

BY THE spring of 1949, Seiko was ready to go to school. Most of the wealthy families near us sent their children to a private school which they felt had higher scholastic standards than the public schools.

Mother thought Seiko should go to this school.

"I can afford it," I said, "but I object to an exclusive school for her. We should try to improve our public schools."

Mother replied, "I agree, but I don't think you should sacrifice the child for a principle when you know there are better schools."

Reiko said, "It's not that Seiko should learn to speak the most polite language, but you should hear the language spoken by some of the children at public school. It is really vulgar."

"Sooner or later," I contended, "she will hear all kinds of things. Surely we can give her at home what is lacking in the school."

Finally it was settled that she was to go to a public school only a ten-minute walk from our house.

Although grammar-school education is compulsory in Japan, the children are required to take a test before entering the first grade. On her examination day I took Seiko to the School. Inside the two-story wooden building, the parents waited at the back of the room while the children were seated in small chairs at low desks. The young man teacher gave each child a piece of paper and instructed them to draw a boy.

Some of the children were quick; some were completely at a loss. Several worried mothers tried to help their children from the side.

Seiko drew very slowly, but I could see that she was forming the recognizable outline of a boy wearing a cap and a pair of short trousers. From the serious expression on her face I knew she was feeling the weight of this new experience without fully comprehending its meaning.

The principal of the school and more than half the teaching staff were men. Seiko's class of about forty boys and girls was in the charge of a young man just out of normal school. It was one of three classes into which the first-graders were divided, and every other week it met in the afternoon instead of the morning because of the lack of classroom space. This school could not obtain an appropriation from the government for new buildings because so many other schools had been completely destroyed during the war and these had priority. The roof of the auditorium leaked and there was no heat in the winter months but, everything considered, it was better equipped than the average.

All Seiko's classmates wore Western-style clothes to school—the girls one-piece cotton or rayon dresses and the boys short pants and shirts or high-necked student uniforms. Instead of shoes, which were extremely expensive, most of them wore *geta*, a kind of Japanese footwear made of wood (the best *geta* is made of paulownia, very light and soft). Seiko was proud of her American-made clothes, sent by my friends in America. Before leaving the house in the morning, she would look at herself in the mirror just as I used to do when I was a child.

[240]

On the days when she had classes in the morning, I walked with her to school on my way to the office. Reiko remarked, "Nobody can doubt she is your child. She looks exactly like you in the picture taken upon your graduation from Shaker Heights School when you weighed about twenty more pounds than you do now." Seiko had always been a very healthy child, a little taller and heavier than others her age. Inouye-*san*, a newspaper friend, liked to joke: "You must be feeding her on the black market." The children nicknamed her "female Tarzan," but this did not seem to bother her in the least.

Walking to school one morning, I asked Seiko, "Who sits next to you in class?"

"Sato-*san*."

"Do you always sit next to him?"

"No, we change around. But a boy and a girl always sit next to each other."

This was indeed different from my school days when the boys sat on one side of the room and girls on the other. Seiko's teacher was apparently doing his best to practice coeducation, with which he himself was unfamiliar.

The Occupation's democratization program made it necessary to rewrite all the school text books. Not all the new texts were ready and teachers were obliged to mimeograph copies. No longer were there classes in morals and calligraphy, and no longer did the school day start with bowing toward the Imperial Palace.

Now we had a new set of national holidays. The first Seiko encountered was Constitution Day on May 3, the second anniversary of the day when the new Constitution had become effective. Seiko came home after the ceremony at school and reported, "Mommie, the principal said we celebrate because Japan was defeated."

"I am sure he did not say exactly that," I told her hastily, and then paused to think how to explain the meaning of the new Constitution to a six-year-old. In exasperation I said, "I'm afraid you will have to be a little older in order to understand it."

This was the first of several incidents which made me aware that the problems of my daughter's education were more complex than I had expected. So when I was asked to attend a meeting of parents to discuss the forming of a PTA, I accepted gladly. There had been

[241]

a parents' association even in prewar days, but now all schools were encouraged to form a new one on the American pattern.

About fifty parents of children in all six grades were present that night. Nearly one-third were women, who sat together on one side of the room. The draft of a constitution was up for discussion and the men were doing all the talking. So far as I could see, all the pertinent points had been covered; so, like the other women, I just listened—until the chairman turned toward us and said in a politely condescending tone, "How about some suggestions from the mothers?"

At this the woman next to me whispered to her neighbor on the other side, "Women don't understand such things as a constitution. That is men's business. Don't you think so?"

Her tone of near-indignation compelled me to speak up—to let her know that women too could discuss such matters if they tried. To the surprise of the chairman, I raised my hand and pointed out that the wording in a certain article was obscure and needed clarification. Then, feeling slightly self-conscious, I sat down.

It was partly due to this incident, I think, that a group of mothers called upon me and asked permission to nominate me for vice-president of the new PTA. "Our association has been managed by the same people for many years," one of them said, "and we have never had a woman in such an office. We badly need someone to represent us." I could not refuse.

These women went about for the next two weeks with astonishing vigor and earnestness, urging other reluctant ones to come to the general meeting to vote for officers. Most of my supporters were in the late twenties or early thirties, with only a minimum of schooling.

It was pouring rain that Sunday morning when the general meeting was held, but the school auditorium was packed, with more than half of the seats occupied by women. This seemed to upset the former officials of the association. One of them, a mustached man of about fifty wearing a kimono, was outspoken in expressing his displeasure. It was alarming, he said, how democracy was being misunderstood, particularly by women. He added that running for office was not a woman's task. This was meant for me as I was the only woman up for election.

Whispers of indignation were heard from the women, though

none of them stood up to object. They showed their disapproval further by not applauding.

In the lively discussion which followed I could draw a line between the opinions of those men who were below forty years of age and those who were older. The older men resisted any move for change. Although women did not participate in the discussion, except for myself, they applauded enthusiastically when the younger men spoke. Almost all of the women favored changes.

The noon hour passed, yet these mothers stayed. When the election was finally held by secret balloting, a new set of officers was elected by an overwhelming majority.

I was nervous when I stood up to make my acceptance speech, and keenly aware of my responsibilities to Seiko and her generation. At the end of the meeting, a woman teacher came up to congratulate me. Her face glowed when she said, "This could never have happened before. It gives us hope, too, that we may be able to improve our status in the teaching profession."

85 ~

IT WAS with stunned gratitude that I had received in September 1948 Laura Lou's invitation to spend a year in the United States. Aside from the legal difficulties to be met in traveling abroad, since Japan was still technically at war with the Allied nations, I had my responsibilities at home, particularly toward Seiko. Reiko was scheduled to be sent to the United States from the Japanese YWCA for study the following year, and it would mean leaving six-year-old Seiko with Mother, who was aging rapidly. This hardly seemed fair.

I weighed the matter for several days before I talked to Mother and Reiko. Mother did not hesitate for a moment, but said, "This is a rare opportunity for you to see Japan from outside. You have been too engrossed in the changes taking place here. Don't worry about Seiko. I'll take care of her."

It was typical of her not to say a word about the burden put upon her.

Early in November SCAP announced that Japanese would be permitted to go to the United States for the purpose of studying or training in religious or cultural fields provided they were sponsored by an institution or an individual in the United States. I immediately notified Laura Lou, and soon received from her an official invitation which I transmitted, along with a formal application, to the Occupation authorities.

I did not tell Seiko about my plans, feeling that it would be unwise until everything was definitely settled. Weeks and months passed. Apparently I was being thoroughly investigated as to my background and associations. The neighborhood children, who had always played with Seiko at our house because she had more toys than others, suddenly stopped coming. The parents, I discovered, had become frightened when they were questioned by the police concerning me. But they were reassured when I called upon the families in our Neighborhood Association (the wartime geographical unit remained for rationing food) and explained my plan to go to America.

A year after Laura Lou's invitation first reached me, I finally received permission to make the trip. It was not easy to break this news to Seiko. After having put her to bed one evening, I sat beside her *futon*, held her hand and said, "Mommie has something to tell you, Seiko."

Then I paused. I was determined to tell her in such a way that she would be prepared to face the coming year not with a lonely heart, but with courage and hope. Taking a long breath, I started my carefully prepared speech, "Brookman-*san* has invited me to come to America for a year of study. It is very important for Mommie to study again. You understand that, don't you? This coming winter, next spring, and the summer will be gone before I return. You will be in the second grade then." I looked into her big brown eyes. "You will be brave and be a good girl with Grandmother, won't you?"

Suddenly tears rushed down my cheeks, beyond my power to control. I had been afraid to see her tears, but it had never occurred to me that I would be the one to lose composure. Now for the first time I understood the tears on Mother's face when I had departed for America seventeen years before. I realized that I was going to miss Seiko perhaps more than she would miss me.

Seiko did not say a word. Abruptly she turned her head toward the pillow. Seeing her black silky hair gently vibrate, I knew she, too, was crying.

What was I to do? Seiko depended upon me completely, which was natural considering that I had held her during so many bombardments and had been the bread-earner in the family since her babyhood. Her faith in me was infinite. Whenever she was asked what she wanted to be when she grew up, she would invariably reply with pride, "I am going to be like Mommie—go downtown and type and study," as though this were the highest human achievement. There is nothing which hurts more than to be trusted beyond one's power. How much better, I thought, if she knew my weaknesses and limitations, and was prepared to challenge and accuse me.

Sitting there beside her, I recalled a question once put to me: "What makes you want to live in this world?" I had answered after some deliberation, "Because I believe humanity ultimately progresses." This belief, I understood now, was inseparably related to my feelings of responsibility, hope and aspiration for her, and to her faith in me. Because Seiko believed in me, I had to believe in the world and humanity; if I did certain things, surely the world would be a better place for her generation to live in. It was she who had saved me from becoming cynical.

For Seiko's sake I could not and must not repeat the mistakes of Mother's generation. War and what follows war, I had learned, is destructive of all distinctively human values. But what path to choose in a society which was being torn in two?

Perhaps if I get away from Japan for a while, I may find an answer, I thought. Seiko had gone to sleep now and my tears had dried.

With renewed determination, I decided to go to America, for I wanted to believe in tomorrow for Seiko.